Creating Worldwide Software

Software

*Solaris International
Developer's Guide
2nd Edition*

*Bill Tuthill
David Smallberg*

The publisher offers discounts on this book when ordered in bulk quantities. For more information, contact Corporate Sales Department, Prentice Hall PTR, One Lake Street, Upper Saddle River, NJ 07458.
Phone: 800-382-3419; FAX: 201-236-7141.
E-mail: corpsales@prenhall.com.

Editorial/production supervision: *Kathleen M. Caren*
Cover designer: *Talar Agayson*
Cover design director: *Jerry Votta*
Manufacturing manager: *Alexis R. Heydt*
Marketing manager: *Stephen Solomon*
Acquisitions editor: *Gregory G. Doench*
Sun Microsystems Press publisher: *Rachel Borden*

10 9 8 7 6 5 4 3 2 1

ISBN 0-13-494493-3

Sun Microsystems Press
A Prentice Hall Title

Table of Contents

≡

11. Communicating Network Data   169

C. OpenWindows and DevGuide   285

D. XView Programming   295

E. OLIT Programming   311

List of Tables

List of Figures

Preface

The globe is not shrinking, it just seems that way. Improved telecommunications and air travel have accelerated the flow of goods, services, and capital worldwide. Despite this, computer systems have been slow to evolve, often being limited to a single language or culture.

Creating Worldwide Software presents a blueprint for building global products that can be easily adapted to international market conditions, both now and in the future.

Intended Audience

This book is intended for software developers and engineering managers who want to design and develop global products and applications for UNIX® platforms. It specifically covers Sun Microsystems' Solaris™ environment. Many chapters assume knowledge of the C programming language, and a few chapters discuss X11 Window System® toolkits under CDE (Motif®) and OpenWindows™. Some chapters do not require any programming background.

All operating system information pertains to SunOS™ 5.x, whereas all window system information pertains to CDE x.x and OpenWindows 3.x, where x is a number from one on up. Most of the information in this book also pertains to all UNIX systems with X Window System and Motif library interfaces.

As much as possible, this guide is standards based, except when existing standards are lacking or deficient. When you engineer software that conforms to standards, you can rest assured that it will be portable to many operating systems and hardware platforms, and that vendors cannot change interfaces on a whim.

The scope of hardware coverage is for SPARC® and Intel® x86 machines. For the most part, support for these two processor architectures should be identical, but a note appears when this is not the case.

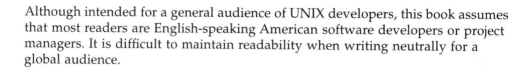

Although intended for a general audience of UNIX developers, this book assumes that most readers are English-speaking American software developers or project managers. It is difficult to maintain readability when writing neutrally for a global audience.

Book Organization

The material in this guide is organized as follows:

- Chapter 1, *Winning in Global Markets* presents the worldwide market potential for internationalized software products. It also defines key notions of global software design, such as internationalization and localization. These concepts are critical to understanding the rest of this book.

- Chapter 2, *Understanding Linguistic and Cultural Differences* enumerates some of the cultural differences that global software design must resolve.

- Chapter 3, *Encoding Character Sets* examines how to encode character sets for any language.

- Chapter 4, *Establishing Your Locale Environment* describes how an end user specifies a desired locale and how a software developer can make an application become locale aware. Support for basic locale-specific features such as time, date, monetary, numeric, sorting, and character processing are discussed.

- Chapter 5, *Messaging for Program Translation* describes how to prepare your application to handle localized program messages. It also demonstrates how to create and install user message catalogs after they have been translated.

- Chapter 6, *Displaying Localized Text* looks at font, user interface, and printing issues associated with localized text.

- Chapter 7, *Handling Language Input* familiarizes you with various input methods for different languages.

- Chapter 8, *Working with CDE* presents an overview for setting your locale in a CDE environment and discusses how software developers can make use of an international graphical user interface builder.

- Chapter 9, *Motif Programming* explains how to write internationalized Motif and CDE applications and provide graphical user interfaces.

- Chapter 10, *X11 Programming* discusses the internationalization features supported by X11 and how to internationalize an X Windows program.

- Chapter 11, *Communicating Network Data* discusses various issues of interoperability and data exchange for distributed computing.

Creating Worldwide Software

- Chapter 12, *Writing International Documentation* provides some guidelines for writing documents that can be readily translated.

- Chapter 13, *Product Localization* discusses business issues that you should consider before deciding to localize a product. It also examines how a system locale definition might be created.

- Chapter 14, *Standards Organizations* enumerates the standards bodies and published standards that affect global software design.

- Chapter 15, *Internationalization Checklist* summarizes software internationalization requirements and provides a "do and don't" checklist for developers.

- Appendix A, *Languages, Territories, and Locale Names,*" lists accepted locale names for language and territory.

- Appendix B, *Locale Summaries and Keyboard Layouts,*" provides locale-specific information for a wide range of locales and illustrates a variety of localized keyboard layouts.

- Appendix C, *OpenWindows and DevGuide,*" presents some issues in window system design and provides an introduction to internationalization using the OpenWindows Developer's Guide, referred to as "DevGuide."

- Appendix D, *XView Programming,*" discusses internationalized window system programming with the XView™ toolkit for East Asia and Western Europe.

- Appendix E, *OLIT Programming,*" talks about window system programming with the OPEN LOOK® Intrinsics Toolkit (OLIT) for East Asia and Western Europe.

   Note that SunSoft has end-of-lifed both XView and OLIT, although XView remains in widespread use.

- Appendix F, *Example Program,*" provides a complete source code example of an internationalized Motif application.

- Appendix G, *Annotated Bibliography,*" describes recommended further reading

- Appendix H, "Glossary," defines special terms used throughout this book.

Conventions Used in This Book

The following table describes typeface changes and symbols used in this book.

Table PR-1 Typographic Conventions

Typeface	Description	Examples

`AaBbCc123`
`fixed-width`
	The names of commands, reference manual pages, or files and directories; any output appearing on-screen	Use `ls -a` to list all files.
		See the `ls(1)` manual page.
		Edit your `.login` file.
		`You have mail.`
		`system%`

`AaBbCc123`
`fixed-width`
`bold`
	What you type, contrasted with on-screen computer output	`system%` **`su`**
		`password:`
		`#`

AaBbCc123 *italics (variable)*	Command-line placeholder: replace with a real name or value	To delete a file, type `rm` *filename*
AaBbCc123 *italics (emphasis)*	Book titles, new words or terms, or words to be emphasized	See Chapter 6 of *User's Guide*. These are called *class* options. You *must* be root to do this.
Code samples are included in boxes and may display the following:		
%	UNIX C shell prompt	`system%`
$	UNIX Bourne shell prompt	`system$`
#	Superuser prompt, either shell	`system#`

About the Authors

Bill Tuthill learned UNIX while doing graduate work in Comparative Literature at U.C. Berkeley. Finding computers more interesting than literary theory, he left school and began programming. After several years, he became a Technical Writer for Sun Microsystems. He survived the transition from small to large company, but could not survive the transition to SVR4. While writing the first edition, Bill worked on European localizations and participated in the Unicode effort.

David Smallberg is a consultant specializing in software development and training. He has conducted seminars and workshops on internationalization, standard C, and C++ on three continents and hopes to reach the other four soon.

Acknowledgments

Many people contributed to the design, writing, review, editing, and production of this book. SunSoft would particularly like to acknowledge the following people for their contributions:

Gail Yamanaka, the project leader and book coordinator, who should have been listed as this book's third co-author.

Vartan Piroumian, for extensive and helpful review comments on almost every chapter.

SunSoft Global Products Engineering: Ienup Sung, Shinobu Matsuzuka, Hiroshi Watanabe, Hidetoshi Tajima, Nelson Ng, Alexander Gelfenbain, Hideki Hiura, Shripad Patki, Melissa Biggs, Ed Julson, Nancy Rains, and Jean Cunnington.

SunSoft Asian Localization Center: Ken Lee, Eric Li, Changhoon Joon, and Ko-haw Nieh.

SunSoft European Localization Center: Ann Fitzpatrick, and Tom Garland.

SunSoft Japanese Localization Center: Akira Ohsone, Tomonori Shioda, and Masayoshi Okutsu.

Sun Press: Rachel Borden, John Bortner, and Karin Ellison.

SunSoft OS Internationalization Group: Robbin Kawabata, Bing-Meng Hong, Kenjiro Tsuji, and Walter Tsai.

Also: Willie Jow, Larry Miller, Andrea Vine, Dave Huang, and James Wade.

Winning in Global Markets   1

Imagine yourself as a Frenchman living in Paris. You want to purchase a desktop publishing application for your computer, so you visit a local store that offers a wide selection of software. The salesman demonstrates a word processing package developed in the United States. This software provides an English user interface, uses English commands, and offers keyboard shortcuts based on English mnemonics. The package can't display accented French characters and has no options for displaying French currency or the appropriate date format. You may decide to buy this software and struggle with the little English you know. More likely, you will pass up this product and buy an application that supports French better, even if the French product has fewer features.

Small modifications can make a big difference in capturing market share. The user in the example above probably would have been willing to make concessions for this product if the software developer had added some French functionality. But the software was disagreeable because it did not display French characters or display the appropriate time and monetary formats.

1.1 International Software Markets

This chapter describes how software companies are working to support new and expanding global markets and discusses software design approaches that can help you produce worldwide software.

Computer software has become a tool that many people use in everyday life. Computing helps them both at work and at home. Software is readily available and easily used because it conforms to their native language and conventions.

American users expect that an application purchased in their country will use the dollar sign ($) for the currency and the month/day/year short format (*mm/dd/yy*) to express the date. Similarly, French users expect that the application they purchase in their country will use the Franc symbol (F or FF) for currency and the day/month/year short format (*dd/mm/yy*) to express the date. However, since software is often developed with only local users in mind, international users are often disappointed.

1

In many countries it is difficult to sell computer hardware and software that does not support the prevailing language or national customs. Most major industrialized nations today require that software distributors offer applications to support their local standards and language. For example, Japan, Germany, and France have either government or industrial requirements. Even less regulated industrial countries, such as Korea, Taiwan, and parts of Latin America, have established national standards and possess growing software markets requiring international support.

It should be obvious that software must meet the needs of international users to be marketed around the globe. This requires effort and investment.

Many software vendors who make the requisite investments are able to capture significant worldwide market share by selling their products internationally. Companies like Sun Microsystems currently generate more than half their revenue from sales outside the U.S.

As an example of worldwide market potential, let's look at the worldwide software market as reported by International Data Corporation (IDC). Figure 1-1 shows IDC estimates that 53% of software revenues in 1999 will come from outside the U.S. The fastest growing markets at present are in the rest of world (ROW) category, which includes Eastern Europe, South and Southeast Asia, Russia, and Latin America.

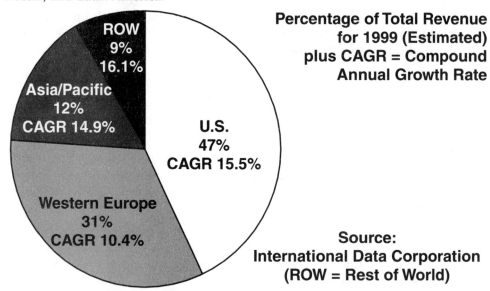

Figure 1-1   Worldwide Software Revenues by Geographic Region

The international software market has grown exponentially during the last decade. For example, the Japanese software industry has expanded from 30% to 45% on a sales value basis. The Japanese software market grew from US$370 million in 1986 to over a US$1 billion by 1990. Such rapid growth, the result of software usage by many people in all industries, exemplifies the need for custom applications tailored to fit the needs of local markets.

Figure 1-2 charts international revenues for some of the major U.S. computer corporations and indicates the growth of international revenue. This information comes from corporate annual reports.

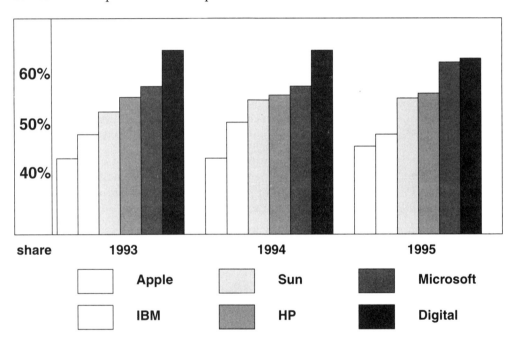

Figure 1-2   *International Revenue as Percentage of Total Revenues*

1.1.1 Benefits of International Products

Here are some benefits that international products provide:

- For end users
  - Ease of use through local language translations
  - Products for worldwide use, especially for multinational companies
  - Translated software and documentation, which are especially valuable to commercial end-users

- For developers
  - Ease of creating global applications
  - Wider and more diverse customer base
- For software vendors
  - Broader market for most products
  - Ability to expand internationally

There are two different approaches to providing global products: customization and internationalization/localization. These approaches are discussed below.

1.2 Customization—the Old Approach to Worldwide Software

In the past, developers often created software with hardcoded linguistic and cultural conventions. Such software worked well for the native local market, but usually fell short of expectations when shipped to an international market.

The old approach to providing worldwide applications consisted of having software redeveloped and specially rewritten for a specific language or region, called a *locale*. We will refer to this old approach of retrofitting software for a particular locale as *customization*. Customization often required:

- Hiring software developers who were familiar with the target language
- Modifying the original source code by replacing hardcoded language strings and cultural conventions with hardcoded language and conventions of the target market, and recompiling the code

For a simple, single locale case, this might work well particularly if the target language is culturally similar to the native language. The original developers are impacted only minimally, since the product is merely handed over to a new development team. But if it is desirable to extend support to multiple markets and have every release of every software product individually customized for each country, then the development and maintenance costs could be staggering. Moreover, international markets would receive software upgrades significantly later than the local market.

Here are the disadvantages of customized software:

- Customized products ship much later than the original product, often resulting in reduced product marketability or sales.
- Duplicate development resources are necessary.

- Redundant source code makes it harder to maintain products over time.
- It is difficult to expand support for new languages.

How can this work be done more efficiently? The solution is *internationalization*.

1.3 Internationalization—the New Approach to Worldwide Software

Internationalization is a way of designing and producing software that can be easily adapted to local markets. Unlike customized software, which must be largely revised or rewritten before it can be used with different languages and customs, internationalized software does not require revision. It is able to support any number of language markets without change.

The recommended approach to providing worldwide software is a two-phase process: after being internationalized, software undergoes *localization*. Internationalization is done only once and applies to all languages. Internationalized products are then localized (or adapted) to different languages and cultures. Fortunately, this can be done with minimal effort. In effect, internationalization enables localization.

For example, in an internationalized application, translated program messages do not reside in the executable image but in a language-specific message database. Data files specifying culture-specific formats for time, currency, and numbers also exist. End users only need to set their environment to get the proper messages and format conventions for their language and culture. As a result, customers gain control of an application's language and cultural behavior.

Think of internationalization as a way of *generalizing* software so it can handle different user needs, especially various cultural or linguistic conventions. Localization is a method for making the generalized application more specific again.

Internationalized software has these properties:

- It supports new languages and cultures without changes to the source code.
- It does not require recompiling when you add support for a new language.
- It is provided as an executable image that dynamically retrieves language and culture-specific data (or shared objects) at runtime.
- It strives for the goal of having one shrink-wrapped package that can run anywhere in the world.

- It is cost-effective, since good international design requires relatively little incremental effort, and avoids the huge costs associated with retrofits.

Solaris is internationalized, providing the infrastructure and interfaces you need to create internationalized software. Chapters 3 through 10 describe the interfaces for international support built into Solaris and discuss the preferred methods for programming these interfaces.

Internationalization is often abbreviated as i18n in English speaking countries because in English there are 18 letters between *i* and *n* in the word. Globalization might have been a better term, but the computer industry has already settled on internationalization.

1.4 Localization

Whereas internationalization makes software readily portable between languages or regions, localization adapts software for a specific language or region. Localized software is adapted to culturally specific elements of a country or language. An application that is translated without first being internationalized is said to be a "customized" application (see page 4). Internationalized applications do not need redevelopment when they are localized.

Localization involves both translating software messages and establishing on-line information to support a specific language or region. International software uses on-line information or dynamically linked libraries to modify program behavior at runtime, in accordance with specific cultural requirements. Products can have different levels of localization:

- Full localization—provides complete localization support
- Partial localization—provides localization support only in some aspects, for example, a localized user interface without localized documentation

Localization is often abbreviated as l10n because in English there are 10 letters between *l* and *n* in the word.

1.4.1 Full Localization

A *full localization* should meet all possible cultural expectations, linguistic realities, and national requirements for the target locale. Chapter 2, *Understanding Linguistic and Cultural Differences*, discusses some of the most important locale-specific considerations.

Japanese Solaris is an example of a full localization, providing:

- Japanese language support (fonts, text display, input, and printing)

- Localized user interface and translated program messages
- Translated manual pages and on-line help
- Translated hard-copy documentation
- Translated product packaging

1.4.2 Partial Localization

A *partial localization* meets only some of the linguistic requirements, cultural expectations, and national standards for a target locale. Two partial localizations may be incomplete in different ways. Partial localization is usually less expensive than full localization. Many software distributors partially localize an application to determine the demand for the product in a specific market. If demand is high enough, they fully localize the application for that market.

For each target market you will need to determine the amount of localization necessary, based on marketing factors for the geography. Companies frequently create partial localizations for small, emerging markets, but these products meet only the minimum acceptable requirements. Full localizations are typically recommended for mature markets. See Chapter 13, *Product Localization*, for more details on localization planning.

Regardless of the level of localization, you should always consider developing fully internationalized products, so your company can be prepared to enter any worldwide market.

Solaris products provide both full and partial localizations for different locales. See Appendix A, *Languages, Territories, and Locale Names* for a list of supported locales in recent Solaris releases.

1.5 Advantages of Internationalization and Localization

The two-phase internationalization and localization approach allows you to enter new markets quickly. It simplifies software maintenance significantly, since there is only one *base product* for all locales. Moreover, it allows nearly simultaneous releases around the globe, since localizing is much easier than customizing or rewriting software.

Here are the principal reasons for choosing the internationalization approach:

- Permits quick and easy entry into new markets—localization is fast.
- Simplifies maintenance—there is a single source code base.

- Ensures software consistency—products operate the same everywhere.

- Is cost effective—because it saves time for supporting multiple locales.

Here are the challenges inherent in the internationalization approach:

- *Retraining*—Many software developers will need some training to write internationalized code. Developers that have written software for their own language and culture are often unaware that they have hardcoded in many linguistic and cultural assumptions that limit the software's usefulness in other parts of the world.

- *Working with localization developers*—Since the final product is the result of both the internationalization and localization pieces working together, a large amount of coordination is typically involved in producing the final product. This requires teamwork to ensure that international software works with localized data. Improper actions on either side will produce poor quality results. Internationalization bugs are especially troublesome because a problem is often propagated to every localized product.

- *Performance*—Internationalization involves generalizing software. There is a trade-off for making software robust enough to handle any locale. At times internationalized code might be a bit slower than code that is tuned to a specific set of linguistic or cultural rules.

- *Not good for simple cases*—If software only handles one other locale, it might be faster, easier, and less costly in the short-term to use a customization approach. However in the long-term, your company will still incur the overhead of maintaining duplicate source trees, and perhaps duplicate development teams, over the life of a product.

1.6 Basic Steps in Internationalization

An internationalized application's executable image is portable between regions and languages. The key is to avoid hardcoding any linguistic or cultural assumptions into your application. To internationalize software:

- Use the interfaces described in this book to create worldwide software, which can be modified dynamically without program recompilation.

  - Have your application set the locale according to user preference.

  - Use the appropriate character encoding methods.

  - Call standard library routines to display time, numbers, and currency.

  - Enclose user-visible strings in standard messaging routines.

  - Take stock of cultural differences for character display and input.

- Remove from your code any hardcoded dependencies on any one locale.
- Revise documentation to make material easier to translate.

To use a localized version of a product, users set an environment variable or select a locale from a window-system menu. The product then displays user messages in their translated form, and also formats date, time, and currency according to the locale-specific conventions.

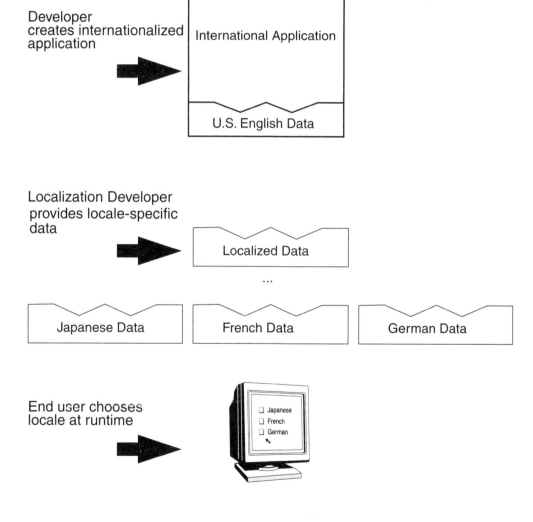

Figure 1-3   Internationalization and Localization Flowchart

1

1.7 Conforming to Standards

Many standards bodies are developing guidelines for internationalized software. Practices described in this book conform to various ANSI, IEEE, ISO, and X/Open™ standards. The following standards bodies provide internationalized programming interfaces:

- ANSI—American National Standards Institute
- ISO—International Organisation for Standardisation
- IEEE—Institute of Electrical and Electronics Engineers
- Open Group—a worldwide UNIX industry consortium

The ANSI/ISO standard for the C programming language specifies many common interfaces for writing international code. ISO has established many standards for coded character sets, and other standards that affect locale naming. The IEEE's standard for portable operating systems (POSIX) specifies some common library interfaces for international code and several administrator and user commands that set or create different locales.

Open Group is in the forefront of setting international standards for UNIX and X Window System vendors. Successive releases of the *X/Open Portability Guide* have established several important new standards for C libraries and interfaces and, more recently, for user commands and administrative utilities.

Where possible, this book recommends practices that have been accepted as standard. If you are interested in more information about the various standards, see Chapter 14, *Standards Organizations*.

1.8 Summary

As computers progress into all sectors of the world economy, the need for locale-specific functionality is increasing. Users today expect an easy-to-use solution; internationalization and localization are necessary steps to meet users' needs.

The main goal of internationalization is to have one executable image that can run anywhere in the world. The internationalized binary should dynamically retrieve locale-specific data and shared objects at runtime. Key concepts to remember when developing applications for the worldwide market are:

- Internationalization represents a paradigm shift—instead of customizing software for specific markets you should create generalized software, which can then be localized for an arbitrary number of markets.

- Standardize where possible; adapt where necessary. There are many standard application programming interfaces (API) available that will help you internationalize your application. If no standard API is available you may be forced to create your own interface for handling localized data.

The international software market has become increasingly important for companies that want to expand their market share. As the world becomes more integrated, users seek ways to find compatibility in computing software across multilingual and multicultural barriers. To remain competitive, developers must enhance their software to suit local styles, standards, and conventions.

The international market is wide open for developers who are willing to make the necessary enhancements to their applications. If you follow the steps outlined in this book, your product will be compatible with all the languages and cultures supported by the Solaris environment.

Understanding Linguistic and Cultural Differences

Suppose you were evaluating software products for preparing reports for your business. One product you are considering has excellent features and price, but it was developed in the (fictional) country of Elbonia for only the Elbonian market. A typical report printed by this product, shown in Figure 2-1, contains numbers, dates, and monetary amounts. You have no control over their style of presentation or the language used. If you had a choice, would you buy this product?

			12/10/96
Pani i Drazlik Vendu op			
at 12 oktub 1996			
Vendo	**Rombla**	**Uro Zinu**	**Tonslo**
Adams	6.45.322	13.48	2.038,83kn ZN
Colinas	1.78.904	15.06	1.05.079,56kn
Chavez	2.89.126	16.56	15.337,75kn
Vu	4.02.007	17.07	259,03kn ZN
Volstad	10.62.998	13.47	10.324,62kn

Figure 2-1   Elbonian Report

As this example illustrates, different countries in the world use different conventions for writing. The language used is the most obvious, but there is considerable variation in styles for expressing dates, times, and numbers, addressing correspondence, conveying ideas via images, and so on. You should not code these conventions directly into your application; instead, an internationalized product in conjunction with localized data should produce the appropriate results.

2

This chapter presents the major areas of variation:

- *Writing system differences*. Each language has a character set and conventions for writing direction, punctuation, and sorting. See *Writing System Differences* on page 14.

- *Formatting differences*. Some writing differences stem not from language, but from cultural conventions. Varying ways of representing times, dates, numbers, and monetary amounts are presented in *Formatting Differences* on page 23.

- *Other cultural differences*. For nonlinguistic issues, such as varying connotations of symbols and colors, see *Other Cultural Differences* on page 27.

Chapters 4 through 6 provide coding practices you can follow to produce software that can handle these differences. Appendix B lists conventions used for specific languages.

2.1 Writing System Differences

The most visually apparent differences between the way people around the world communicate are in the writing systems they use. Variations that arise from languages and the manner in which they are written involve:

- Character sets
- Writing direction
- Word delimiters
- Hyphenation and line breaks
- Punctuation
- Sort order
- Word order in sentences
- Inflections

2.1.1 Character Sets

A *character set* is a set of symbols used in a writing system. (In contrast, a *codeset*, discussed in Chapter 3, is an assignment of a number to each character in a character set.)

Writing systems fall into two categories: *phonetic* systems, which attempt to express sounds, and *ideographic* systems, which express meanings.

2.1.2 Phonetic Writing Systems

The writing systems of most languages are an approximate representation of the sounds of the language. The system uses an *alphabet* if each symbol more or less stands for a fundamental sound, or a *syllabary* if each symbol represents a syllable. For example, the word "ma" is expressed in the Latin alphabet as two letters: "m" and "a." In the Japanese Hiragana syllabary, the one symbol ま represents the syllable. Alphabets typically contain twenty to forty letters; syllabaries may have 100 to 200.

2.1.2.1 European Scripts

Most languages of Western European origin use the Latin alphabet in their written form. Many other countries with no prior writing system have adopted systems based on the Latin alphabet as well. English uses 26 unadorned letters, but other languages use additional letters (for example, "æ") or letters with diacritics, such as "é" or "ü." By contrast, Russian and many other Slavic languages use the Cyrillic alphabet.

The Latin, Cyrillic, Greek, and Armenian alphabets are the only major writing systems that distinguish between uppercase and lowercase. For some languages, there are anomalies when converting between cases. In German, the uppercase equivalent of "ß" is the two-letter sequence "SS". In French (except in Canada), "e", "é", and "ê" have the same uppercase form, "E", so a conversion from lowercase to uppercase and back again may not yield the original string.

Table 2-1 shows the phonetic scripts of Europe and some of the languages that use those scripts.

Table 2-1   European Scripts

Phonetic Script	Language
Latin	English, Spanish, Portuguese, Malay-Indonesian, French, German, Vietnamese, Italian, Turkish, Tagalog, Swahili, Polish, Swedish, Hungarian, Hawaiian, Croatian, Afrikaans, ...
Cyrillic	Russian, Ukrainian, Bulgarian, Serbian, Macedonian, Mongolian, Byelorussian, ...
Greek	Greek
Armenian	Armenian
Georgian	Georgian

2.1.2.2 Middle Eastern Scripts

Arabic and Hebrew use alphabets and are written from right to left. However, numerals are written from left to right; the sentence "We shipped 1,234 units" would be written "stinu 1,234 deppihs eW" if English followed this convention. Languages using the Arabic and Hebrew alphabets are listed in Table 2-2.

Table 2-2   Middle Eastern Scripts

Phonetic Script	Languages
Arabic	Arabic, Urdu, Farsi (Persian), Pashto, Kazakh, Kashmiri, Sindhi, Kirghiz, ...
Hebrew	Hebrew, Yiddish

2.1.2.3 East Asian Phonetic Scripts

Most modern Korean is written using an alphabet. Instead of appearing in a linear sequence, however, the letters making up each syllable are arranged to fit in a square cell.

Japanese uses both ideographic and syllabic characters. Chinese uses only ideographs, except that text for children may use an alphabet as a pronunciation guide. For foreigners, both Japanese and Chinese have Latin alphabet transliteration systems. Table 2-3 shows the phonetic scripts used in East Asia.

Table 2-3   East Asian Phonetic Scripts

Phonetic Script	Language
Hangul	Korean
Hiragana	Japanese
Katakana	Japanese
Bopomofo (Zhuyin)	Chinese
Latin	Japanese (Hyojunshiki and Hepburn transliterations)
Latin	Chinese (Pinyin and Wade-Giles transliterations)

2.1.2.4 Indic Scripts

The Devanagari script, used originally to write Sanskrit, is the script for a few modern languages of India. Other Indic languages use derivatives of Devanagari. The writing systems of most Southeast Asian languages, from Myanmar (Burma) to Cambodia, are more distant derivatives of Devanagari. Indic scripts are listed in Table 2-4.

Table 2-4   Indic Scripts

Phonetic Script	Language
Devanagari	Hindi, Marathi, Nepali, Sanskrit
Bengali	Bengali, Assamese
Gujarati	Gujarati
Gurmukhi	Panjabi
Oriya	Oriya
Telugu	Telugu
Tamil	Tamil
Kannada	Kannada
Malayalam	Malayalam
Sinhalese	Sinhala
Tibetan	Tibetan, Dzongkha
Khmer	Khmer (Cambodian)
Burmese	Burmese
Lao	Lao
Thai	Thai
Javanese	Javanese

2.1.2.5 Context Dependency in Alphabetic Scripts

In some alphabets, letters change their form depending on their context. The Greek letter sigma is "ς" at the end of a word, "σ" elsewhere. Arabic letters have different forms depending on whether they are at the beginning of a word, in the middle, at the end, or in isolation. Thai has vowels that are written before, after, above or below the preceding consonant. There are also diacritics and tone marks that can appear above or below consonants and vowels.

Section 6.6, *Complex Text Languages*, on page 100, discusses many of these issues further.

2.1.3 Ideographic Writing Systems

Some languages use scripts with symbols that do not capture the pronunciation of the language. Instead, each symbol, called an *ideograph* or *ideogram*, generally represents one morpheme. (A morpheme is the smallest unit that has a meaning, be it a word or part of a word; in English, "redevelopment" is composed of the morphemes "re-," "develop," and "-ment." In Chinese, the ideogram 明 represents the morpheme "bright.") The best-known example of an ideographic script is the one developed in China that was adopted by and adapted for other East Asian languages as well. Chinese, Japanese, and Korean currently use this system. Vietnamese used the Chinese writing system until it was supplanted by an alphabetic script (Latin) 150 years ago.

The Chinese ideographic system, called Hanzi in Chinese, Kanji in Japanese, and Hanja in Korean, has tens of thousands of ideographs. In a particular language, say, Japanese, many ideographs with different meanings may have exactly the same pronunciation. Furthermore, one ideograph may be pronounced in several ways, depending on context.

Several hundred characters appear in a smaller, or stylized, form as part of many ideographs. If an ideograph is not a root character, it usually consists of two or more of these so-called *radicals*, two being most common. The character 明, for example, is composed of the two radicals 日, and 月. The analysis of characters into component radicals is the basis of several sorting schemes.

The ideographic scripts of East Asia are enumerated in Table 2-5. Most ideographs have the same form in all of the scripts. Because of various national simplification efforts, however, some characters have different forms in different scripts.

Table 2-5   Ideographic Scripts

Ideographic Script	Language
Hanzi (Traditional)	Chinese (Taiwan)
Hanzi (Simplified)	Chinese (PRC)
Kanji	Japanese
Hanja	Korean

The following subsections note a few characteristics of the writing systems for East Asian languages. Diagrams of keyboards used to input these languages appear in Appendix B, *Locale Summaries and Keyboard Layouts*.

2.1.3.1 Chinese

There are many dialects in Chinese which are mutually incomprehensible. Remarkably, they all make use of the same grammar and writing system. Therefore, speakers of Cantonese and Mandarin who may be unable to converse with each other can communicate perfectly in writing.

The *Traditional Chinese* writing system, used in the Republic of China (Taiwan), uses over 48,000 Hanzi characters, although many are rare. The People's Republic of China (PRC) has over the years simplified and eliminated many of the traditional characters to form *Simplified Chinese*, in which there are about 7,000 commonly used simplified Hanzi characters; emerging standards for Simplified Chinese number Hanzi characters in the tens of thousands.

2.1.3.2 Korean

Although most modern Korean is written using the Hangul alphabet, many Hanja ideographs appear in newspapers as well as academic and government publications. Of the tens of thousands of Hanja characters, everyday Korean uses about 5,000.

2.1.3.3 Japanese

Japanese text consists of three different scripts mixed together: Kanji ideographs derived from Chinese, and two phonetic scripts, Hiragana and Katakana.

Kanji are generally used for the root part of nouns, verbs, and adjectives. Grammatical markers and inflections are written in Hiragana. Katakana is generally used for borrowed words of non-East Asian origin.

There are tens of thousands of Kanji, but the number commonly used has been declining steadily over the years. Computer systems must support more than 10,000 because users require conformance to Japan Industry Standard (JIS) character encodings.

2.1.4 Writing Direction

While the varieties of character sets are the most obvious differences between writing systems, other writing conventions, such as writing direction, vary as well. For example, most languages are written left-to-right in rows from the top to the bottom of the page. However, the Arabic and Hebrew scripts are written from right to left. East Asian languages are traditionally written top-to-bottom in columns from the right side to the left side of the page, although now left-to-right, top-to-bottom is quite common.

2.1.5 Word Delimiters

In many writing systems, words are separated by a space character. In East Asian languages and Thai, however, there is often no delimiter between words. Identifying word boundaries in these languages can require detailed language-specific knowledge.

2.1.6 Hyphenation and Line Breaks

A sentence that is too long to fit on one line must be broken into multiple lines. In many languages, the preferred breaking point is at a word boundary. If that is not satisfactory, a word may be split in the middle, often with a hyphen or other indication after the first part, to denote that the word is continued on the next line.

Hyphenation rules vary from language to language. In Chinese, a line break can occur in the middle of a word, with no hyphen alerting the reader to the split. English allows mid-word splits, usually at syllable boundaries, but not always: most style guides forbid a word like "aboard" to be split into "a-" and "board". In German, hyphenating a word may cause a letter to change. For example, "ck" becomes "k-k", so a word like "necken" is split into "nek-" and "ken."

Special rules often apply to punctuation. In most languages, a line cannot start with a sentence-ending punctuation symbol, a close parenthesis, or a closing quotation mark. If fixed-width text is displayed with justified margins, some conventions allow punctuation symbols to spill into the margin area.

2.1.7 Punctuation

Both the position and the type of punctuation symbols can vary among languages. In Spanish, "¿" and "¡" can appear at the beginnings of sentences, while in Finnish, colons (:) can occur inside words. Greek uses a semicolon (;) at the end of a question. Items in a list are separated by commas (,) in some languages, and semicolons in others.

2.1.8 Sort Order

Conventions for sorting vary widely across languages. Languages may have different rules for collating the same characters. For example, the character "ö" sorts with the ordinary "o" in German, but sorts differently in Swedish, where it is the last letter of the alphabet. Even though "ø" and "ö" are distinct letters in Swedish, they collate together, since "ø" is the Danish and Norwegian equivalent of "ö."

The following subsections present some additional complications. Software solutions to the collation problem are described in Section 4.4, *Collation*, on page 54.

2.1.8.1 One-to-Many and Many-to-One Mappings

In most collating schemes, you can determine the order of two strings by examining them character by character. When you come to the first point of difference, the order of the characters there determines the order of the strings. In English, "head" precedes "heart" because "d" precedes "r."

This method fails for some languages. For sorting purposes German effectively maps the one character "ß" to the two-character string "ss." so the following strings are in ascending order:

> weise
> weiß
> weissagen
> weißen

Vietnamese goes the other way and treats some multiple-character sequences as one character when sorting. The strings "th" and "tr" sort as units after "t," for instance, so these words are in correct order:

> ti
> tu
> thu
> tru

Traditionally, Spanish also used such a many-to-one mapping: the digraph "ch" collated after "c," and "ll" followed "l." However, in 1994 the Association of Spanish Language Academies changed hundreds of years of tradition by voting to treat the digraph "ch" as "c" followed by "h," and "ll" as "l" followed by "l."

2.1.8.2 Multilevel Sorting

Often, differences between some characters are ignored in one phase of sorting, but then used at a secondary level to break ties. An English dictionary ignores uppercase and lowercase distinctions, except to break ties:

> green
> Green
> greenhouse

In French, accented and unaccented forms of a letter sort together initially, and then the accents are considered at a secondary level:

et
étire
étiré
être
étude
eux

2.1.8.3 Sorting Ideographs

Users of phonetic scripts have no problem memorizing the usually arbitrary order of the characters in that script. If a person is to determine order in a script with tens of thousands of ideographs, however, there must be some systematic collating scheme. The two most common schemes are based on the form or the pronunciation of the characters.

A form-based system analyzes the written form of the character. A typical Hanzi ideograph consists of two or more radicals. There are only a few hundred radicals, and rules determine which radical is to be considered the primary radical in the character. All ideographs with the same primary radical sort together. Ties are usually broken by considering the number of strokes needed to write the character.

Another scheme sorts all ideographs with the same pronunciation together. A secondary sort may be based on stroke count. A computer application may need to be able to sort both by form and by pronunciation.

2.1.9 Word Order

The order of words in the written form of a language reflects the order in which they are spoken. In English and Japanese, for example, adjectives precede the nouns they modify; in Spanish and Vietnamese, the adjective generally follows the noun. The basic sentence structure in some languages is subject-verb-object, while in some others it is subject-object-verb. Word order may become an issue if your application programmatically displays end-user messages in the local language.

2.1.10 Inflections

In many languages, words take on different forms depending on their grammatical context. In modern English, the only major inflections are the singular/plural forms of nouns and the few verb forms (play/plays/played/playing). Many languages have inflections based on grammatical case, gender, and number. In some, verbs change form depending on the way the speaker obtained the information conveyed or on the degree of completion of an action. Some languages (including Old English) distinguish nouns as being singular, dual, or plural. There are languages where modifiers may take a dozen different forms, depending on the class of the noun they modify. Inflections are another case in which your application may need to take special precautions when programmatically generating end-user messages.

2.2 Formatting Differences

While many writing differences stem from language, some arise from cultural conventions. This section discusses variations in representing time, date, numbers, currency, and measurements in different locales.

2.2.1 Time Formats

Time can be represented by both a 12-hour clock and a 24-hour clock. The hour and minute separator can be either a period (.) or a colon (:). Some countries attach letters to the time indicating that it is a time, but this is not strictly necessary. Table 2-6 exemplifies some of the ways to express one minute before midnight.

Table 2-6   Time Formats

Country	Format
Canada	23:59
Finland	23.59
Germany	23.59 Uhr
Japan	23時59分
Norway	Kl 23.59
U.K.	11:59 PM

Of course, even within one country, several time formats may be used. Time zone splits can occur between and within countries. A time zone can be described in terms of how many hours it is ahead of or behind Greenwich Mean Time (GMT). Note that this number is not always an integer. For example, Newfoundland is in a time zone that is half an hour different from the adjacent time zone.

Daylight Saving Time (DST) or Summer Time starts and ends on different dates that vary from country to country, and some places do not observe DST at all. A displayed time may have to include an indication about whether DST is in effect.

2.2.2 Date Formats

Table 2-7 shows some of the date formats used around the world. As with time formats, there may be several date format variants in common use within one country.

Table 2-7   Date Formats

Country	Convention	Example
Denmark	dd-mm-yy	13-08-97
Finland	dd.mm.yyyy	13.08.1997
France	dd/mm/yyyy	13/08/1997
Germany	dd.mm.yyyy	13.8.1997
Japan	yyyy年 mm 月dd日	1997年08 月13日
Norway	dd.mm.yy	13.08.97
Sweden	yyyy-mm-dd	1997-08-13
U.K.	dd/mm/yy	13/08/97
U.S.	mm/dd/yy	08/13/97

With a new century upon us, there is potential confusion in a date expressed as 01/02/03. The international date standard ISO 8601, *Representation of Dates and Times*, specifies yyyy-mm-dd or yyyymmdd. A date written this way is unlikely to be misunderstood and has the benefit of being in a form ideal for sorting.

2.2.3 Calendars

A number of variations can occur with calendars.

- The starting point for counting years may differ.

  The Gregorian calendar, which is used in most of the world, starts from the year the early Christian church believed that Jesus was born. The Islamic calendar starts from the year of Hegira, Mohammed's flight from Mecca to Medina. In Japan, years are reckoned by using an era name chosen for each emperor and the year of the emperor's reign. For example, 1996 is the eighth year of the Heisei era, which is the era created when Akihito ascended to the throne in 1989.

- First day of the week may differ.

Canadians and Americans consider Sunday as the first day of the week; Germans and Scandinavians call Monday the first day of the week. You need to be aware of this issue if you want to lay out a calendar properly. In addition, a number of countries list weeks column by column, instead of row by row as in the U.S.

- Number of days and months in a year may differ.

Many cultures use lunar calendars, usually based on 12 lunar cycles. To keep in sync with the solar year, many of these calendars have a schedule of leap days or leap months. For instance, the Gregorian calendar uses a 12-month, 365-day system with 366 days in a leap year. The Islamic calendar has 12 months but only 354 or 355 days. The Hebrew calendar can have either 12 or 13 months. The Iranian national calendar is based on 12 months of fixed length.

Also note that some cultures pay more attention than others to particular properties of a date. In most countries, a person would not be able to tell you what week of the year it is. However, businesses in many northern European companies express dates by week numbering, as in "the beginning of week 37."

Many computer systems support not only the Gregorian calendar, but also calendar variations that are compatible with the Gregorian calendar month and day structure, such as Japanese Emperor Time (since the months, their lengths, and the leap day rule are the same as in the Gregorian calendar). Table 2-8 lists some countries where a non-Gregorian calendar is in common use. Many of these countries use the Gregorian calendar as well.

Table 2-8   Non-Gregorian Calendars

Country	Calendar
Arabic countries	Islamic
China (PRC)	Chinese
Iran	Islamic, Iranian
Israel	Hebrew
Japan	Japanese Emperor
Taiwan	Republic of China, Chinese
Thailand	Buddhist

2.2.4 Numbers

The United Kingdom and the United States are two of the few places in the world that use a period to indicate the decimal place. Many other countries use a comma instead. The decimal separator is also called the *radix* character. The U.K. and U.S. use a comma to separate thousands groups, many other countries use a period, and some countries separate thousands groups with a thin space. Table 2-9 shows some commonly used numeric formats.

Table 2-9   Numeric Conventions

Country	Large Number
Belgium	1.234.567,89
Finland	1 234 567,89
India	12,34,567.89
Japan	1,234,567.89
South Africa	1 234 567.89
U.S.	1,234,567.89

In India, the portions of a number to the left of the thousands are separated in groups of two, not three. Traditionally, Japanese separates not thousands, but ten thousands, so that one million would be written 100,0000. This usage is declining in popularity somewhat.

2.2.5 Currency

Currency units and presentation order vary greatly around the world. Table 2-10 lists monetary formats in some countries. As with time and date formats, one country may use several formats.

Table 2-10   Monetary Conventions

Country	Currency	Example
Canada (English)	Dollar ($)	$1 234.56
Canada (French)	Dollar ($)	1 234.56$
Denmark	Krone (kr)	kr.1.234,56
Finland	Markka (mk)	1.234,56 mk
France	Franc (F)	F1.234,56
Germany	Deutsche Mark (DM)	1.234,56DM
Italy	Lira (L)	L. 1.234,56

Table 2-10   Monetary Conventions

Country	Currency	Example
Japan	Yen (¥)	¥1,234.56
Norway	Krone (kr)	kr 1.234,56
Portugal	Escudo ($)	1.234$56
Spain	Peseta (Pts)	1.234,56Pts
Sweden	Krona (Kr)	1234.56KR
U.K.	Pound (£)	£1,234.56
U.S.	Dollar ($)	$1,234.56

Note that local and international symbols for currency can differ. For example, the designation for the French franc is "F" in France but this is often written as "FRF" internationally to distinguish it from other francs, such as the Swiss franc or the Malagasy franc. International currency designations are specified in ISO 4217, *Codes for the Representation of Currencies and Funds*.

Be aware also that a *converted* currency amount may take up more or less space than the original amount. To illustrate: at exchange rates prevailing in 1996, U.S. $1,000 can become L. 1.507.000.

2.2.6 Measurements

Most countries now use the metric system of measurement. However, the United States, parts of Canada, and the United Kingdom (albeit unofficially) still use the imperial (English) system. The symbols for feet (') and inches (") are not understood in all countries. Remember to convert actual measurements and not just the measurement symbols.

2.3 Other Cultural Differences

Many other differences in locales must be considered: titles and addresses, images, symbols, sounds, colors, product names, and so forth.

2.3.1 Titles and Addresses

Titles like Mr., Miss, Mrs., and Ms. or their equivalent are common in some countries, but are not used in others. In some cultures, though, omitting an honorific like "Dr." is a social blunder.

The order of people's names varies. In some countries, a person's family name comes last (John Smith); in others, it comes first (in the Vietnamese name Dương Quỳnh Liên, "Dương" is the family name, "Liên" the given name, and "Quỳnh" the "middle" name).

Address formats differ from country to country. In many countries, the postal code includes letters as well as numbers and may precede the name of the city. The city name may come before the street address, which in turn may come before the addressee's name. Here are a U.S. and a Russian address:

Mary Smith
11001 Wilshire Boulevard #403
Los Angeles, CA 90024

125036 Москва	city
Улица Кирова 23	street
Квартира 13	apartment
Камаров, В. И.	name

2.3.2 Images

Images are the visual language of a culture. Like words, images don't always translate. What we recognize in our culture may have little or no meaning in another. Graphical interfaces are especially susceptible to this problem.

For example, Figure 2-2 is an icon image of a trash can which was originally employed in the Apple® interface. This was an acceptable user interface image in the U.S.; however, British users indicated it looked much more like a British postal box than a British trash can.

Figure 2-2   Trash Can Icon Recognized in the U.S.

A trash can in Thailand may be recognizable if depicted as a wicker basket with flies, as shown in Figure 2-3.

Figure 2-3   Localized Trash Can Icon

Similarly, Sun Microsystems found that the icon chosen for the SunView™ electronic mail product was problematic. The image in Figure 2-4 was confusing to some urban dwellers even in the U.S. who were unfamiliar with rural American mail boxes.

Figure 2-4   U.S. Rural Mailbox Icon

A number of educational studies have concluded that many images do not convey the same meaning in all cultures. Some users will recognize an image, but they will not associate it with the originally intended concept. For example, a casual choice of a chrysanthemum in an image means nothing special to an American; in France, though, that flower is associated with funerals, and in Japan, with the imperial family.

To succeed in an international market, images must be carefully selected and designed. Designers must be sufficiently aware of differences among cultures to recognize images that are culturally specific and isolate them during the internationalization process. To do this, designers must work with international experts to determine whether images in a product are universally recognized and understood.

What is *comprehensible* to a culture may differ from what is *acceptable*. Because social norms vary greatly among cultures, what is acceptable in one culture can be a gaffe in another. In particular, be careful when designing images that contain religious symbols (such as crosses or stars), representations of the human body, women in any but the most conservative of poses, and almost any hand gesture.

Of course, your design work is simpler if you do not have to use the same image everywhere in the world. In that case, you can use a localized image for each culture.

2.3.3 Symbols

Commonly used symbols in one culture often have no meaning or a different meaning in another. A product using a Red Cross icon for help would not be acceptable in Islamic countries, where a red crescent would be more appropriate An "**X**" as a prohibitive symbol is not recognized as such in Egypt.

2.3.4 Sounds

While laughter is universally recognized, some sounds are not. Sirens in Italy don't wail like those in the United States. The hoot of an owl may connote nighttime in some cultures, death in others. A voice used to give certain instructions is expected to be female in some countries; in other countries, it should be male, while for many it doesn't matter.

Many computer programs emit an audible signal if a user makes an error. In some cultures, this may cause embarrassment. A Japanese user whose computer beeps frequently in an office environment may feel that other workers will doubt his or her competence.

2.3.5 Colors

The interpretation of color varies significantly across cultures (see Table 2-11). For instance, red in the United States means danger; in China, it means happiness. Similarly, yellow in the United States means cowardice, but in Egypt, it means prosperity. If developers choose to use colors to convey information to users (say, *red* error messages or *yellow* warning messages), the colors must be appropriately translated during the localization process. Table 2-11 summarizes some cultural associations of color. While the table oversimplifies matters somewhat, the point remains that color associations are by no means universal.

Table 2-11   Some Cultural Associations of Color[1]

	Red	**Blue**	**Green**	**Yellow**	**White**
U.S.	danger	masculinity solidity	safety	cowardice	purity
France	aristocracy	freedom peace	criminality	transience	neutrality
Egypt	death	virtue faith truth	fertility strength	happiness prosperity	joy

Table 2-11   Some Cultural Associations of Color[1]

	Red	**Blue**	**Green**	**Yellow**	**White**
India	life creativity		prosperity fertility	success	death purity
Japan	anger danger	villainy	future youth energy	grace nobility	death
China	happiness	heavens clouds	Ming dynasty heavens clouds	birth wealth power	death purity

1. *from* Russo, Patricia, and Stephen Boor, "How Fluent is Your Interface?" 1993, *ACM Computer Human Interface Proceedings*.

2.3.6 Product Names

A common oversight when planning products for an international market is choosing product names that do not translate well in other cultures. For example, Rolls Royce planned to name one of their new cars the "Silver Mist" until someone pointed out that "Mist" in German means manure. The oil company Enco changed its name to Exxon because "enko" in Japanese means "engine trouble". A product could fail because its name fails to consider the language idioms and the cultural context of the target market.

2.3.7 Paper Sizes

In each country, most text is printed on paper cut to one of a few standard sizes. Most countries use ISO standard sizes, the U.S., Canada, and Latin America being notable exceptions. Section 6.5, *Paper Sizes*, on page 100 discusses this in more detail.

2.3.8 Keyboard Differences

Keyboards in one country may have characters that are not present on keyboards in another. The positions of keys may also vary. See Appendix B for illustrations of different keyboard layouts.

2

2.4 Summary

Internationalized software should avoid implicit cultural assumptions. Instead, it should look up localized data at runtime. In the following list of areas of cultural variation that we have discussed, we note where in this book you can learn about the standard interfaces for accessing this localized data. Unfortunately, standard interfaces don't exist for all areas; in those cases, you will have to invent your own methods.

Be careful not to embed assumptions about these conventions in your code, at the risk of limiting your potential market:

- Character sets (see Chapter 3, *Encoding Character Sets*)
- Writing direction
- Word delimiters
- Hyphenation and line breaks
- Punctuation
- Sort order (see Section 4.4, *Collation*, on page 54)
- Word order (see Section 5.4.5, *Use Dynamic Messaging with Care*, on page 86)
- Inflections
- Time and date formats (see Section 4.3.1, *Time and Date Formats*, on page 52)
- Calendars
- Currency and numbers (see Section 4.3.2, *Monetary and Numeric Formats*, on page 53)
- Measurements
- Titles and addresses
- Images and symbols
- Sounds
- Colors
- Product names
- Paper sizes
- Keyboard layouts

Encoding Character Sets 3

Recall that a *character set* is a set of symbols in a writing system and that different writing systems contain different numbers of symbols. A *codeset* is an assignment of a numeric value to each symbol in the character set. A codeset is also referred to as a *coded character set*.

This chapter surveys the codesets you will encounter the most on a Solaris system. Topic areas include:

- **Codesets for alphabetic writing systems**. Alphabetic writing systems use relatively small character sets. Each character can be coded by using one byte. See *Single Byte Codesets* below.

- **Codesets for ideographic writing systems**. Ideographic writing systems, common for East Asian languages, contain thousands of characters. Most characters must be encoded using more than one byte. See *Multiple Byte Codesets* on page 36.

- **Universal codesets**. Many problems with processing multilingual text can be reduced if one codeset represents all scripts. See *Universal Codesets—Unicode and ISO 10646* on page 41.

Notice that we follow the common modern convention of assuming that the word *byte* denotes an 8-bit byte. Some documents use the word *octet* for this meaning.

Before you can even consider supporting multiple byte codesets, your application must correctly handle single byte codesets, so we examine them first.

3.1 Single Byte Codesets

One of the most widely used codesets is ASCII. Many developers in English-speaking areas have acquired some thought patterns that stem from using the ASCII codeset: only 7 bits of a byte contain a text character, the lowercase letters range from "a" to "z," and so forth. These properties do not hold true in most other codesets.

3

Since ASCII maps characters into the range 0 through 127, only seven bits of a byte are needed for a code. Many a programmer striving for compactness has packed other information into the most significant bit of each text byte. This practice is not possible in any other commonly used codeset, since they use all eight bits for code values.

ASCII is not the only codeset used for U.S. English. The U.S. EBCDIC codeset maps characters into the 0 through 255 range. Unlike ASCII, adjacent characters in the English alphabet may not map to consecutive codes.

Recall that a codeset is an assignment of a numeric value to each character of a character set. If the codes fall in the range 0 through 255, then each will fit in a single 8-bit byte.

The ISO 8859 series of standards extends ASCII to support alphabetic languages other than U.S. English. Each code in these codesets fits in a single byte. Table 3-1 shows the ISO 8859 standards and the languages whose scripts they encode.

Table 3-1   *Single Byte ISO Codesets*

Standard	Languages Covered in Addition to English
ISO 8859-1	Western European - Danish, Dutch, Faeroese, Finnish, French, German, Icelandic, Italian, Norwegian, Portuguese, Spanish, Swedish
ISO 8859-2	Eastern European - Albanian, Czechoslovakian, German, Hungarian, Polish, Rumanian, Croatian, Slovene
ISO 8859-3	Southeastern European - Afrikaans, Catalan, Dutch, Esperanto, German, Italian, Maltese, Spanish, Turkish
ISO 8859-4	(superseded by ISO 8859-10) Northern European - Danish, Estonian, Finnish, German, Greenlandic, Lappish, Latvian, Lithuanian, Norwegian, Swedish
ISO 8859-5	Eastern European (Cyrillic based) - Bulgarian, Byelorussian, Macedonian, Russian, Serbian, Ukrainian
ISO 8859-6	Arabic
ISO 8859-7	Greek
ISO 8859-8	Hebrew
ISO 8859-9	Western European (plus Turkish, minus Icelandic) - Danish, Dutch, Faeroese, Finnish, French, German, Italian, Norwegian, Portuguese, Spanish, Swedish, Turkish
ISO 8859-10	Northern European (plus Faeroese and Icelandic) - Danish, Estonian, Faeroese, Finnish, German, Greenlandic, Icelandic, Lappish, Latvian, Lithuanian, Norwegian, Swedish

Table 3-1   Single Byte ISO Codesets

Standard	Languages Covered in Addition to English
ISO 8859-11	(proposed) Thai
ISO 8859-12	(proposed) Celtic
ISO 8859-13	(proposed) Pacific Rim

In each of these single byte codesets, an ASCII character is encoded by a byte whose most significant bit is 0, and whose seven low-order bits are the same as the ASCII encoding for that character. Those characters not in the ASCII set are assigned codes with 1 as the most significant bit.

Because of Western Europe's economic and technological leadership, the standard encoding for its languages is the most widely used of the ISO 8859 series. For example, by default, newer PROM monitors, OpenWindows, and CDE provide fonts for ISO 8859-1. Table 3-2 shows the non-ASCII characters included in ISO 8859-1. The code A0 represents a nonbreaking space, and AD encodes a soft hyphen.

Table 3-2   Non-ASCII Characters in ISO 8859-1

	A	B	C	D	E	F
0	NBSP	°	À	Ð	à	ð
1	¡	■	Á	Ñ	á	ñ
2	¢	²	Â	Ò	â	ò
3	£	³	Ã	Ó	ã	ó
4	¤	´	Ä	Ô	ä	ô
5	¥	µ	Å	Õ	å	õ
6	¦	¶	Æ	Ö	æ	ö
7	§	·	Ç	×	ç	÷
8	¨	¸	È	Ø	è	ø
9	©	¹	É	Ù	é	ù
A	ª	º	Ê	Ú	ê	ú
B	«	»	Ë	Û	ë	û
C	¬	¼	Ì	Ü	ì	ü
D	SHY	½	Í	Ý	í	ý
E	®	¾	Î	Þ	î	þ
F	¯	¿	Ï	ß	ï	ÿ

3

3.2 Multiple Byte Codesets

The nonalphabetic scripts used in East Asia have tens of thousands of characters, far too many to map to a single byte. Consequently, Chinese, Japanese, and Korean all require *multibyte* codesets for language processing. Several codesets are in common use for each language. We will first look at encodings in general and then examine Extended UNIX Code (EUC).

3.2.1 Multibyte Strings and Wide Character Strings

Because one character may be represented by more than one byte, be careful in the following discussion to distinguish between the words *character*, which denotes an element of some writing system, and *byte*, which is an 8-bit unit of storage. Note that despite the name, the C language type char is the same as a byte for our purposes.

The C standard provides two ways for representing strings. One is as an array of chars terminated by a null byte. Each character in the string is encoded as a sequence of one or more bytes. This is the *multibyte* representation. Many multibyte encodings are variable-length, so that different characters may be encoded as byte sequences of different length. Notice that despite the name, single byte codesets as we have used them are also multibyte representations, where each code happens to be one byte long.

A string may also be represented as an array of *wide characters*. Several standard headers define the type wchar_t, which is a fixed-size integer type large enough to hold any code value in any supported codeset. In Solaris 2.x, each wide character is four bytes long; in many other systems, a wide character is two bytes. A wide character string is terminated by a null wide character. Standard C supports wide character constants (such as
L'\0'
) and wide character strings (L"Hello"). Figure 3-1 shows the same Japanese string represented in both a multibyte and a wide character form.

Creating Worldwide Software

7 月 1 4 日

37	B7	EE	31	34	C6	FC	00

Multibyte representation

7 月 1 4 日

00	00	00	37	30	00	1B	EE	00	00	00	31	00	00	00	34	30	00	23	7C	00	00	00	00

Wide character representation

Figure 3-1   Multibyte and Wide Character Representations

Why are there two ways to encode a string? Multibyte strings are the more visible representation. They are used for data stored in files or sent to other processes, for file names, and system names. Output devices expect multibyte strings; input methods deliver multibyte strings to a program. If you simply read strings, do minimal processing on them, and write them out, then you should be able to use only the multibyte representation. Multibyte codes are also called *file codes*.

Because multibyte encodings can be variable length, intensive text processing can be difficult to program. Tasks such as editing and parsing are often easier if each character occupies one element of an array. For these jobs, you convert a multibyte string to wide character format (using a library routine), do the processing on the wide character representation, and then convert the result back when needed. Wide character codes are also called *process codes*.

Some text processing tasks may not be apparent in your program. Motif's TextField and TextEdit widgets, for example, allow a user to edit text while entering it. Motif library code does the processing. Section 9.3, *Character Encoding and Text Formats,* on page 132, explains that you can create the widget as a wide character widget for better performance.

3.2.2 Extended UNIX Code (EUC)

Solaris has adopted EUC from AT&T's Multi-National Language Supplement (MNLS). Four EUCs for multibyte codesets are currently supported: Japanese EUC, Korean EUC, Simplified Chinese EUC, and Traditional Chinese EUC.

For each language, EUC consists of four sub-codesets, three of which may be multibyte, and two of which must be announced by 8-bit control codes called single-shift characters. EUC's primary codeset (codeset 0) is used for ASCII. Up to three supplementary codesets (codesets 1, 2, and 3) are assigned to different codesets in each of the four supported East Asian locales. (For this discussion, a *locale* consists of those aspects of the runtime environment of a program that determine the linguistically sensitive behavior of that program.) For example, the Japanese locale using EUC assigns the supplemental codesets to the Japanese Industrial Standard codesets JIS X 208, JIS X 201, and JIS X 212.

Codeset 0 is single byte, with the most significant bit set to zero. The supplementary codesets can be single- or multibyte, with the most significant bit set to one. Codesets 2 and 3 have a preceding single-shift character, known as SS2 and SS3 respectively, where SS2 = 0x8E (10001110) and SS3 = 0x8F (10001111). There is no SS1.

Differentiating among codesets is done as follows: If the most significant bit is 0, the codeset is ASCII. If the most significant bit is 1, the byte is checked for SS2 or SS3 to determine codeset. The length (in bytes) of characters from that codeset is retrieved from a database governing character classification associated with the particular version of EUC.

Table 3-3 summarizes the preceding information.

Table 3-3   Representation of EUC Codesets

Codeset	EUC Representation
0	0xxxxxxx
1	1xxxxxxx *or*
	1xxxxxxx 1xxxxxxx *or*
	1xxxxxxx 1xxxxxxx 1xxxxxxx
2	SS2 1xxxxxxx *or*
	SS2 1xxxxxxx 1xxxxxxx *or*
	SS2 1xxxxxxx 1xxxxxxx 1xxxxxxx
3	SS3 1xxxxxxx *or*
	SS3 1xxxxxxx 1xxxxxxx *or*
	SS3 1xxxxxxx 1xxxxxxx 1xxxxxxx

Whether codesets 1, 2, and 3 are single byte, double byte, or triple byte depends on the locale. Codeset 1 could be used to represent ISO Latin-1, but this is not the usual practice in East Asian locales.

EUC divides the codeset space into graphic and control characters. Graphic characters are those that can be displayed. Special characters include control characters, unassigned characters, and the space and delete characters. Control characters are characters other than graphic characters, whose occurrence may initiate, modify, or stop a control operation. Table 3-4 indicates the single byte special characters.

Table 3-4   EUC Special Characters

Special Character	EUC Representation
Space	00100000
Delete	01111111
Control codes (Primary)	000xxxxx
Control codes (Supplementary)	100xxxxx

SS2 and SS3 are examples of supplementary control codes.

The particular EUC encodings for the four supported East Asian scripts are detailed in Table 3-5. The supplementary codesets are filled with codes derived from various national standards.

Table 3-5   East Asian EUC Encodings

EUC Definition for Japanese Solaris		
Codeset	**EUC Representation**	**Assigned Codeset**
0	0xxxxxxx	ASCII
1	1xxxxxxx 1xxxxxxx	JIS X 208 (Kanji, Hiragana, Katakana, Latin, Cyrillic, graphic)
2	10001110 1xxxxxxx	JIS X 201 (half-size Katakana)
3	10001111 1xxxxxxx 1xxxxxxx	JIS X 212 (less common Kanji)

EUC Definition for Korean Solaris		
Codeset	**EUC Representation**	**Assigned Codeset**
0	0xxxxxxx	ASCII
1	1xxxxxxx 1xxxxxxx	KSC 5601 (Hanja, Hangul, Latin, Cyrillic, graphic)
2	10001110 1xxxxxxx	not used
3	10001111 1xxxxxxx	not used

Table 3-5   East Asian EUC Encodings

EUC Definition for Simplified Chinese Solaris

Codeset	EUC Representation	Assigned Codeset
0	0xxxxxxx	ASCII
1	1xxxxxxx 1xxxxxxx	GB 2312 (Hanzi, Latin, Cyrillic, graphic)
2	10001110 1xxxxxxx	not used
3	10001111 1xxxxxxx	not used

EUC Definition for Traditional Chinese Solaris

Codeset	EUC Representation	Assigned Codeset
0	0xxxxxxx	ASCII
1	1xxxxxxx 1xxxxxxx	CNS 11643-86 (Hanzi, graphic)
2	10001110 1xxxxxxx 1xxxxxxx 1xxxxxxx	CNS 11643-86 (less common Hanzi)
3	10001111 1xxxxxxx	not used

The wide character type wchar_t is four bytes long in Solaris 2.x. The mapping from multibyte EUC to wide character form is not the same in every Solaris release. This is not usually a problem, since wide characters are designed for convenient internal processing by an application and are not written to external files.

Use the dumpcs(1) command if you want to see the multibyte or wide character code values assigned to each character in the current locale.

Remember that the characters represented by a multibyte or wide character string depend on the current locale. For example, the two-byte sequence F6 DF represents the two-character sequence "öß'" in the German locale (which uses ISO Latin-1). In each of the four locales using East Asian EUCs, the sequence represents one character and, in fact, a different character in each locale. This means that with EUC, there is no easy way to process data in a mixture of languages, such as German and Chinese.

Non-UNIX personal computers generally do not use EUC. Encoding schemes like PC-Kanji (or Shift-JIS) for Japanese, Big 5 for Traditional Chinese, and Johap for Korean are more common. These schemes do not have some of the properties of EUC. For example, in these systems, a byte with 0 as the most significant bit may not necessarily represent an ASCII character; instead, it may be the second byte of a multibyte character.

The problems of inconsistent encodings for one language and inconsistent encodings between languages spurred work on a universal codeset, one that would encode all the world's characters in one codeset.

3.3 Universal Codesets—Unicode and ISO 10646

Work on the universal codeset known as Unicode began in 1989, resulting in the formation of the Unicode Consortium and the publication in 1991 and 1992 of the two-volume work *The Unicode Standard*. Unicode was merged with ISO 10646, the ISO universal codeset standard, producing Unicode 1.1. Further revisions resulted in Unicode 2.0 in 1996. You can visit the Unicode Consortium on the Web at http://unicode.org.

Unicode remedies several serious problems in multilingual computer programming: the overloading of fonts to encode character semantics, the use of inconsistent character encodings based on conflicting national standards, and the complexity involved in codeset switching and announcement mechanisms. However, Unicode causes another problem: ASCII and ISO Latin-1 files are instantly twice as large and are incompatible with older files.

3.3.1 Universal Codeset Support in Solaris

To permit backward compatibility with existing applications and file systems, Solaris 2.6 and later support a UNIX file-system safe transmission format for Unicode called UTF-8. The ISO 10646 standard includes an annex describing UTF (Unicode Transmission Format), which is optional, not normative. UTF is a variable-length encoding scheme in which characters in the ASCII set are represented in one byte. UTF is not file-system safe, since one byte of a multibyte character might be the code for "/", the pathname separator character. UTF-8 encodes characters in a file-system safe way, so it is sometimes called FSS-UTF. Internet RFC 2044 is an easily accessible specification of UTF-8.

Table 3-6 illustrates the UTF-8 encoding scheme. Specifically, UTF-8 encodes ISO 10646 values in the range 0 to 7FFFFFFF (hex), using multibyte characters of lengths 1, 2, 3, 4, 5, and 6 bytes. For all encodings of more than a single byte, the initial byte determines the number of bytes used, and the most significant bit in each byte is set. Every byte that does not start 10vvvvvv is the start of a character sequence. Note that the number of high-order 1 bits in the initial byte signifies the number of bytes in the multibyte character.

Table 3-6   UTF-8 Multibyte Encoding Scheme

Bytes	Bits	Hex Min	Hex Max	Byte Sequence in Binary
1	7	00000000	0000007F	0vvvvvvv
2	11	00000080	000007FF	110vvvvv 10vvvvvv
3	16	00000800	0000FFFF	1110vvvv 10vvvvvv 10vvvvvv
4	21	00010000	001FFFFF	11110vvv 10vvvvvv 10vvvvvv 10vvvvvv
5	26	00200000	03FFFFFF	111110vv 10vvvvvv 10vvvvvv 10vvvvvv 10vvvvvv
6	31	04000000	7FFFFFFF	1111110v 10vvvvvv 10vvvvvv 10vvvvvv 10vvvvvv 10vvvvvv

The Unicode value is simply the concatenation of the v bits in the multibyte encoding. The bits column indicates how many v bits are involved. When there are multiple ways to encode a value, for example, code point 0, only the shortest encoding is legal.

Under UTF-8, files containing nothing but ASCII remain the same size as before. Files containing characters in any of the ISO 8859 codesets, including Arabic, Cyrillic, Greek, and Hebrew, require two bytes for those characters. All other scripts, including most of those used in Asia, require three bytes currently.

The main goal of UTF-8 support is to provide existing applications with a method to represent and display multiscript text.

Starting with Solaris 2.6, an additional set of locales that use the UTF-8 encoding will be introduced. These locales will be identical to the current locales except that they will be defined with the UTF-8 encoding. Using these locales, users will be able to include the full range of Unicode characters in their applications and files. Library functions such as mbstowcs(3) and wcstombs(3) will convert strings between UTF-8 multibyte and wide character forms.

The window system will be updated to be able to display the UTF-8 multiscript text. The system libraries' multibyte handling routines will be modified to handle the UTF-8 encoding. Once these steps are performed, all current multibyte-capable, wchar_t-based applications (including system utilities) will be able to process UTF-8 text. Additionally, conversion utilities and library functions that convert between the EUC of existing locales and the new UTF-8 encoding will be provided.

The result will be Western European, East Asian, and Eastern European locales that can share data without requiring codeset conversion. Furthermore, Unicode and UTF-8 support will pave the way for the implementation of new locales to serve emerging markets.

3.4 Summary

The variety of languages in the world has led to a variety of encodings for the characters used by those languages. We have examined these aspects of encoding in this chapter:

- The ASCII codeset uses seven bits per character.
- The ISO 8859 series extends ASCII to encode many alphabetic scripts using eight bits per character.
- The ideographic scripts of East Asian languages require more than one byte per character.
- Multibyte strings are `char` arrays. A sequence of one or more bytes encodes each character in the language. The length of the sequence may be different for different characters.
- Wide character strings are arrays of elements of type `wchar_t`. One `wchar_t` element can hold the encoding of any character in the language.
- Since each wide character is the same size, you can perform intensive text processing tasks more easily on wide character strings than on multibyte strings.
- The same sequence of bytes may be the encoding of different characters in different locales.
- Unicode and ISO 10646 define one codeset that encodes almost all of the world's characters.

Now that we have looked at linguistic and cultural differences in Chapter 2 and encoding systems in Chapter 3, we can begin in the following chapters to explore how internationalized software can address these issues.

Establishing Your Locale
Environment

The previous chapters introduced many of the areas of difference among the languages and cultures of the world. How can you write programs that accommodate these differences? This chapter describes some specific steps that you should take to internationalize your applications. Topics covered include:

- *Locales*. A locale models the conventions used by a language and territory. See *Locales* below.

- *Enabling locale-specific behavior*. Your program needs to take explicit action to become aware of the user's preferred locale. See *How to Make Your Program Locale Aware* on page 50.

- *Formats*. Facets of a locale affect the formatting of times, dates, monetary amounts and numbers. See *Formats* on page 52.

- *Sorting*. Alphabetic ordering varies by locale. See *Collation* on page 54.

- *Character classification*. Many algorithms need to classify characters as being digits, uppercase or lowercase letters, etc. For the standard classification functions to use, see *Character Classification* on page 61.

- *Codeset independence*. The same language may be encoded using different codesets. To write applications that do not depend on the particular codeset used, see *Codeset Independence (CSI)* on page 63.

- *Limitations on characters used for Solaris objects*. Some objects known to the operating system must be named by using a limited character set. See *Solaris Object Naming Rules* on page 68.

4.1 Locales

The key concept for internationalized application programs is that of a program's *locale*. The locale is an explicit model and definition of a cultural convention and native-language environment. The notion of a locale is explicitly defined and included in the library definitions of the ANSI/ISO C and C++ language standards and thus the X/Open CAE specifications. You can reference POSIX P1003.2 or the X/Open Portability Guide, Issue 4 (XPG4), for further information on locale as defined in a UNIX system.

4.1.1 Locale Naming Conventions

According to the XPG4 convention, a locale name takes the form:

language_territory.codeset@modifier

An installation may allow any of *_territory*, *.codeset*, and *@modifier* to be omitted. In Solaris, the language names are represented by the two lowercase letters defined by ISO 639 (Appendix A has a list). Territory names are represented by the two uppercase letters defined by ISO 3166 (again, see Appendix A). There is no standard for naming the codeset or modifier.

The codeset field indicates how characters are to be encoded. (Chapter 3 discussed encoding.) No Solaris locales use the modifier field, but its intent is to enable support for locales that differ in ways other than those implied by the other three fields.

As an example of a locale name, English as used in the U.S. represented in ASCII could be en_US.ASCII. Swiss German using ISO 8859-1 as the codeset for representing characters could be de_CH.iso8859-1. Since the codeset of choice for Western European languages is ISO 8859-1, your installation could allow de_CH to be used as well. Often, only the language code need be given if the territory is that in which the language originated. For example, de could be the name of the locale for German as used in Germany.

Solaris follows the XPG4 convention but does not allow every combination of present or absent locale name elements. For example, fr is valid for French, but fr_FR is not. British English is en_GB, not en. Appendix A lists the accepted Solaris locale names.

The standard C language requires that there be a locale named C; the same locale is also called POSIX. All implementations define one locale as the default locale, to be invoked when no environment variables are set or are set to the empty string. Most UNIX systems, including Solaris, use this C locale as the default locale.

The C locale generally follows the conventions of U.S. English. For example, the period (.) is the decimal separator. One of the major differences between the C locale and the U.S. English locale (en_US) is that the string used to represent monetary amounts is the empty string instead of the dollar sign ($).

To find out what locales are installed on your system, run the `locale`(1) command with the `-a` option. If a locale you want is not listed but is supported by your operating system, you should be able to obtain it from your vendor. When installing packages or a product localized for the locale, you may also need to install the locale itself. In the worst case, you may have to create the locale yourself (see Section 13.3, *Creating a Locale Definition,* on page 198).

4.1.2 Selecting a Locale

Suppose you are an Italian-speaking user. You would normally set the locale once only at login time and never change it. If you log in using `dtlogin` in CDE (Common Desktop Environment), you would select the Italian choice from the Options menu in the login screen (see Section 8.1, *Setting the Locale in CDE,* on page 121 for information about logging in under CDE). Otherwise, you would set the LANG environment variable in your login shell:

```
% setenv LANG it
```

As a typical user, you would put this setting in your `.login` file and probably never think about it again. Nothing you do during any login session would ever motivate you to later change the locale.

If you are a developer of an internationalized application, however, you may very well want to change locales during the course of a login session for test purposes. If you type a command like

```
% setenv LANG fr
```

your locale will be changed to French. This will affect every program you run after this, including the shell itself:

```
% setenv LANG fr
% cat < nonexistentfile
nonexistentfile: Ce fichier ou ce répertoire n'existe pas
```

If instead you want the locale set for only one command, you can use the env(1) command:

```
% echo $LANG
en_US
% env LANG=fr date
lundi, 14 juillet 1997, 12:34:56 PDT
% echo $LANG
en_US
```

Here, the date(1) command was run in the fr locale, with no permanent effect on the LANG variable.

A common problem is to run an application in a locale without having all the resources, such as fonts, that the application needs for that locale. The following example illustrates a related error. A cmdtool window started up in an English locale will not display Japanese characters, because the Japanese EUC codes for Kanji characters are interpreted as ISO 8859-1 codes:

```
% env LANG=ja date
1997Ç⁻07·î14Æü (·î) 12»p34Ê56ÉÃ PDT
```

The boldface characters in the response are incorrect; they should have been Kanji. See Section 6.2.2, *Fonts for East Asian Languages,* on page 95, for details about this problem.

4.1.3 POSIX Locale Categories

The locale consists of a number of categories for which there are language-dependent formatting or other specifications. A program's locale defines its codesets, date and time formatting conventions, monetary conventions, decimal formatting conventions, and sort (collation) order.

The locale categories are listed in Table 4-1.

Table 4-1   POSIX Locale Categories

Locale Category	Description
LC_CTYPE	Controls the behavior of character handling functions. For example, this category affects the behavior of isalpha().
LC_TIME	Determines date and time formats, including month names, days of the week, and common full and abbreviated representations.
LC_MONETARY	Specifies monetary formats like currency symbol, monetary thousands separator, monetary decimal point, etc.
LC_NUMERIC	Determines the decimal separator (or radix character) and the thousands separator.
LC_COLLATE	Controls sorting order for a locale and string conversions required to attain this ordering.
LC_MESSAGES	Controls the choice of message catalogs (user message translations).

The aspects of a locale controlled by LC_MESSAGES are discussed in Chapter 5, *Messaging for Program Translation*. The remaining categories are the subject of Section 4.3, *Formats,* Section 4.4, *Collation*, and Section 4.5, *Processing Character Data*.

Ordinarily, you set the locale by using the LANG environment variable only. In that case, all of the Table 4-1 categories use that same setting. However, you can override the setting for a category by setting an environment variable whose name is that of that category. For example,

```
% env LANG=zh_TW LC_MESSAGES=C textedit
```

runs the editor in a predominantly Traditional Chinese locale. Chinese text can be entered, and Chinese fonts are available for display. However, button labels, menu items, error texts, and other messages will be the defaults used in the C locale, which means they will be in English. This ability to override by category can be useful when testing an application in a locale whose messages you cannot read.

Setting the `LC_ALL` environment variable overrides `LANG` and all categories. You probably never want to set it: because it is so rarely used, you may forget that you set it and then wonder why setting `LANG` later has no effect on the locale. Table 4-2 summarizes the precedences of the environment variables.

Table 4-2   Locale Environment Variable Precedence

Precedence	Variable
Highest	LC_ALL
Middle	LC_CTYPE
	LC_TIME
	LC_MONETARY
	LC_NUMERIC
	LC_COLLATE
	LC_MESSAGES
Lowest	LANG

4.2 How to Make Your Program Locale Aware

An application begins in the C locale. When a program explicitly sets its locale, usually to the locale determined by environment variables, it enables itself to behave according to the conventions of that locale.

4.2.1 Setting the Locale

The standard C function called `setlocale()` initializes language and cultural conventions:

```
#include <locale.h>
int main() {
  if (setlocale(LC_ALL, "") == NULL)
    fprintf(stderr, "Warning: cannot set locale. Continuing in "
                    "the default locale\n");
  ...
}
```

Use `LC_ALL` as the first argument to set all six locale categories. The empty string argument indicates that the application should set the categories as dictated by the `LANG` and `LC_*` environment variables, using the precedence listed in

Table 4-2. If `setlocale()` fails, it returns a NULL pointer and leaves the locale unchanged. In this example, the call may fail because the user set `LANG` to an unsupported locale name.

Your application can call `setlocale()` with a particular locale category as the first argument, but this is uncommon and generally not useful.

A process has only one locale. If you are writing a multithreaded application, be careful: if one thread sets the locale with `setlocale()`, all threads continue in the new locale.

An application using the X Toolkit Intrinsics does not normally call `setlocale()` directly. Instead, it calls `XtSetLanguageProc()` (see Section 9.2, *Locale Announcement,* on page 131).

4.2.2 Saving and Restoring the Locale

An application may need to change locales temporarily to process data in a different locale. You can save the current locale, change to a new locale, and change back later:

```
#include <locale.h>
#include <string.h>
int main() {
  char *oldlocale;
  . . .
    /* query the old locale */
  oldlocale = strdup(setlocale(LC_ALL, NULL));
    /* change to the C locale */
  setlocale(LC_ALL, "C");
  . . .
    /* restore the old locale */
  setlocale(LC_ALL, oldlocale);
  free(oldlocale);
  . . .
}
```

Despite its name, `setlocale()` called with a NULL pointer as its second argument does not actually set the locale. Instead, it returns a pointer to a string describing the current locale. This string is in static storage, so we duplicate it. (The `strdup()` function is not in the ANSI/ISO C library, but is commonly available; it produces a dynamically allocated duplicate of its string argument.) To change the locale, we pass `setlocale()` either the string `"C"` or the value returned by a previous query call.

4

The text of the string returned by the query is implementation dependent. Under some Solaris releases, for example, if all locale categories have the same value, say, zh_TW, then the string will have that value. If at least one category has a different value, then the string is a /-separated list of the values of the six categories. For example, if LANG=de but LC_MESSAGES=sv, then the string would be de/de/de/de/de/sv. Recognizing this format is useful for debugging, but your programs should not depend on any particular format.

4.3 Formats

As discussed in Chapter 2, many different formats are employed throughout the world to represent date, time, currency, numbers, and units. These formats should not be hardcoded into your program. Instead, programs should call setlocale(), then call the various locale-specific format routines. This leaves format design to localization teams for each locale.

4.3.1 Time and Date Formats

To produce time and date formats valid in many locales, use the strftime() library routine, whose behavior depends on the LC_TIME category. First, get the system time by calling time(), then populate a tm structure by calling localtime(). Pass this structure to strftime(), along with a format for date and time, plus a holding buffer:

```
#include <locale.h>
#include <stdio.h>
#include <time.h>
int main()
{
    time_t    now;
    struct tm *tm;
    char      buf[100];

    setlocale(LC_ALL, "");
    now = time(NULL);
    tm = localtime(&now);
    strftime(buf, sizeof(buf), "%c", tm);
    printf("%s\n", buf);
    return 0;
}
```

The %c format yields the local form of the date and time. Also, %x produces the local date form (numeric), and %X yields the local time form. If you try out the above program, your results will look something like this:

```
% env LANG=de a.out
Di 14 Jul 97, 12:34:56 PST
% env LANG=fr a.out
mar 14 juil 97, 12:34:56 PST
```

4.3.2 Monetary and Numeric Formats

The only way to properly represent monetary amounts using the facilities of Standard C is to laboriously build a string using information extracted from an lconv structure returned by localeconv(). Fortunately, XPG4 standardizes a function analogous to strftime(), named strfmon(), whose behavior depends on the LC_MONETARY category. This program uses strfmon() to format monetary amounts:

```
#include <locale.h>
#include <monetary.h>
#include <stdio.h>
int main()
{
  double cost;
  char   buffer[100];
  setlocale(LC_ALL, "");
  scanf("%lf", &cost);
  strfmon(buffer, sizeof(buffer), "%n\t%i", cost, cost);
  printf("%s\n", buffer);
  return 0;
}
```

As with strftime(), the formatted string is placed in a buffer. The %n format item formats the amount in the locale's national format, and %i uses the international currency code specified in ISO 4217:

```
% echo 12345.678 | env LANG=en_US a.out
$12,345.68       USD12,345.68
% echo 12345,678 | env LANG=sv a.out
12.346 kr        12.346 SEK
```

The behavior of the %f format item for scanf() and printf() is affected by the LC_NUMERIC category. Swedish uses a comma (,) as the radix character and a period (.) as the thousands separator, so scanf() expects a comma where an English speaker would use a period. Be careful here: scanf() in the Swedish locale (or any similar locale) will stop reading upon encountering a period, just as it would stop at a comma in the C locale.

4.4 Collation

Chapter 2 noted that alphabetic ordering varies from one language to another. For example, in Spanish "ñ" immediately follows "n." In German the letter "ß" is collated as if it were "ss." Swedish has additional unique characters "å," "ä," and "ö" following "z." Danish and Norwegian have additional characters "æ," "ø," and "å" following "z."

4.4.1 Ordering Strings—Replace strcmp() with strcoll()

The traditional library routine for comparing strings, strcmp(), remains unchanged. It compares two strings byte by byte, using the byte values to determine the ordering. Even in English, strcmp() places "a" after "Z." This ordering is often unacceptable.

By contrast, the standard library routine strcoll() compares two strings according to the comparison rules for the current locale. In the U.S. English locale, for example, "a" and "A" collate before "b" and "B." Fortunately, strcoll() takes exactly the same parameters and returns the same values as strcmp(). Unfortunately, strcoll() does a lot more work and is consequently slower.

To speed up applications that compare the same strings frequently, use strxfrm() to transform strings into coded arrays of bytes that can be collated correctly with strcmp(). Using this approach, you pay the cost of examining strings according to the locale's collating rules only once per string.

The coded form that strxfrm() uses is implementation dependent. To determine the number of bytes needed for the coded form, call strxfrm() this way:

```
char    sourceString[100];
size_t n;
...
n = strxfrm(NULL, sourceString, 0) + 1; /* "+ 1" for the null byte */
    /* The transformed string will require n bytes */
```

The following program reads lines of standard input into an array, then sorts the array, using qsort() and strcoll():

```
/* strcoll_demo.c */
#include <stdio.h>
#include <stdlib.h>
#include <string.h>
#include <locale.h>
#include <time.h>

struct sortstring {
  char *text;
} strings[50000];
int nstrings = 0;

int compare(const void *vp1, const void *vp2)
{
  const struct sortstring *sp1 = vp1, *sp2 = vp2;
  return strcoll(sp1->text, sp2->text);
}

int main()
{
  char buffer[1000];
  clock_t start;
  setlocale(LC_ALL,"");
  while (fgets(buffer,sizeof(buffer),stdin) != NULL)
    strings[nstrings++].text = strdup(buffer);
  start = clock();
  qsort(strings, nstrings, sizeof(strings[0]), compare);
  printf("%.2f\n", (clock() - start)/(double)CLOCKS_PER_SEC);
  return 0;
}
```

The calls to clock() are for measurement purposes. Sorting and searching are operations where the same string is compared many times. At the expense of space, we may be able to improve running time by transforming each string once only into a form that we can compare by using strcmp(). Differences from the strcoll() version are indicated in boldface:

```
/* strxfrm_demo.c */
#include <stdio.h>
#include <stdlib.h>
#include <string.h>
#include <locale.h>
#include <time.h>

struct sortstring {
  char *text;
  char *codedtext;
} strings[50000];
int nstrings = 0;

int compare(const void *vp1, const void *vp2)
{
  const struct sortstring *sp1 = vp1, *sp2 = vp2;
  return strcmp(sp1->codedtext, sp2->codedtext);
}

int main()
{
  char buffer[1000];
  int k;
  clock_t start;
  setlocale(LC_ALL,"");
  while (fgets(buffer,sizeof(buffer),stdin) != NULL)
    strings[nstrings++].text = strdup(buffer);
  start = clock();
  for (k = 0; k < nstrings; k++)
  { strxfrm(buffer, strings[k].text, sizeof(buffer));
    strings[k].codedtext = strdup(buffer);
  }
  qsort(strings, nstrings, sizeof(strings[0]), compare);
  printf("%.2f\n", (clock() - start)/(double)CLOCKS_PER_SEC);
  return 0;
}
```

Table 4-3 shows the result of running these programs in several locales on the same 25,000-line file.

Table 4-3   Comparison of `strcoll()` and `strxfrm()` Performance

Locale	Output (run time in seconds) of	
	strcoll_demo	strxfrm_demo
en_US	3.76	2.32
de (German)	5,88	2,32
it (Italian)	3,56	2,31

Note that the German and Italian output use a comma as the decimal separator. The initial pass through the data calling `strxfrm()` and `strdup()` pays off.

4.4.2 Searching for Strings

In your zeal to write internationalized code, don't get carried away and use `strcoll()` everywhere you would have used `strcmp()` before. If you are searching for a string in a table, you usually want your program to find a match only if the strings are identical. In most languages, the only way two strings could collate equally is if they are identical. If you test either `strcoll()` or `strcmp()` for a zero return value, your program will work.

Swedish, however, is an example of a language where different strings may collate equally. In the Swedish locale, "ø" and "ö" are distinct letters, but collate together. If you were looking up "bø" and used `strcoll()` to compare it against "bö" in a table, your program would consider the strings to match. Had you used `strcmp()`, they would not match, since they are not byte-for-byte identical.

4.5 Processing Character Data

4.5.1 Maintaining Data Integrity

By default, your system should boot up in 8-bit mode, which means that all system interfaces are passing single byte character data intact. If your system is not running in 8-bit mode, simply type the command `stty cs8 -istrip` in a shell or command window; better yet, set this up in a startup file such as your `.profile` or `.cshrc` file.

To process single byte characters correctly within an application, you should follow these coding practices, which we elaborate on in the following sections:

- Make software 8-bit clean.
- Watch for sign extension problems.

You should, of course, test your program with 8-bit non-ASCII characters. Chapter 7 shows how you can input such characters even from a U.S. keyboard.

4.5.1.1 Make Software 8-Bit Clean

Code that explicitly uses the most significant bit of a `char` for its own purposes is said to be 7-bit dirty. Such 7-bit dirty code often involves setting and clearing flags, as shown below:

```
#define INVERSE_VIDEO 0x80               /* bad practice */
char c;
...
c |= INVERSE_VIDEO;
```

Find another way to encode this information. If you want to associate a flag with a particular character, you could declare a structure:

```
struct FlaggedChar {
    char ch;
    char flags;
} c;
...
c.flags |= INVERSE_VIDEO;
```

Alternatively, you could use a data type for c that is longer than a `char` :

```
#define INVERSE_VIDEO 0x8000
unsigned short c;
...
c |= INVERSE_VIDEO;
```

Code that assumes characters are only seven bits long is dirty. Here's an example of masking off the most significant bit on the assumption that it's a parity bit:

```
c = string[i] & 0x7F;                    /* bad practice */
```

A useful exercise is to search your program for constants like 0x80, 0x7f, 0200, 0177, 128, and 127. When you see them, or macros #defined to them, in character-handling code, you almost surely have a problem.

Rewrite code that assumes characters fall in the range 0–127:

```
static int hashtable[128];                    /* bad practice */
```

You need to extend the range of such tables, as shown in the code below:

```
#include <limits.h>
static int hashtable[UCHAR_MAX+1];
```

On all ANSI/ISO C conforming systems, <limits.h> defines UCHAR_MAX as the maximum value of an unsigned character, almost always 255.

4.5.1.2 Watch for Sign Extension Problems

According to the C standard, whether a char is signed or unsigned is implementation dependent. Code that widens a char to other lengths may be 7-bit dirty. For a C compiler that treats the char data type as signed, a char variable that holds an 8-bit character with the most significant bit set will have that bit propagated during assignment. Needless to say, a negative integer might cause problems later on:

```
int i;
char c = 0xA0;
i = c; /* i is now negative */
```

Do not pass a char to a function that specifies a short, int, or long parameter if the parameter is not used simply as a char. This is bad practice because of the sign extension problem. For example, in the following code, the parameter i is initialized to -96, the result of converting ch to an int by sign extension:

```
void f(int i)
{
    int a[1000];
    a[i+50] = 0;      /* negative array index if i is -96 */
}
int main()
{
    char ch = 0xA0;
    f(ch);
    ...
```

Since i could safely be any integer from -50 to 949, we can't resolve the problem by changing its type to char or unsigned char. We must either declare ch to be unsigned char or call the function with a cast:

```
f((unsigned char) ch);
```

It would seem that the sign extension problem could be solved by changing all declarations of unadorned chars to unsigned chars. Unfortunately, the C library declares many functions as accepting char * arguments. The following code fragment will probably cause your compiler to emit a warning about passing an unsigned char * to a char * parameter, even though the function performs the proper action:

```
#include <string.h>
/* <string.h> defines strcpy(char *, const char *); */
int main()
{
    unsigned char s[100];
    strcpy(s,"Hello");
    ...
```

Some C compilers have an option that lets you specify whether or not unadorned chars should be treated as unsigned. Even this solution must be used carefully: code that depends on a char being signed would no longer work. Such a program may use the `char` simply to hold a small signed integer, not a value from some codeset. If the program had been developed under an older C compiler, the `signed char` type would not have been available.

4.5.2 Character Classification

It is a common software practice to process characters according to certain characteristics they possess. It often helps to classify characters, for instance, by whether they are numeric, uppercase, lowercase, white space, or punctuation. Knowing the characteristic or *character classification* can simplify your character processing.

Since different character sets possess different sets of characteristics and each character set can be associated with a different codeset, you cannot make assumptions based on the encoded value. For example, in ASCII, the 26 English lowercase letters map to 26 consecutive code values, so to test whether a character is a lowercase letter, you could do the following:

```
if (c >= 'a' && c <= 'z')/* bad practice */
```

Hardcoding conditional information based on the values of a codeset is bad internationalization programming practice.

In other codesets, such as U.S. EBCDIC, there are nonletter characters with codes between those for "a" and "z." In most languages supported by ISO Latin-1, there are lowercase letters whose codes are outside the range spanned by the codes for "a" and "z." For example, even though "ß" comes between "s" and "t" in the German alphabet, its code value (0xDF) is well after that of "z" (0x7A).

If you `#include` the header `<ctype.h>`, you can use the macros and library routines listed in Table 4-4 to test character properties without hardcoding particular characters.

Table 4-4   Character Test Functions

Function	True if character is a ...
`isalpha(c)`	letter
`isupper(c)`	uppercase letter
`islower(c)`	lowercase letter
`isdigit(c)`	digit from 0–9
`isxdigit(c)`	hexadecimal digit from 0–f

Table 4-4   Character Test Functions (Continued)

Function	True if character is a ...
isalnum(c)	alphanumeric (letter or digit)
isspace(c)	white space character
ispunct(c)	punctuation mark
isprint(c)	printable character
iscntrl(c)	control character
isascii(c)	7-bit character
isgraph(c)	visible character

The right way to test for a lowercase letter is thus:

```
if (islower(c))
```

Be careful. These functions apply only to characters encoded by a single byte. For East Asian languages, you use different functions, such as iswdigit(), which we discuss later in Section 4.5.3, *Codeset Independence (CSI)*.

The two <ctype.h> functions for case conversion are listed in Table 4-5.

Table 4-5   Case Conversion Functions

Function	Converts a character...
toupper(c)	to upper case
tolower(c)	to lower case

Here also there is a pitfall for the unwary. Many programmers expect the toupper() function, for example, to behave like this:

```
if (argument is a lowercase letter)            /* wrong */
  return the uppercase equivalent;
else
  return the argument;
```

In fact, it behaves like this:

```
if (argument is a lowercase letter and
      there is a single byte upper case equivalent)
   return the uppercase equivalent;
else
   return the argument;
```

The uppercase equivalent of the German "ß" is the two-character sequence "SS", so `toupper('ß')` yields `'ß'`. This means that you cannot reliably change a string from lowercase to uppercase simply by applying `toupper()` to each character. There is no standard function for converting a string from one case to another.

4.5.3 Codeset Independence (CSI)

Suppose you wrote a program that is 8-bit clean and correctly uses multibyte strings so that you can handle English, French, Japanese, and Korean by using ISO Latin-1 or an East Asian EUC as appropriate. If your code contains a fragment like this, you may have a portability problem in the future:

```
char s[1000];
char *p;
fgets(s,sizeof(s),stdin);    /* get a line of input */
p = strchr(s,':');           /* find colon */
if (p != NULL)               /* if found, */
   *p = '\0';                /*    replace with null byte */
```

The problem lies with the `strchr()` function: it looks for the first occurrence of the *byte* ':' in the multibyte string s. In EUC codesets, this is fine, since the byte 0x3A (the code for ':') cannot be part of a multibyte character. If you port your program to a system that uses another codeset, this guarantee may not hold (it doesn't for PC-Kanji, for example). Your code depends on a particular property of EUC codesets. If you want your program to be portable to Asian PC systems, you must write it in a codeset-independent manner.

Codeset independence (CSI) can be achieved by making no assumptions about character encodings that are not guaranteed by the C standard. The assumptions guaranteed by the standard are few:

- The null byte 0x00 is not part of any multibyte character; it marks the end of a multibyte string.

- The next character in a multibyte string can be determined by examining no more than MB_CUR_MAX bytes. This macro is defined in <stdlib.h> and is an expression whose value depends on the current locale.

- The worst case value for MB_CUR_MAX is MB_LEN_MAX. This macro is a constant independent of the current locale.

The Standard C library provides functions for converting between multibyte and wide character representations. Amendment 1 to ISO C added a host of wide character string manipulation functions, most of them analogous to the <string.h> functions for char strings, the <stdio.h> functions for character string I/O, and the <ctype.h> functions for character classification.

To access wide character functions , use the header <wchar.h> or <wctype.h>. With releases of Solaris prior to 2.6, you must also link with the libw library by passing the -lw option to the compiler or linker.

The functions whose names start with str in <string.h> (the so-called str*() functions) have analogues whose names start with wcs. The is*() classification functions in <ctype.h> correspond to isw*() functions for wide characters. The wide character I/O routines have the letter w in front of c (for character-based routines) or s (for string-based routines). There are the wsprintf() function for wide character formatting and the wsscanf() function for wide character input interpretation.

If you let the library routines do your text processing, you will be less likely to write codeset-dependent programs. Table 4-6 lists the Solaris 2.x library routines you should use.

Table 4-6   Character Library Routines

Library Routine	Description
Multibyte Handling	
mblen()	Get length of multibyte character
mbtowc()	Convert multibyte to wide character
wctomb()	Convert wide character to multibyte character
mbstowcs()	Convert multibyte string to wide character string
wcstombs()	Convert wide character string to multibyte string
Wide Characters	
wcscat()	Concatenate wide character strings
wcsncat()	Concatenate wide character strings to length *n*

Table 4-6   Character Library Routines (Continued)

Library Routine	Description
wsdup()	Duplicate wide character string
wcscmp()	Compare wide character strings
wcsncmp()	Compare wide character strings to length *n*
wcscpy()	Copy wide character strings
wcsncpy()	Copy wide character strings to length *n*
wcschr()	Find character in wide character string
wcsrchr()	Find character in wide character string from right
wcslen()	Get length of wide character string
wscol()	Return display width of wide character string
wcsspn()	Return span of one wide character string in another
wcscspn()	Return span of one wide character string not in another
wcspbrk()	Return pointer to one wide character string in another
wcstok()	Move token through wide character string
wcswcs()	Find string in wide character string
Wide Formatting	
wsprintf()	Generate wide character string according to format
wsscanf()	Interpret wide character string according to format
Wide Numbers	
wcstol()	Convert wide character string to long integer
wcstoul()	Convert wide character string to unsigned long integer
wcstod()	Convert wide character string to double precision
Wide Strings	
wscasecmp()	Compare wide character strings; ignore case differences
wsncasecmp()	Compare wide character strings to length *n*; ignore case
wcscoll()	Collate wide character strings
wcsxfrm()	Transform wide character string for comparison
Wide Standard I/O	
fgetwc()	Get multibyte char from stream, convert to wide char
getwchar()	Get multibyte char from stdin, convert to wide char

Table 4-6   Character Library Routines (Continued)

Library Routine	Description
fgetws()	Get multibyte string from stream, convert to wide char
getws()	Get multibyte string from stdin, convert to wide char
fputwc()	Convert wide char to multibyte char, put to stream
putwchar()	Convert wide char to multibyte char, put to stdin
fputws()	Convert wide char to multibyte string, put to stream
putws()	Convert wide char to multibyte string, put to stdin
ungetwc()	Push a wide character back into input stream
Wide Ctype	
iswalpha()	Is wide character letter
iswupper()	Is wide character uppercase
iswlower()	Is wide character lowercase
iswdigit()	Is wide character digit
iswxdigit()	Is wide character hex digit
iswalnum()	Is wide character alphanumeric
iswspace()	Is wide character white space
iswpunct()	Is wide character punctuation
iswprint()	Is wide character printable
iswgraph()	Is wide character graphic
iswcntrl()	Is wide character control
iswascii()	Is wide character ASCII
isphonogram()	Is wide character phonogram
isideogram()	Is wide character ideogram
isenglish()	Is Latin alphabet wide char from supplementary codeset
isnumber()	Is wide character digit from supplementary codeset
isspecial()	Is special wide character from supplementary codeset
towupper()	Convert wide character to uppercase
towlower()	Convert wide character to lowercase

The routines in Table 4-7 are specific to EUC encodings. Do not use them if you want to write CSI applications:

Table 4-7   Codeset-Dependent Routines

Library Routine	Description
getwidth()	Get codeset information on EUC and screen width
euclen()	Get EUC byte length
euccol()	Get EUC character display width
eucscol()	Get EUC string display width
csetlen()	Return number of bytes for an EUC codeset
csetcol()	Return columns needed to display EUC codeset

Let us now look at examples of how to use these routines. In the examples that follow, assume the following declarations:

```
char s[100];          /* holds a multibyte string */
wchar_t ws[100];      /* holds a wide character string */
size_t n;
char *p;
wchar_t *wcp;
```

To dynamically allocate a string long enough for a copy of a multibyte string:

```
n = strlen(s);
p = (char *) malloc(n+1);   /* add one byte for the null byte */
```

In no codeset is the null byte allowed except as the end-of-string marker, so strlen() is codeset independent. Notice that malloc() expects to be passed a number of bytes, not characters.

To find the first occurrence of ':' in a multibyte string:

```
p = strchr(s,':');           /* bad practice -- not CSI */
```

Some codesets don't assure you that ':' may not be one byte of a multibyte character. A better way to find the ':' is this:

```
mbstowcs(ws,s,100);        /* convert s to ws */
wcp = wcschr(ws,L':');   /* find wide ':' in ws */
```

(To be even better, this code should check for errors.) The first statement converts the string from multibyte format to the easier-to-process wide character format. The third argument 100 is the maximum number of wide characters to store in ws; we might also have specified it as sizeof(ws)/sizeof(ws[0]). The second statement looks for the wide character constant L':' in ws. What comes next depends on our application. We might do further processing with the wide character string, or we might want to convert some portion of the wide character string back to multibyte format for output.

To output a wide character string in multibyte form:

```
wcstombs(s,ws,sizeof(s)/sizeof(s[0]));     /* convert ws to s */
printf("%s",s);

  or simply

printf("%S",ws);
```

The first way converts the wide character string to multibyte form for ordinary printing with the %s format. The second way uses the %S format item, which expects the corresponding argument to be a pointer to a wide character string. The printf() function writes the sequence of multibyte characters that correspond to the wide characters in the string.

4.5.4 Solaris Object Naming Rules

Not every object in Solaris 2.x can have names composed of arbitrary characters. The names of the following objects must be composed of ASCII characters.

- User name, group name, and passwords
- System name
- Names of printers and special devices
- Names of terminals (/dev/tty*)
- Process ID numbers

- Message queues, semaphores, and shared memory labels
- Shell variables and environment variable names

The following may be composed of ISO Latin-1 or EUC characters:

- File names
- Directory names
- Command names
- Mount points for file systems
- NIS key names and domain names

The names of NFS® (Sun's distributed computing file system) shared files should be composed of ASCII characters. Although files and directories may have names and contents composed of characters from non-ASCII codesets, using only the ASCII codeset allows NFS mounting across any machine, regardless of locale.

4.6 Summary

Here is how an application should establish a locale and properly handle formats and collation:

- Call `setlocale()` to set the locale before doing any locale-specific processing.
  - For a multithreaded process, call `setlocale()` before creating any threads.
  - For a GUI application, call `XtSetLanguageProc()` instead of `setlocale()`.
- Use `strftime()` to format times and dates.
- Use `strfmon()` to format monetary amounts.
- Use `strcoll()` or `strxfrm()`/`strcmp()` to order strings.
- Use `strcmp()` to determine whether two strings are equal.

Messaging for Program Translation 5

One of the most critical tasks in software internationalization is providing messages that can be translated easily. Messages are what users see first: help text, button labels, menu items, usage summaries, error diagnostics, and so forth.

This chapter shows you how to write an application containing messages that can be easily localized. Your program consults an external catalog of messages to determine which strings to display for a user. You provide one message catalog for each locale you support, but there is only one version of the program.

The ease of message localization can vary greatly. In a noninternationalized application, engineers fluent in a language must translate every explicit string that could be seen by a user, then recompile the code. In an internationalized application, a lookup function retrieves any user-visible strings from a message catalog: a text database that is easy to compose, translate, and access.

In a well-designed application, nontechnical people can translate message files into their native languages. Because the contents of a message catalog are separate from application code, text can be selected by locale at runtime without altering the code itself.

5.1 Two Methods of Messaging

Two similar (but incompatible) methods for international messaging in Solaris are `catgets()` from the XPG4 standard and `gettext()` from the POSIX.1b and UniForum proposals. The primary difference between them is the way that messages in the catalog are indexed: in essence, you pass `catgets()` a message number, but you pass `gettext()` a string.

Since there are two messaging schemes to choose between, which should you use? Each has its strengths and weaknesses, and adherents to argue for it. There's a lot to be said for standardization, though. X/Open considered both and chose `catgets()`. For maximal portability of your application to other platforms, then, we recommend that you use `catgets()`.

5

This chapter presents the issues involved with messaging:

- *Messaging using **catgets()***. For the steps involved in enabling messaging using the XPG4 scheme, see *Messaging using catgets()* on page 72.

- *Messaging using **gettext()***. For the steps involved in enabling messaging using the nonstandard scheme, see *Messaging using gettext()* on page 79.

- *Problem areas*. Some common pitfalls are discussed in *Problem Areas* on page 83.

- *Messaging in languages other than C*. If you are writing applications in a language other than C, you can still create and access message catalogs. See *Other Programming Languages* on page 88.

5.2 Messaging Using `catgets()`

When creating internationalized applications, developers usually write text strings (error messages, text for buttons and menus, and so forth) in their native language, for later translation into other languages. Solaris lets you use any language as native.

Here are the steps to internationalize and localize text handling:

1. Change source code to `#include <nl_types.h>`, then call `catopen()` to open a message catalog and call `catgets()` to retrieve strings from the catalog.

2. Extract native language text strings from the `catgets()` calls and store them in a source message catalog. You must assign each message a unique number that will appear in both the source catalog and any `catgets()` call that refers to that message.

3. Translate the strings in the source message catalog into a target language.

4. Transform the translated source message catalog into a binary message catalog, using the `gencat(1)` utility. Install the binary catalog.

Creating Worldwide Software

5.2.1 Locating Message Catalogs

After you have established the locale, you will want to open the appropriate message catalog immediately, so that any startup problems that produce error messages will do so in the proper language. Use `catopen()` for this:

```
#include <locale.h>
#include <nl_types.h>
nl_catd catd;
int main()
{
  (void) setlocale(LC_ALL,"");
  catd = catopen("demo", NL_CAT_LOCALE);
     . . .
}
```

The `catopen()` function looks for the message catalog according to these rules:

1. The locale used is the value of `LC_MESSAGES` as established by `setlocale()`. (The only other choice for `catopen()`'s second argument is 0, meaning that locale used is the value of the `LANG` environment variable.)

2. The first argument and the `NLSPATH` environment variable are used to locate the catalog. (If the first argument contains `/`, `LC_MESSAGES` and `NLSPATH` are ignored, and the first argument is taken to be the absolute path name of the catalog. You almost never want to do this.)

The `NLSPATH` variable is a colon-separated list of filename patterns, for instance:

```
/usr/lib/locale/%L/LC_MESSAGES/%N.cat:/tmp/%N.%L.cat
```

In these patterns, `catopen()` replaces `%N` with its first argument, and `%L` with the prevailing locale. If the locale is set to French, for example, then `catopen()` uses the file named `/usr/lib/locale/fr/LC_MESSAGES/demo.cat` if it exists. Failing that, it will try `/tmp/demo.fr.cat`. The first pattern in this example is the same one that `catopen()` uses if `NLSPATH` is not set. The second pattern is one a developer might use while testing an application's messaging ability.

Although you need not name a message file after its application, this convention is recommended. It simplifies maintenance to have `catopen()`'s first argument be the same as the application name.

The header <nl_types.h> defines the (integral) type nl_catd. The return value of catopen(), a *catalog descriptor*, should be stored in a variable of this type, since it will be passed to every catgets() call that looks up messages in the selected catalog. Because you use this variable throughout a program, declare catd globally.

If catopen() fails, it returns (nl_catd)-1. Of course, a good application should test for this and note the error. However, you can safely pass this failure value in calls to catgets(), which will simply return the default strings you provide instead of the localized strings.

An open catalog consumes system resources: a file descriptor and some memory for indexes into the catalog. When your program exits, these resources are automatically released. If you want to release them explicitly, call catclose():

```
catclose(catd);
```

5.2.2 Use catgets() Function

To retrieve strings from a message catalog, you call catgets(), passing it the catalog descriptor returned by catopen(), an index into the catalog to select the message string, and a default string to use instead if there's a problem. The index is the troublesome part of the catgets() interface, so we'll examine it first.

In essence, to use catgets() you must assign a number to each message your program will produce. This requirement alone accounts for the most noticeable change in appearance between a noninternationalized and an internationalized version of a program. It can also lead to a maintenance headache if these numbers are not well managed. The only support the XPG4 messaging scheme gives you is the ability to partition your messages into sets. You may, for example, decide that the button label "Edit" is message number 37 of set number 4. How many sets you use, and what you use them for, is up to you. On some projects, each developer uses a different set number; on others, each subsystem of an application is given its own set number.

Here is an example of how to use catgets():

```
/* Assume catd is the return value of catopen() */
printf(catgets(catd, 3, 27, "Invoice\n"));
```

If all is well, `catgets()` will retrieve message number 27 of set number 3 from the message catalog referred to by `catd`, returning a `char *` value pointing to the message. If there is no message 27 in set 3, or if there is no set 3, or if `catd` is −1, then `catgets()` returns its last argument, the default string. The intent is that message 27 of set 3 in the catalog is a translation of "Invoice\n"; if the translation is unavailable, the program will use the English "Invoice\n", since that's better than nothing.

Although not true for Solaris, on some platforms `catgets()` returns a pointer to storage that may be overwritten on each call. This implies that for maximal portability, you must use or copy the value returned by one call of `catgets()` before you call it again:

```
char buffer[100];
char *p, *q;
  /*
   * This is not portable:
   */
printf("%s %s", catgets(catd, 1, 1, "Name"),
                catgets(catd, 1, 2, "Age"));
  /*
   * This is not portable either:
   */
p = catgets(catd, 1, 1, "Name");
q = catgets(catd, 1, 2, "Age");
printf("%s %s", p, q);
  /*
   * This is portable, provided buffer is big enough:
   */
strcpy(buffer, catgets(catd, 1, 1, "Name"));
printf("%s %s", buffer, catgets(catd, 1, 2, "Age"));
```

5.2.3 Create the Source Message Catalog

Once you know what your messages are, create a source message catalog for your native language. Suppose the following program fragment shows all the messages some program will produce:

```
printf(catgets(catd, 1, 1, "Hello"));
printf(catgets(catd, 3, 4, "Age: %d\n"), age);
makeButton(catgets(catd, 1, 4, "Quit"));
```

5

XPG4 specifies a format for source message catalogs. For this program, here is a possible English source message catalog:

```
$ This line starts with "$ ", so it is a comment
$ We will use " as a delimiter for strings
$quote "
$ Notice that message numbers need not be in a contiguous range
$set 1
1 "Hello"
4 "Quit"
$ Notice that set numbers need not be in a contiguous range
$set 3
4 "Age: %d\n"
```

After each $set line, list the messages in that set in increasing order of message number. The set groups themselves must also be in ascending order of set number. The header <limits.h> defines NL_SETMAX, the maximum set number allowed; NL_MSGMAX, the maximum message number; and NL_TEXTMAX, the maximum number of bytes in a message text. The gencat(1) manual page specifies the syntax of a source message catalog.

Notice that the English message texts in the source catalog are the same as the default strings in the catgets() calls in the program. This is almost always the case, of course: if the English message catalog cannot be located, then the default messages are the same as if the catalog had been opened successfully.

Whoever translates the messages in your catalog will probably not know the context in which those messages appear. Usually, the translators are not programmers, although you can expect that they have some training and can recognize the common characteristics of message strings. For example, you can assume that in the following, the translators know that %s represents some string:

```
1 "%s cannot be opened."
```

However, you cannot assume the translator knows that the %s above will be replaced by a file name. In some languages, this may be significant, since the word for "opened" may be translated differently depending on whether what can't be opened is a file, a window, or a network connection.

Creating Worldwide Software

To enable good translations, you should include comments in your message catalogs for any strings that might cause difficulty:

```
1 "%s cannot be opened."
$ %s is a file name

2 "Read"
$ This is a past participle, not a present tense verb
```

The genmsg(1) utility for creating source message catalogs became available in Solaris 2.6. This utility examines a source program file for calls to catgets() and builds a source message catalog from the information it finds. Here is an example:

```
% cat example.c
  ...
  /* NOTE: %s is a file name */
  printf(catgets(catd, 5, 1, "%s cannot be opened."));
  /* NOTE: "Read" is a past participle, not a
           present tense verb */
  printf(catgets(catd, 5, 1, "Read"));
  ...
% genmsg -c NOTE example.c
The following file(s) have been created.
        new msg file = "example.c.msg"
% cat example.c.msg
$quote "
$set 5
1       "%s cannot be opened"
  /* NOTE: %s is a file name */
2       "Read"
  /* NOTE: "Read" is a past participle, not a
           present tense verb */
```

Running genmsg on the program source file named example.c produced a source message catalog named example.c.msg. By specifying the -c option with an argument of our choosing (we chose the string NOTE), we caused genmsg to include comments in the catalog. If a comment in the source program contains the string we specified, that comment will appear in the message catalog after the next string extracted from a call to catgets().

You can use genmsg to automatically number the messages within a message set. Refer to the genmsg(1) manual page for more information.

5.2.4 Translate the Source Message Catalog

For each language your application will support, you must have strings in the source message catalog translated to that language. For test purposes, you could change the message texts to a made-up language. Here's an example:

```
$quote "
$set 1
1 "XxxHelloYyy"
4 "XxxQuitYyy"
$set 3
4 "XxxAge: %dYyy\n"
```

These "translations" are readable by a tester who knows only English. The translated strings are longer than the English strings to simulate translation to a language where strings may be of a different length than in English. This lets you test that table alignments won't be messed up, that button labels won't exceed the size of the button, and so forth. Another test file could be English with all the vowels deleted, to see if layouts are affected by shorter strings.

The genmsg(1) utility has options that cause it to automatically transform message strings as it produces a message catalog.

5.2.5 Generate the Binary Message Catalogs

For each translated source catalog, generate a binary message catalog. The binary catalog is the one your application will consult at runtime. Use the XPG4 gencat utility to generate the binary catalog. If your Korean source message catalog is named demo.ko.msg, you would say:

```
% gencat demo.ko.cat demo.ko.msg
```

The second argument is the source catalog, and the first is the binary catalog that will be created. Having successfully produced the binary catalog, you can install it in its final destination (/usr/lib/locale/ko/LC_MESSAGES/demo.cat).

While testing your application, you may not want to install the catalog in its production location; indeed, you may not have the permissions to do so. You can leave the binary catalog wherever you like, since you can set your NLSPATH so that your application can find the catalog. Someone who knows only English and wants to test the demo application in Italian might first "translate" the English source message catalog as in the previous section, and then do the following:

```
% gencat demo.it.cat demo.it.msg
% env LANG=it NLSPATH=/tmp/%N.%L.cat demo
```

Italian locale rules will be used for date formats, collation, and so forth. However, the messages will still be readable by the Italian-illiterate tester, since they will be in English surrounded with "Xxx" and "Yyy", rather than in Italian.

If your application does not seem to be finding the translated messages correctly, as evidenced by your seeing the default strings or the wrong translated strings, consider the following common oversights:

- Did you establish the locale *before* you called catopen()?

- Are your NLSPATH environment variable and the arguments to catopen() right? (For example, if the first argument to catopen() is "demo.cat" and NLSPATH is ./locale/%L/LC_MESSAGES/%N.cat,then catopen() will look for demo.cat.cat.)

- Are your catgets() calls referring to the right set and message numbers? If you added, deleted, or changed message numbers in your catgets() calls but failed to revise, regenerate, and reinstall your message catalog, the numbers may be out of sync.

5.3 Messaging Using **gettext()**

Where catgets() uses numbers to index message catalogs, gettext() uses strings; that is the main difference in their approaches to the messaging problem.

The steps for text handling using gettext() are similar to those for catgets():

1. Change source code to #include <libintl.h>, then call textdomain() to open the message catalog and call gettext() to retrieve strings from the catalog. In releases of Solaris prior to 2.6, the object program must be linked with the -lintl flag.

2. Use the xgettext(1) utility to extract native language text strings from the gettext() calls and store them in a source message catalog.

3. Translate the strings in the source message catalog into a target language.

4. Transform the translated source message catalog into a binary message catalog, using the msgfmt(1) utility. Install the binary catalog.

5.3.1 Locating Message Catalogs

Use textdomain() to open a message catalog. The pathname of gettext() message catalogs must end with *locale*/LC_MESSAGES/*domain*.mo, where *locale* is the current locale—the value of LC_MESSAGES as established by setlocale()—and *domain* is the argument you pass to textdomain().

Unless you call bindtextdomain() to change the domain, the complete path is /usr/lib/locale/*locale*/LC_MESSAGES/*domain*.mo. In fact, this is where Solaris system messages for libraries and utilities that use gettext() reside. The following program fragment opens a message catalog named /usr/lib/locale/*locale*/LC_MESSAGES/demo.mo:

```
#include <locale.h>
#include <libintl.h>
int main()
{
  setlocale(LC_ALL,"");
  textdomain("demo");
  ...
}
```

Many applications do not require root permission for installation and thus cannot place their messages in /usr/lib/locale. Moreover, most applications need messages in their own directory hierarchy to simplify export across a network. So, most applications should use the Solaris routine bindtextdomain() to associate a path name with a message domain. Here's a sample invocation:

```
  char *path;
#ifdef TEST
  path = "/tmp";
#else
  path = getenv("APPLICATIONHOME");
#endif
  bindtextdomain("demo", path);
  textdomain("demo");
```

If you compile the program with TEST defined, then the catalog will be found in /tmp/*locale*/LC_MESSAGES/demo.mo; if TEST is undefined, the catalog will be found in $APPLICATIONHOME/*locale*/LC_MESSAGES/demo.mo.

5.3.2 Surround Strings with `gettext()`

Although it is not portable, `gettext()` is much easier to use than `catgets()`.
All you really have to do is go through your programs, enclosing literal strings
inside `gettext()` calls. Here is `demo.c`, a short example:

```
#include <stdio.h>
#include <locale.h>
#include <libintl.h>
int main()   /* demo.c */
{
   (void) setlocale(LC_ALL, "");
   bindtextdomain("demo", "/tmp");
   textdomain("demo");
   printf(gettext("Hello\n"));
   printf(gettext("Goodbye\n"));
   return 0;
}
```

The first `gettext()` looks in the catalog `/tmp/`*locale*`/LC_MESSAGES/demo.mo`
for the translated string corresponding to the English string `"Hello\n"`. It
returns a pointer to the translated string if it finds it; otherwise, it returns the
index string `"Hello\n"`. You compile the program with

```
% cc demo.c -o demo          (for Solaris 2.6 and later)
                             or
% cc demo.c -o demo -lintl   (for Solaris releases prior to 2.6)
```

You can partition your messages among different domains. When you call
`textdomain()`, you establish the domain used by all calls to `gettext()` until
you next call `textdomain()`. If you want to change domain for just the next call
of `gettext()`, use `dgettext()` instead. This would be appropriate for a library
product, as it is the best way to ensure a known domain. (Library calling
sequence cannot be guaranteed, since different domains may be mixed together at
random.) The library developer chooses the domain name.

5

The following two examples retrieve the same strings but have different effects on the text domain. The first example does not change the current text domain. The second example changes the current text domain to `library_error_strings`, then retrieves the alternate language string of `wrongbutton`.

```
message = dgettext("library_error_strings", "wrongbutton");
```

or

```
textdomain("library_error_strings");
message = gettext("wrongbutton");
```

5.3.3 Create the Source Message Catalog

After writing an application, create a text domain by extracting `gettext()` strings and placing them in a file with the alternate language equivalent.

Once you have enclosed all user-visible strings inside `gettext()` wrappers, you can run the `xgettext` command on your C source files to create a message file. This produces a readable `.po` file (the portable object) for editing by translators. For test purposes, you can use `xgettext`'s `-m` option to simulate a translation by adding a prefix string to each message.

```
% xgettext -m TRNSLT: demo.c
% cat messages.po
domain "demo"
msgid "Hello\n"
msgstr "TRNSLT:Hello\n"
msgid "Goodbye\n"
msgstr "TRNSLT:Goodbye\n"
```

The `domain "`*domainname*`"` line states that all following target strings until another `domain` directive belong to the *domainname* domain. Each `msgid` line contains the index string passed to `gettext()` and is followed by a `msgstr` line containing the translated string. The manual page for `msgfmt(1)` specifies the syntax of the `.po` file.

If you anticipate translators having difficulty translating a message, comment it, using lines starting with #. An effective way to do this is to place comments for the translator into your application source code, then use the `-c` *tag* option of `xgettext(1)` to place these comments into the `.po` file.

5.3.4 Create the Binary Message Catalog

Run `msgfmt` on the `.po` source file to produce a binary `.mo` file (the message object), which should be installed under the `LC_MESSAGES` directory. Here's a sample interaction on `demo.c`:

```
% msgfmt demo.po
% su
Password:
# mv demo.mo /usr/lib/locale/test/LC_MESSAGES
```

5.4 Problem Areas

5.4.1 Don't Overdo Messaging

You should not blindly wrap every string literal in your program in a call to `catgets()` or `gettext()`. In general, you only need to message strings that users see. Do not message strings containing system commands or file names, such as `"sort"` or `"/dev/tty"`. Be careful when messaging strings inside `sprintf()`, which is often used to build up path names or command lines. You probably don't need to message strings used only for debugging. Because integers and decimal numbers are not strings, they don't need messaging, either.

5.4.2 Be Aware of Programming Language Restrictions

Not every context allows you to replace a string literal with a call to a function. Converting the noninternationalized declaration

```
static char *greeting = "Hello";
```

to

```
static char *greeting = catgets(catd,1,1,"Hello");
```

produces an illegal C declaration. One way to fix it is:

```
static char *greeting;
int main()
{
  /* establish locale and open catalog, and then: */
  greeting = catgets(catd,1,1,"Hello");
}
```

If this were a C++ program instead of a C program, the declaration with initialization would be legal. However, you must control the order of initialization of static objects so that greeting is not initialized until after the locale has been established and the message catalog opened.

5.4.3 Prepare for Variations in Text Length and Height

If strings must be stored in an array, be sure to declare arrays large enough to hold any possible translation. Messages in German are often longer than in English; messages in Chinese may be shorter, even accounting for multibyte encoding. A good rule of thumb is that a string might double in length, although very short strings might be even longer in translation (e.g., English "Edit" is German "Bearbeiten"). Use strncpy() to avoid overrunning an array:

```
strncpy(msg, catgets(catd,1,1,"Hello"), sizeof(msg));
```

Displayed characters in translated messages may be of different length and height than the original messages. East Asian language ideographs are usually taller and wider than Roman characters.

Window system resource files specify height and width of panel buttons and such. The AppBuilder and DevGuide tools employ these facilities. In some cases, it's best to use implicit object positioning, letting the window system decide where to place things. See Chapter 9 for more details.

5.4.4 Avoid Compound Messages

Creating easily translated messages is an art form that involves more than just inserting catgets() calls around strings. Remember that word order varies from language to language, so complex messages can be very difficult to translate properly. A common-sense guideline is to avoid compound messages with more than two %s parts whenever possible.

There are two approaches to messaging: *static* and *dynamic*. Static messaging simply involves looking up strings in a message catalog, with no reordering taking place. Dynamic messaging also involves looking up strings in a message catalog, but those strings are reordered and assembled at runtime. International standards provide an ordering extension to `printf()` for implementing dynamic messaging.

The advantage of static messaging is simplicity. Use it whenever possible. However, avoid splitting strings across two `printf()` statements, which makes messages difficult to translate. Remember that the ANSI/ISO C preprocessor will paste together two consecutive string literals into one long literal:

```
    /* bad */
  printf(catgets(catd,1,1,"This is a very, very, very, very "));
  printf(catgets(catd,1,2,"long string that I want to display"));
    /* good */
  printf(catgets(catd,1,1,"This is a very, very, very, very "
                          "long string that I want to display"));
```

Translation problems can arise with compound messages, especially when more than one sentence could be produced at runtime. Here is some code that would be difficult to translate:

```
/* poor practice: multipart compound message */
printf("%s: Unable to %s %d data %s%s - %s",
func, (alloc_flg ? "allocate" : "free"),
count, (file_flg ? "file" : "structure"),
(count == 1 ? "" : "s"), perror("."));
```

Quite apart from being poor programming practice, this fragment of code would be much clearer to the reader and much easier to translate if it were split into separate print statements inside an `if-else` block that would select the correct message at runtime:

```
if (alloc_flg)
    if (file_flg)
        printf("Unable to allocate %d file\n", count);
    else
        printf("Unable to allocate %d structure\n", count);
else
    if (file_flg)
        printf("Unable to free %d file\n", count);
    else
        printf("Unable to free %d structure\n", count);
```

The issue of making the objects plural is not addressed in this example because pluralization in many languages involves more than just adding "s" to the end of a word.

5.4.5 Use Dynamic Messaging with Care

Dynamic messaging is used when the exact content or order of a message is not known until runtime. Unless done carefully, dynamic messaging causes translation problems. If the positional dependence of keywords is hardcoded into a program, code needs to be changed before messages can be successfully translated. Obviously, this defeats the purpose of internationalization.

XPG4 defines an extension to the `printf()` family that permits changing the order of parameter insertion. Solaris also supports this extension. For example, the conversion format `%1$s` inserts parameter one as a string, and `%2$s` inserts parameter two. The entire format string is parameter zero.

Here's a small example of how these extensions can be used. This `printf` statement has position-dependent keywords because the verb must come before the object.

```
/* poor practice: position-dependent keywords */
printf("Unable to %s the %s.\n",
(lock_flg ? "lock" : "find"),
(type_flg ? "page" : "record"));
```

This could produce any of four messages in English:

```
Unable to lock the page.
Unable to find the page.
Unable to lock the record.
Unable to find the record.
```

Here are those four messages translated into German. Note that the verb ("sperren" or "finden") must follow, not precede, the object ("Seite" or "Rekord").

```
Das Programm kann die Seite nicht sperren.
Das Programm kann die Seite nicht finden.
Das Programm kann den Rekord nicht sperren.
Das Programm kann den Rekord nicht finden.
```

German syntax requires different word order, so the program's keywords must be reversed. Here is that `printf` statement written for dynamic messaging:

```
printf(catgets(catd,1,1,"Unable to %s the %s\n"),
    (lock_flg ? catgets(catd,1,2,"lock") :
                catgets(catd,1,3,"find")),
    (type_flg ? catgets(catd,1,4,"page") :
                catgets(catd,1,5,"record")));
```

The German message catalog would then appear as follows:

```
1 "Das Programm kann %2$s nicht %1$s.\n"
2 "sperren"
3 "finden"
4 "die Seite"
5 "den Rekord"
```

This example might not work on other vendors' systems because of multiple `catgets()` calls within one expression.

Consider carefully the effects of dynamic messaging. You might have to reposition parameters during translation. Often this fact isn't recognized until translation actually begins, by which time it's already too late—the software would have to be laboriously rereleased.

5.4.6 Manage Message Indices

When you use the `catgets()` messaging scheme, you must ensure that you don't assign the same set number/message number combination to different messages. This can be a problem in a multiperson project. Here are some guidelines for managing the message numbers.

- Use a different message set number for each subsystem or for each developer. This localizes potential conflicts, making them easier to find and fix.

- Do not change a message number once it has been assigned to a message. If a message is deleted, do not reuse its number. This makes successive versions of a message catalog more consistent. Suppose that a localizer has already translated a source message catalog. If a new version of that catalog arrives for translation, much less work needs to be done if unchanged messages can be quickly identified.

- Use a tool to assign message numbers. An automated process is less likely to assign duplicate numbers than a manual one. The `genmsg(1)` tool that became available in Solaris 2.6 has an option that automatically numbers those messages in each set that have not already been assigned numbers.

- Appoint a central numbering authority. Making one entity responsible for managing message numbers helps ensure that consistent procedures are followed.

5.5 Other Programming Languages

The Desktop Korn Shell, `dtksh`, in CDE has built-in `catopen`, `catgets`, and `catclose` commands. Here is an example:

```
catopen CATD demo
catgets msg1 $CATD 3 7 'Hello there'
catgets - $CATD 3 7 'Hello there'
catclose $CATD
```

Using the `LANG` and `NLSPATH` environment variables and the name `demo` (which will be substituted for `%N` in `NLSPATH`), `catopen` opens the message catalog and sets `CATD` to the catalog ID. The calls to `catgets` look for message 7 of set 3, returning `Hello there` if it can't find it. The message is stored in the variable `msg1` in the first call and written to standard output in the second. The `catclose` command releases the resources acquired by `catopen`.

Solaris provides a gettext(1) command to retrieve translated messages from a catalog for use in shell programming. This command reads the TEXTDOMAIN environment variable for the domain name and the TEXTDOMAINDIR environment variable for the path name to the message database.

At the time of this writing, the Working Paper for the C++ standard specifies a library class messages with member functions open(), get(), and close(). These functions' behaviors are implementation defined, but the interface suggests that the most common implementation will be based on the catgets() scheme.

FORTRAN and Pascal are not normally provided with catgets() or gettext() wrappers, but those could be written if needed.

5.6 Summary

To internationalize and localize text handling in an application, follow these steps:

1. Decide whether you will use the standard catgets() scheme or the nonstandard gettext() scheme.

2. Open the message catalog after establishing the locale.

3. Call catgets() or gettext() to retrieve strings from the catalog.

4. Extract native language text strings to form the source message catalog. Comment those strings that may cause translation difficulty.

5. Translate the strings in the source message catalog into a target language.

6. Transform each translated source message catalog into a binary message catalog.

7. Install the binary message catalogs when you install the application.

Displaying Localized Text 6

In Chapter 4, we saw how to encode and process the characters used by various languages. This chapter examines the issues involved in displaying those characters. Since localized text may be of different sizes in different languages, displaying localized text may affect the layout of your user interface.

For many of your applications, you may find that there is little you need to do within your program to enable the correct display of localized text. Your program's capabilities depend on your system's capabilities. For example, if your system does not support scripts written from right to left, your program will not be able to display Arabic or Hebrew without your building that support from scratch.

In this chapter, we look at these issues:

- *Resource files*. Attributes of your application's display that may vary from one locale to another should be specified in an external resource file, not in the program code. See *Resource Files* on page 92.

- *Fonts*. When you display a text string, an appropriate font must be available to your application. See *Fonts* on page 93.

- *Text display width*. Your output layout may depend on the lengths of strings you display, which will vary from language to language. Your program needs a way to determine these lengths. See *Text Display Width* on page 96.

- *User interface layout*. The size and positioning of buttons and menus should adjust to the size of text they contain. See *User Interface Layout* on page 99.

- *Paper sizes*. Text displayed on paper must fit on the page. See *Paper Sizes* on page 100.

- *Complex text languages*. Correctly rendering text in languages such as Arabic or Thai requires extra support from the system. See *Complex Text Languages* on page 100.

6

6.1 Resource Files

Someone using your application sees the text strings it produces and, in a graphical user interface (GUI) environment, menus, control buttons, icons, and other window objects. These objects have attributes such as size, color, and location. If different locales require different values for these attributes, where do you specify them so they can be localized? Here are some possibilities:

- Code the attribute values in the source program. This requires that separate versions of the source program must be produced for each locale, making our goal of one application binary for all locales unachievable.

- Have users specify attribute values on the command line at runtime. This puts an unreasonable burden on users.

- Put attribute values in a file that the application consults at runtime. This is the preferred solution.

When an internationalized application needs locale-specific information, it should get it from an appropriate file. A program running in a Spanish locale would refer to a file localized for that locale, for example. The one application binary may be packaged with many localized files, one for each supported locale.

Actually, the information needed for a particular locale is spread over several files:

- *Application-independent localization files.* We saw in Chapter 3 that information about date and time formatting or string collation for a particular locale is in files under the directory /usr/lib/locale/*localename*. These files are generally not your responsibility and are not packaged as part of your application.

- *Message catalogs.* Your application must display its messages in the user's language. For each locale you support, a message catalog for that locale contains appropriately translated strings. Chapter 6 discusses the details.

- *Resource files.* The X11 Resource Manager consults resource files for window object attributes such as size, color, and location.

As, say, an English-speaking Canadian developer, you would not be expected to create all the localized files yourself. Rather, you produce a message catalog and a resource file for the en_CA locale only. The part of your organization responsible for localization creates the localized versions for other locales.

A typical entry in a resource file is one specifying the background color for the window in which the application is running:

```
*background: gold
```

In some locales, a different color might be more appropriate. Each locale's resource file usually has a name in one of these forms:

```
/usr/lib/X11/localename/app-defaults/applicationname
/usr/openwin/lib/locale/localename/app-defaults/applicationname
/usr/dt/app-defaults/localename/applicationname
```

The resource manager consults the environment variable XFILESEARCHPATH to find the resource file. This variable is a colon-separated list of file name patterns. Here's an example with two patterns:

```
% echo $XFILESEARCHPATH
./app-defaults/%L/%N:/usr/openwin/lib/locale/%L/app-defaults/%N
```

In each pattern, the resource manager will replace %L by the current locale and %N by the application name. You might set the variable this way to test that your application is picking up the right resource file. If your application is named MyApp, then you could install the resource file in ./app-defaults/it/MyApp to test the Italian locale. A simple way to prove that the right file is found is to change a resource such as background color.

One important application resource is the set of fonts used to display text. This is the subject of the next section.

6.2 Fonts

We have seen earlier that a codeset is a mapping from the characters of a writing system to numeric values. In order to display text, we need to map those numeric codes into glyphs. A *glyph* is a visual representation of a character. Any one of the following glyphs, for example, represents the character lowercase g: *g* **g** **ɡ** g. Glyphs that have properties in common are organized into fonts. The glyphs forming the characters of this *word*, for example, are drawn from a 10-point Palatino bold italic font. More formally, a *font* is a mapping from a codeset to a set of glyphs. Table 6-1 shows that just as one language may be encoded in more than one way (e.g., English in ASCII or U.S. EBCDIC), several fonts may be available to display characters encoded in one codeset (e.g., Palatino or Helvetica to display ASCII). Furthermore, different fonts may map the same code value to different glyphs. For example, the first font in the table would map the code 0x50 (ASCII uppercase P) to **P**, while the third would map 0x50 (U.S. EBCDIC ampersand) to **&**.

Table 6-1   *Examples of Fonts for Different Codesets*

Language	Codeset	Font
English	ASCII	10-point Palatino bold for ASCII
English	ASCII	24-point Helvetica italic for ASCII
English	U.S. EBCDIC	10-point Palatino bold for U.S. EBCDIC
French	ISO 8859-1	10-point Palatino bold for ISO 8859-1
. . .	. . .	. . .

Because ASCII is a subset of ISO 8859-1, many systems that provide ISO 8859-1 fonts do not separately provide ASCII fonts. It is the responsibility of localization teams to acquire and provide required fonts. All Solaris systems include ISO 8859-1 fonts. Starting with Solaris 2.6, the base Solaris release includes fonts for ISO 8859-2, 8859-4, 8859-5, 8859-7, and 8859-9 as well. Solaris locales for Asia include appropriate localized fonts.

6.2.1 Selecting Fonts

The X window system uses a naming scheme for fonts that encodes many characteristics of a font in its name. The X Logical Font Description (XLFD) name of one particular font is

```
-linotype-palatino-bold-r-normal--10-100-72-72-p-57-iso8859-1
```

Notice that the font's codeset, ISO 8859-1, is part of the name. The xlsfonts(1) command lists available fonts. Here is one way to find Palatino fonts, for example:

```
% xlsfonts | grep palatino
-linotype-palatino-bold-i-normal--0-0-0-0-p-0-iso8859-1
-linotype-palatino-bold-i-normal--0-0-72-72-p-0-iso8859-1
-linotype-palatino-bold-i-normal--10-100-72-72-p-56-iso8859-1
[additional lines omitted]
```

To see what a font looks like individually, run the `xfontsel`(1) command and choose a font by selecting a combination of attributes. Figure 6-1 shows an example.

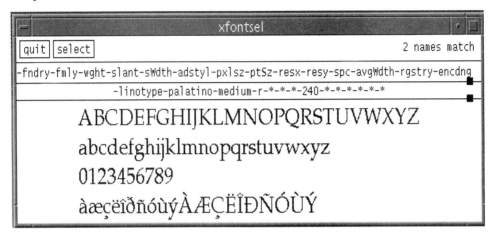

Figure 6-1   Example of `xfontsel`

The `xfd`(1) utility displays the glyphs in a font. For more information about X11 fonts in general, see the `X11`(7) manual page.

6.2.2 Fonts for East Asian Languages

East Asian languages complicate the font picture. We saw in Chapter 3 that Japanese EUC, for example, uses four different codesets to represent characters: ASCII, JIS X 0201, JIS X 0208, and JIS X 0212. On most systems, no one font is available to display all the encodings. Instead, a collection of at least three fonts is needed: one for JIS X 0201, one for JIS X 0208, and one for JIS X 0212. (JIS X 201 has most ASCII glyphs.) In the X Window System, such a collection is a *font set* at the Xlib level, or a *font list* at the Motif level. (These terms are explained more fully in Section 9.4.1, *Specifying Font Lists*, on page 133.)

You specify the fonts for your application with the Motif `fontList` resource. The Japanese resource file for your application might contain a list of three fonts:

```
*fontList:\
-sun-gothic-bold-r-normal--16-140-75-75-c-70-jisx0201.1976-0;\
-sun-gothic-bold-r-normal--16-140-75-75-c-140-jisx0208.1983-0;\
-sun-gothic-bold-r-normal--16-140-75-75-c-140-jisx0212.1990-0:
```

Attempting to display text with inappropriate fonts usually results either in characters disappearing or in wrong characters being displayed. For example, if a Korean application tries to display characters encoded using Korean EUC when no Korean fonts are available, it is quite likely that characters from the non-ASCII range of ISO 8859-1 will be displayed instead. Each Korean EUC byte has its most significant bit set. In the usual default ISO 8859-1 font, these bytes represent non-ASCII ISO 8859 characters.

The various East Asian versions of Solaris support industry-standard fonts so that developers and users do not have to create their own. Additional tools, such as FontEditor and FontManager, allow developers and users to edit and create fonts.

6.2.3 X11 Font Types

Solaris stores its X11 font data in `/usr/openwin/lib/X11/fonts`, `/usr/openwin/lib/locale/`*locale*`/X11/fonts`, and `/usr/dt/config/xfonts/locale`, and supports the following font types:

- Bitmapped screen fonts in 75 and 100 dot per inch resolutions, usually in Portable Compiled Format (PCF)

- Some PostScript® fonts in Adobe® Type-3 format and a limited range of scalable outline fonts in Adobe Type-1 format

  Type-1 fonts can be purchased separately and added to the system.

- In Solaris 2.6 and later, Truetype™ fonts

  Truetype fonts can give better results than Type-1 fonts at low screen resolutions. Truetype fonts are often cheaper as well. For high-end publishing however, Type-1 generally gives better results.

- Several fonts in Bitstream's outmoded Speedo format

- A wide range of 57 scalable outline fonts in Folio Font Format (F3), although these fonts will not be supported indefinitely

The FontAdmin tool allows system administrators and users to install, delete, and manage fonts. See the `fontadmin(6)` manual page for details. If you install a font, you may need to adjust your font search path. Use the `xset(1)` command with one of the variants of the `fp` option to do this. To see your current font search path, use `xset -q`.

6.3 Text Display Width

Despite the widespread use of graphical interfaces, many programs continue to lay out text by doing their own length and positioning operations. Such programs assume that the text will be displayed in a fixed-width font (also called a monospaced font), one in which all glyphs have the same width. This is generally a safe assumption: for most writing systems, fixed-width fonts are acceptable, so a computing environment is likely to provide at least one. But there are traps for the unwary. This code fragment attempts to print a string centered in a field 80 columns wide:

```
char mystring[1000];
int n;
...
n = strlen(mystring);                 /* BAD ASSUMPTIONS MADE HERE! */
if (n <= 80) {
    printf("%*s", (80-n)/2, "");      /* print (80-n)/2 spaces */
    printf("%s\n", mystring);
}
else
    string doesn't fit
```

It works correctly for European languages. But as we saw in Chapter 4, a program that assumes one character equals one byte will not work for encodings used for East Asian languages. At the very least, we need to determine how many characters are in the string, not how many bytes:

```
char mystring[1000];
wchar_t wMystring[1000];
int n;
...
    /* convert to wide characters; n = number of wide characters */
    /* BAD ASSUMPTION STILL MADE HERE! */
n = mbstowcs(wMystring, mystring, 1000);
if (n <= 80) {
    printf("%*s", (80-n)/2, "");      /* print (80-n)/2 spaces */
    printf("%s\n", mystring);
}
else
    string doesn't fit
```

Converting the multibyte string to wide characters lets us use `wcslen` to count the characters correctly. But another assumption makes this code still wrong for East Asian languages: we incorrectly assume that one character occupies one display column position. Those languages are invariably written with fixed-width fonts, but in Japanese, for example, a Kanji glyph occupies twice as many columns as a Latin letter, a digit, or a JIS X 0201 half-size Katakana glyph. Figure 6-2 shows a short list of names:

Figure 6-2   Display Columns for Japanese Text

The XPG4 function that computes the number of display columns a string will occupy is wcswidth(3), used as follows:

```
char mystring[1000];
wchar_t wMystring[1000];
int n;
 . . .

mbstowcs(wMystring, mystring, 1000);
n = wcswidth(wMystring);
if (n <= 80) {
   printf("%*s", (80-n)/2, "");     /* print (80-n)/2 spaces */
   printf("%s\n", mystring);
}
else
    string doesn't fit
```

The wcswidth() function makes simple assumptions under Solaris: Chinese, Korean, and Japanese characters (except for half-size Katakana) occupy two column positions; all other characters require only one. These assumptions are consistent with the way these languages customarily appear in print. Since the characters are all written with the same height, there is no function corresponding to wcswidth() for the vertical dimension.

When you use wcswidth(), you are building into your program a requirement that fixed-width fonts be used for text display. For some applications, this requirement may not be valid. In fact, for some writing systems, such as the one used by Arabic and Farsi, fixed-width glyphs are rarely acceptable. In an X11 environment, you can use the Xlib metric functions, shown in Table 6-2, to determine the display size of a string in pixels. (See Section 10.4.2, *Text Extents Functions*, on page 154 for details on these functions)

Table 6-2   Xlib Metric Functions

Function	String Argument Type	Description
`XmbTextEscapement()`	multibyte	Yields the number of pixels in x dimension
`XwcTextEscapement()`	wide character	
`XmbTextExtents()`	multibyte	Yields the number of pixels in the x dimension and bounding box info
`XwcTextExtents()`	wide character	

6.4 User Interface Layout

Window objects include control buttons, menus, labels, and text boxes. The layout of objects containing strings can change from one locale to another because the dimensions of those strings usually change. A control button in English, for example, is often shorter than the equivalent in German. A Japanese button is probably taller than the English equivalent. Even within one language, increasing the size of a font causes the text inside buttons to grow. This can have one of the following effects:

- Button sizes stay the same, possibly resulting in the contained texts being clipped.
- Buttons grow to fit the text, but adjacent buttons may now overlap.
- Buttons grow to fit the text, but the containing window remains the same size, so the buttons are clipped.
- Buttons grow to fit the text and are repositioned so as not to overlap.

The first two effects are symptomatic of the dimensions or positions of the objects being specified as constants somewhere. Hardcoding these in the source code is certainly wrong for an internationalized application. Explicitly putting these constants in a resource file makes localization possible but requires that they be checked and possibly adjusted by the person doing a localization.

The easiest approach is to let the GUI system's geometry manager do the layout. This implicit layout means that not even the resource file need say anything about objects' sizes and dimensions; items will automatically be placed according to built-in rules. Unfortunately, the geometry manager may not place objects where users in some locales would like them to be. In that case, you can always take control of layout explicitly. By measuring strings with the functions of Table 6-2, your application can compute the sizes of objects and position them itself.

Another concern is input. A data entry field of fixed size may be too short to accommodate input strings in some languages. Making the field scrollable can solve this problem.

6.5 Paper Sizes

Just as output to a screen should fit into the window in which it will be displayed, output to be printed should not overrun the edges of the paper. Within each country a small number of paper sizes are commonly used, normally with one of those sizes being much more common than the others. Most countries follow ISO 216, *Writing paper and certain classes of printed matter—Trimmed sizes—A and B series.*

Internationalized applications should not make assumptions about the page sizes available to them. Solaris provides no support for tracking output page size; this is the responsibility of the application program itself. Table 6-3 summarizes the paper sizes in common use.

Table 6-3   Common International Paper Sizes

Paper Type	Dimensions	Countries
ISO A3	29.70 cm x 42.00 cm	Everywhere except U.S., Canada, Latin America, and Japan
ISO A4	21.00 cm x 29.70 cm	
ISO A5	14.85 cm x 21.00 cm	
JIS B4	25.00 cm x 35.30 cm	Japan
JIS B5	17.65 cm x 25.00 cm	
U.S. Letter	8.50 in x 11.00 in	U.S., Canada, and Latin America
U.S. Legal	8.50 in x 14.00 in	
U.S. Ledger	11.00 in x 17.00 in	

6.6 Complex Text Languages

Despite their obvious visual differences, most Latin-based writing systems and East Asian writing systems share several characteristics when being displayed. Both scripts can be written from left to right, and each character can be rendered in the same way, regardless of the characters around it.

Languages that don't fit this model are called complex text languages (CTL). They have one or more of these attributes:

- Context sensitivity. The rendering of a character can vary depending on its position in a word or on neighboring characters. This is true of Arabic, Farsi, Urdu, Thai, Korean Hangul, and many Indic languages.

- Composite characters. Characters are composed of a few base elements. Korean Hangul, Thai, Vietnamese, and many Indic languages have this property.

- Bidirectionality. Text is written from right to left, but may contain substrings written from left to right. This is true of Arabic, Farsi, Urdu, Hebrew, and Yiddish.

For efficient text operations, CTL text strings are usually stored in a "logical" form different from the display form. A system that supports a complex text language must process the logical strings prior to their display.

6.6.1 Context Sensitivity

In some writing systems, a character may take different forms depending on where it is in a word or what characters are next to it. In Arabic, for example, some characters have one form if at the beginning of a word, another in the middle, another if at the end of a word, and a fourth if appearing in isolation, as shown in Figure 6-3. Adjacent characters may be combined to form a single ligature glyph, as depicted in Figure 6-4.

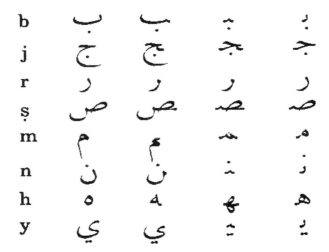

Figure 6-3   Isolated, Initial, Medial, and Final Forms of Arabic Consonants

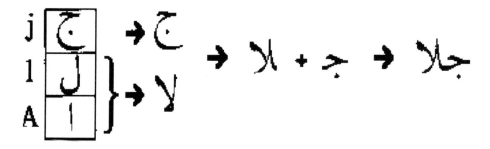

Figure 6-4   The lA Ligature in the Arabic Word jlA.

6.6.2 Composite Characters

Some scripts may have what appears to be many characters that in fact are constructed from comparatively few base elements. Korean Hangul is a prime example. While there are only 14 base consonants and 10 base vowels in the Hangul alphabet, as depicted in Figure 6-5, they can be combined to form syllables in thousands of ways. Each syllable is written in a square cell (Figure 6-6). A few simple rules dictate the positioning of the base components in the cell.

Figure 6-5   Base 14 Consonants and 10 Vowels of Korean Hangul Alphabet

Figure 6-6   Korean Syllables

A system may support languages with composite characters without an analysis of the characters' structure. Display of Korean Hangul in Solaris, for example, relies on 2,350 precomposed characters. Character composition allows for 11,172 combinations, so many possibilities cannot be displayed.

6.6.3 Bidirectionality

A language like Hebrew is written predominantly from right to left. However, numerals are written left to right. Figure 6-7 shows that when Hebrew text is embedded in an English sentence, there may be more than one change of direction.

The address "ירושלים, 1234 בצלאל" should be "בצלאל 5678, ירושלים" instead.

Figure 6-7   Hebrew Text in an English Sentence

6.7 Summary

Do the following to enable your application to correctly display localized text:

- Specify display attributes that may vary from one locale to another in resource files, not in the program code.

- Make sure each localized resource file specifies appropriate attributes. A common oversight is to omit fonts appropriate to the locale.

- Measure text width by passing the text string to a function such as `wcswidth()` or `XmbTextEscapement()`. Do not assume one character occupies one display column position.

- For GUI applications, let the geometry manager do window object layout.

- Remember that paper sizes may vary among locales.

Handling Language Input 7

Many programs are interactive and require some sort of user input, either from the keyboard, the mouse, or some other input device. Internationalized programs must consider how different locales communicate with the program—what the local *input methods* are.

In an internationalized program, you can't assume any particular mapping between keystrokes and input characters. An internationalized program must run in any locale on a single workstation, using a single keyboard. When there are more characters in a codeset than there are on the keyboard, some sort of input method is required for mapping between multiple keystrokes and input characters.

Even if you are not familiar with a different local language, as an international developer, you must test your application's ability to accept localized input. To do this you must know how to input localized text.

- *Input with Localized Keyboards* describes how users can enter text using specialized keyboards designed for European and Asian locales. See *Input with Localized Keyboards* below.

- *Input Methods* shows how to use the Compose key on European keyboards, and phonetic and other input methods on a Japanese keyboard, one of the Asian keyboards. See *Input Methods* on page 109.

- *Input Method Architecture* gives a summary description of how various input methods can be integrated into internationalized X applications. See *Input Method Architecture* on page 118

7.1 Input with Localized Keyboards

One method for inputting local characters is to use localized keyboards. With this approach, keys are mapped to facilitate easy entry of the characters in the local language.

7

7.1.1 European Keyboards

Localized keyboards are available for many European-language locales. Sun, for example, normally delivers international keyboards with country kits, but they are also available separately. Type-5 keyboards have been produced for the languages listed in Table 7-1.

Table 7-1   European SPARC Keyboards

Czech/Slovak	French	Norwegian
Danish	French (Switzerland)	Polish
Dutch	German	Portuguese
English (U.K.)	German (Switzerland)	Russian
English (U.S./Canada)	Hungarian	Spanish
Finnish	Italian	Swedish

The PC-AT101 and PC-AT102 keyboards have been produced for the languages listed in Table 7-2.

Table 7-2   European PC Keyboards

Danish	French	Norwegian
Dutch	French (Switzerland)	Portuguese
English (U.K.)	German	Spanish
English (U.S./Canada)	German (Switzerland)	Swedish
Finnish	Italian	

In addition to providing European characters, the keyboard layout is also localized. As shown in Figure 7-1, the French keyboard uses an AZERTY keyboard layout, not the QWERTY layout found on U.S. English keyboards. German keyboards use a QWERTZ layout. Also note that there are keys with an accent mark above a square; these are referred to as "accelerator keys" and can be used to compose an accented character. They are also called "dead keys" because using these keys does not advance the text cursor. Instead, the accent on the dead key is combined with the character on the next key pressed, resulting in an accented character. To produce the character ê, for example, you would first type the dead key with the accent and then press the e key. This input method is well established, having been used with French typewriters for a hundred years.

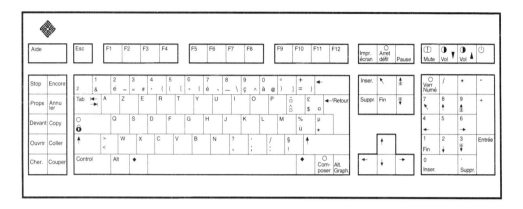

Figure 7-1   French Keyboard Layout

Appendix B shows keyboard layouts for specific locales.

7.1.2 Asian Keyboards

Asian keyboard layouts are based on the U.S. English layout but also have local language markings on the right portion of many keycaps. Sun currently has type-5 keyboards available for the four Asian locales listed in Table 7-3.

Table 7-3   Asian SPARC Keyboards

Japanese	Korean	Simplified Chinese (PRC)	Traditional Chinese (Taiwan)

The PC-AT101 and PC-AT102 keyboards are currently available in the Asian locales listed in Table 7-4.

Table 7-4   Asian PC Keyboards

Japanese	Korean	Simplified Chinese (PRC)	Traditional Chinese (Taiwan)

The Japanese keyboard contains Hiragana characters, the Korean keyboard has Hangul elements, and the traditional Chinese keyboard has Bopomofo symbols and ideographic character components (radicals). Figure 7-2 shows a Japanese keyboard. Note that the keyboard has extra keys next to a narrow space bar. These keys allow the user to switch between different input modes, as discussed on page 110.

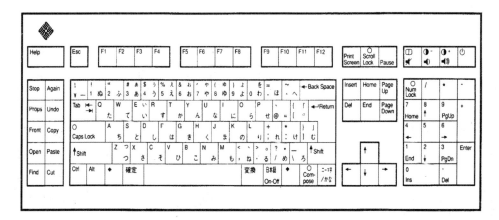

Figure 7-2   Japanese Keyboard Layout

Because of the huge character sets in Asian locales, two or three keystrokes would not be sufficient to produce every possible character in an intuitive way. Also, because characters change within the context in which they appear, a special facility—an input method—is built into the Asian locales for input.

7.1.3 Avoid Managing the Keyboard

Type-5 keyboards have provisions for typing all the ISO 8859-1 characters. If programs use system and window services to read characters, they need only be 8-bit clean. But if programs read /dev/kbd or perform keystroke mapping, they are managing the keyboard. If that's the case, make sure to support the following input methods for all keyboard layouts:

- Entering any character by using a single keystroke. Note that German keyboards switch Y with Z, and French keyboards switch Q and W with A and Z

- Using a dead key accent followed by a given keystroke to produce any valid ISO 8859-1 character

- Pressing the Compose key followed by two additional keystrokes to produce any valid ISO character

Exhaustively testing software that manages the keyboard by trying all keystroke sequences on all country kit keyboards is tedious. If at all possible, use regular OS or window system facilities to manage the keyboard for you. Doing so saves time and gives your software a uniform user interface.

7.2 Input Methods

An input method is a method by which an application directs the user to type, select, and send text to an application. Input methods differ for each language, depending on the language's structure and conventions.

It is important to note that in most cases, there is nothing special you must do in your application code to receive input. If you read a line of input using `fgets()` or you obtain the string from a text widget using `XmTextGetString()`, you will get a multibyte string properly encoded for the current locale. Your program is blissfully unaware of what the user had to do to get those characters to you. The fact that the user started your application in a particular locale is sufficient to cause the system to enable the appropriate input method.

7.2.1 European Input Methods

For European locales, special characters can be produced with the Compose key.

Compose Key on SPARC

The system's input method software lets you use the Compose key on a U.S. English SPARC type-5 keyboard to produce all characters in the standard ISO 8859-1 code set. Such characters are typically composite characters that include diacritical marks. To produce a composite character on the U.S. English keyboard, first press the Compose key. Next, press the key for the desired diacritical mark, and then the key for the desired alphabetical character. You can type the diacritical mark and the alphabetical character in either order. For example, to produce à, press the Compose key, then type a and `(order doesn't matter). Table 7-5 shows a few of the possible Compose key sequences; Appendix B contains the complete list.

Compose Key on x86

On x86 systems, the default compose key sequence for Solaris for x86 is CTRL SHIFT F1. When in compose mode, the system expects two more characters to be typed by the user to generate a character. Press CTRL SHIFT F1 followed by n ~ to produce the Spanish ñ on the screen. If you press the compose key and then press ? twice, the Spanish inverted question mark is displayed.

Table 7-5   Using the Compose Key (SPARC and x86)

Compose Key Sequence		Result	Description
a	´	à	a grave (uses apostrophe)
a	ʹ	á	a acute (uses single quote)
a	^	â	a circumflex
a	"	ä	a umlaut
a	~	ã	a tilde
a	*	å	a angstrom
a	e	æ	ae ligature
c	,	ç	c cedilla (uses comma)
,	,	˛	cedilla (uses comma)
"	"	¨	umlaut/diaeresis (uses double quote)
!	!	¡	inverted exclamation
?	?	¿	inverted question
l	-	£	pound sterling

7.2.2 Asian Input Methods

In English, a user enters text by typing in a sequence of letters to create a word. However, for languages based on ideographic characters, input is more complicated. For example, there are two phonetic scripts in Japanese, Hiragana and Katakana, in addition to the traditional ideographic script, Kanji. In any piece of writing, all three alphabets may be used. Moreover, Romaji (Roman letters) may be used for foreign words.

To handle languages for which there isn't a one-to-one key to character mapping, input methods typically provide features such as the following:

- A control key sequence, which selects the *input mode*

- A pre-edit region, which displays characters as the user enters them but before the user *commits* them

- A lookup choice region, which displays ideographic characters and allows the user to choose one

- A status region, which provides information such as whether conversion is activated and the state or mode of the input method

Text input widgets, in conjunction with some input methods, can also provide advanced, language-specific, pre-editing features. The Motif TextEdit widget, for example, can determine when to commit any uncommitted pre-edit text without the user having to take further action. This technique is known as *implicit commit*.

Example: In a mail application the user enters a message in Japanese and presses a "send" button to dispatch the composed message. If pre-edit text has not been committed to the text buffer and the user's intention is that it be part of the message, then it is useful for the toolkit to intervene and cause a commit to occur before the application processes the buffer and sends the message.

Details of the operations that trigger implicit commit semantics in Motif widgets can be found in the localization documentation for the appropriate languages.

The use of these features varies with the input method. For more information, see the documentation for the input method you are using. Figure 7-3 shows the input method screen regions.

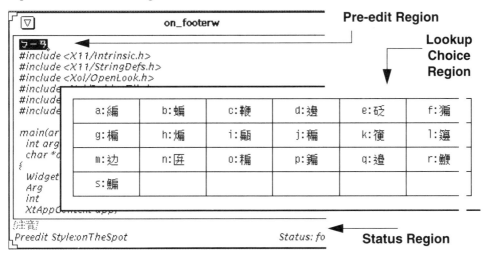

Figure 7-3   *Input Method Screen Regions for* zh_TW *locale*

It is often impractical to map all Asian alphabets and characters onto a keyboard. Recall from Chapters 2 and 4 that many Asian languages have extremely large character sets and some have several alphabets. Input methods are particularly useful for accommodating languages with large character sets.

We will explore an Asian input method, its use, and the user interface associated with it, by using the Japanese language as an example case.

7.2.2.1 Japanese Language Overview

First let's try to understand some basics about the writing system for Japanese. Those familiar with the Japanese language can skip to the next section—*Japanese Language Input Methods.*

Kanji

Japanese uses a combination of four different scripts—*Kanji* characters, *Hiragana* and *Katakana*, and *Romaji*, the Roman alphabet phonetic system. Kanji characters are used to express ideas and concepts and are the key visual elements of written Japanese. The Kanji characters, originally developed in China, were introduced to Japan by Buddhist monks around 600 AD. Since that time they have been stylized and adopted to meet the needs of the Japanese language. Today, the complete set of characters commonly used in Japan is on the order of 6,500.

Most Kanji characters have at least two methods of pronunciation: *on-yomi*, derived from the original Chinese pronunciation; and *kun-yomi* from the native Japanese language. Some Kanji characters have many more than two. The pronunciation of a particular Kanji character depends on the context in which it is used. As we will see, these multiple pronunciations present complexities for computer systems, specifically involving the method of text input.

Hiragana

Hiragana is a set of 83 symbols, called a *syllabary*, that encompass all of the basic syllables used for Japanese pronunciation. These include the five basic vowel sounds—a, i, u, e, o—in combination with initial consonants k, s, t, n, h, m, y, r, and w, and the final consonant, n. The Hiragana syllabary is used in written Japanese to express grammatical parts of speech, verb tenses, and some words for which there is no Kanji character or the Kanji has become obsolete.

Katakana

Katakana is also a phonetic syllabary, but provides a different set of symbols for the same sounds expressed in Hiragana. Since its use is reserved primarily for words of foreign origin, for example, *konpyuuta* (computer), a few additional syllables have been created to deal with sounds that do not exist in the native Japanese language. Katakana is also used to express the multitude of sound and action imitating phrases (onomatopoeia) used by Japanese, such as *batabata* (the sound of running feet). The syllables represented by Hiragana and Katakana are generically called *kana*.

Romaji

Romaji is used to write Japanese sounds with Roman letters. In the example above, *konpyuuta* is a Romaji representation of the Japanese sounds. Romaji is also used for abbreviations of many modern technical terms (for example ASIC), product names (for example NFS), and business names (such as Canon).

A typical Japanese text string consists of a combination of Hiragana, Katakana, and Kanji characters. The Kanji characters are particularly important since they represent the ideas of the language. Figure 7-4 shows the relationship between Romaji, Hiragana, Katakana, and Kanji characters.

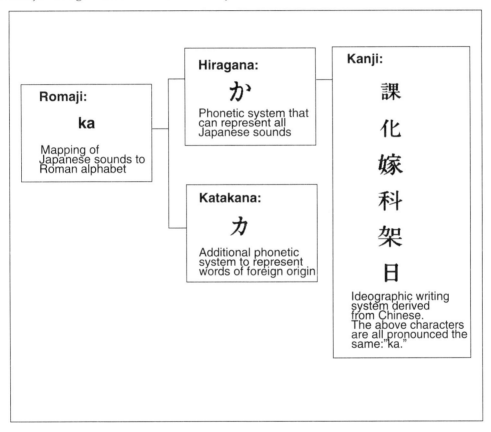

Figure 7-4   Relation of Romaji, Hiragana, Katakana, and Kanji Characters

7.2.2.2 Japanese Language Input Methods

Input methods for Japanese must be capable of producing Hiragana, Katakana, and Kanji characters, each of which can appear in a typical Japanese sentence, as well as occasional Roman characters. Since Japanese uses such a large number of Kanji characters, there cannot be a one-to-one mapping from a keyboard to the Japanese Kanji character set. Additionally, since many Kanji have similar pronunciation, there must be a way of identifying the correct character from among the Kanji homonyms.

Roman, Hiragana, and Katakana characters can be input directly through several input methods:

- ASCII input is used for inputting characters in the Roman alphabet.

- Romaji input uses Roman letters to phonetically spell out Japanese words. Romaji input is automatically converted to its Japanese syllabary equivalent in a pre-edit region on the screen. For example, if the user inputs "h-a" under the Romaji method, it is automatically displayed in a pre-edit region as は .

- Hiragana input maps the Japanese native Hiragana syllabary to the keyboard, as shown in Figure 7-2. For example, by typing the "f" key, a user could input the syllable は [ha].

- Katakana input maps the Japanese Katakana foreign-word syllabary to the keyboard in the same manner as the Hiragana input method. The Katakana syllable ハ [ha] is also input by typing the "f" key.

Entering Kanji characters is accomplished by one of two methods:

- Kana to Kanji conversion—input of a syllabic representation of the Japanese character through the Romaji, Hiragana, or Katakana input method described above. From this syllabic representation of the Kanji, the system provides the user with a list of Kanji having that pronunciation. More detail about this conversion method will be given below.

- Kuten code—direct input of a Japanese character by specifying its numeric value according to a standardized encoding scheme *(Kuten code)*. The user selects the Kuten code input method and types a four digit code number for each Kanji.

7.2.2.3 Switching Between Input Methods

ASCII input is the system default input method. To use any of the Japanese language input methods—Romaji, Hiragana, Katakana, Kuten code, or kana-Kanji conversion—the user must turn the Japanese conversion mode on. This is done by typing a special control character on the standard U.S. English keyboard or the special `Japanese/On-Off` key on the Japanese keyboard. These key combinations are used to toggle the Japanese language input on and off.

When the Japanese language option is turned on, only one input method at a time can be used. The user selects from the various input methods by pressing a special control character sequence on the U.S. English keyboard or a function key on the Japanese keyboard. The Japanese keyboard also includes a key to toggle between Romaji and direct Kana input.

7.2.2.4 Kana to Kanji Conversion

The most direct way of inputting Kanji characters is by using the Kuten code method. For example, to key in the word 幹事 (pronounced *Kanji* and meaning "secretary" or "organizer") using the Kuten code input method, the user would type 3434 and 3B76 for the respective Kanji. However, this method requires extensive knowledge of codeset values and is clearly not user-friendly when dealing with over 6,500 commonly used characters. Although there are trained operators who use this technique effectively, most users employ the Kana-Kanji conversion method described above.

Since there are many Kanji characters with similar pronunciation, Japanese Solaris includes a Conversion Manager responsible for translating the input string to the possible character options, which are stored in a Japanese language user dictionary. When ambiguity arises, the system prompts the user to select the proper conversion from a menu of choices. For example, the word *hashi* in Japanese can be input as h-a-s-h-i (Romaji) or as はし (Hiragana input).

In written Japanese, a user would want to express this word or concept as a Kanji character. In converting the word *hashi* to a Kanji character, however, there are numerous choices or Kanji characters, each pronounced the same way but with different meanings:

- 橋 bridge

- 箸 chopsticks

- 端 edge

The Kanji that a user has in mind will obviously depend on the context of his sentence.

The Conversion Manager displays the multiple ideograph choices that correspond to the phonetic representation input by the user in a look-up choice region. The user has two choices for viewing and selecting characters. The choices can be displayed one-at-a-time in the pre-edit region and scrolled through by key commands until the correct Kanji is found. Alternatively, it is possible to display all candidates at one time and then select the correct one from a list that pops up in a separate window. In either case, the user selects the most appropriate choice and commits it to the pre-edit region.

After the user has completed conversion of the text string, the converted character string is displayed in the application. Japanese Solaris permits Kana-Kanji conversion of contiguous Japanese text strings. The Conversion Manager selects logical groups within the text string to become the *focus*, or portion under consideration for conversion to Kanji. The user can change the syllables under consideration for conversion or shift the focus to other parts of the phrase by using control key combinations.

7.2.2.5 Japanese Language Input Method Regions

Because of the multiple input methods and general ambiguity of Kana-Kanji conversion, the user interface incorporates a number of windows that aid the user in creating Japanese text. These include:

- *Status region*—an active window that displays the selected input mode. The status region provides feedback on the state of the input method—whether the Japanese language input method is activated and if so, whether it is in Romaji, Hiragana, Katakana, or Kuten code input type.

- *Pre-edit region*— an active window that displays the text string as input by the user.

- *Look-up choice region*—an active window that displays the multiple Kanji choices that correspond to a particular phonetic representation input by the user.

An illustration of these regions is shown in Figure 7-5.

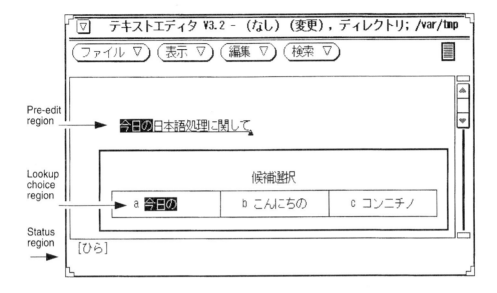

Pre-edit region →

Lookup choice region →

Status region →

Figure 7-5   Status, Edit, and Look-up Regions for Japanese Character Input

7.2.2.6 Japanese Solaris Input Method Server

An Input Method (IM) Server provides an interface between applications and conversion engines. As with the input methods, there can also be differences in the look-up dictionaries. Dictionaries may be suited for specific application or industry segments such as medicine and finance, or they may have different levels of intelligence built in, i.e. able to present the most logical character choices to the look-up region based on the context of the string. Japanese Solaris offers the user a choice of two popular conversion engines—*cs00*, from Ergosoft Technology, and *atok7/atok8*, from Just Systems.

Many of the X toolkit-based applications automatically configure to use the Input Server to perform the functions required for input of Asian text. If you use any of Sun's toolkits (Motif, XView, or OLIT), the input/output conversion process is transparent to the application.

7.2.2.7 Japanese Language Engines

While the Input Method Server provides the interfaces to the Japanese Input Method on behalf of the applications, it is the responsibility of the Japanese Language Engines to do the actual conversions from key inputs to Japanese texts. Japanese Solaris bundles commercially popular language engines, ATOK by Just Systems, for example.

Many of the commercially available engines today have built-in artificial intelligence, by which the conversion can be done as efficiently as possible. For example, engines can understand and learn the relationships among words so that the most appropriate combination of words will be the first candidate for the conversion result.

Dictionaries are as important as the logic part of the language engines. Default standard dictionaries are bundled in Solaris, but utilities are also provided so that users can create their own dictionaries in addition to the default one.

7.3 Input Method Architecture

An internationalized X application gets localized user input by communicating with an input method. Often, a localized input method will establish a connection to another process known as the "input manager" or "input method server." This typically occurs at application startup time. The input method server can provide input method service to multiple X clients that use the same locale. Sometimes an input method server will connect to a third process, the language engine, which performs dictionary lookup and translation from preedit text to composed text.

Here are some advantages of using localized input methods:

- Frees application from having to code in input method/language engine knowledge
- Input method server helps to display composed characters and input method status
- Language engine determines multi-stroke-to-character conversion

Figure 7-6 illustrates the input method server and its relationship to the window system.

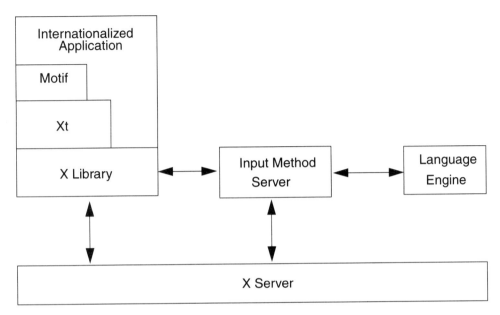

Figure 7-6   Input Method Server and X Windows

7.3.1 X Input Method (XIM)

Most X toolkits such as Motif will automatically create an input method connection when your Motif application uses any text-based widget.

If however, you are creating your own widget that will handle text input, or have a pure Xlib application, you must make the connection to the input method yourself. See Chapter 10 for a discussion of how to do this.

7.4 Summary

As an I18N programmer you should test your applications to make sure they can handle localized text input. You should also create your own localization files in different languages.

Most X toolkits, including Motif, automatically create a connection to the input method server for use by text-based widgets.

Working with CDE 8≣

This chapter describes how to set the user's locale in CDE (Common Desktop Environment) and how to employ App Builder, the CDE Application Builder, for creating graphical applications.

- *Setting the locale* describes how to change the default language, both at login time and for a single application, how to specify custom fonts, and how to change the input method and keyboard map.

- *App Builder* is a development tool that speeds up and simplifies the design and implementation of CDE applications. After you set up visual objects on the screen, App Builder generates user interface code, which you hook up with other modules. See *Using App Builder* on page 125.

- *CDE applications* are internationalized and localized for many languages. The calendar manager, the multimedia mail reader, and the help facility are all worth looking at as examples. See *Other CDE Applications* on page 128

8.1 Setting the Locale in CDE

CDE sets the locale as an option at dtlogin time. This locale applies to an entire login session and may differ from the default system locale. The user's locale is retained for the next dtlogin session, when the user can choose a new locale.

It is difficult to change locales in mid-session. CDE sets the LANG environment variable, but has no interface for setting any separate LC_* categories. (The reason for both is that CDE has no locale properties dialog box, as does OpenWindows).

8.1.1 Default Language at Login

The messages and menus in the initial dtlogin window are displayed in the default locale (possibly set in the /etc/default/init file) or in the previous dtlogin locale. If a default locale has not been set, messages and menus are displayed, using a generic C locale environment. You can change the language from the Options menu in the dtlogin screen.

8.1.2 Logging In to a Language-Specific Session

Logging in to a specific language through the desktop is easy. However, specific hardware requirements such as keyboards and printers may be required to make localized sessions productive. These requirements vary by language, character set, and country. Software and fonts can further increase the effective localization of your system. To log in to a language-specific session:

1. **Use the Options menu in the login screen to select a language.**

    The list of locales includes all the supported languages that are installed.

2. **Log in normally with your name and password.**

8.1.3 Creating or Editing a Language-Specific File

You can create, edit, and print language-specific files. You can also give files language-specific names. However, for system administration files that are shared across a network, file names should contain just ASCII characters, since different systems on the network might be using different locales.

If you have logged in to the desktop in a specific language, all applications are invoked using that language. However, you can still invoke an application with another language, assuming that the locale for that language is installed. If you want to create a file with a different language, start a new instance of Text Editor and specify your desired locale.

♦ **With the env command, set the LANG environment and run dtpad.**

   For example, to run Text Editor in the French locale, type:

```
env LANG=fr dtpad &
```

   where *fr* sets the LANG environment variable for the French locale. Alternatively, you can start Text Editor in the French locale directly:

```
dtpad -xnllanguage fr &
```

You can now enter French characters (if that locale has been installed). You can also use the Text Editor session to edit previously created French files.

8.1.4 Using a Language-Specific Terminal Emulator

The following example uses dtterm and starts a French terminal emulator.

♦ **With the env command, set the LANG environment and run dtterm.**

   For example, to run Terminal in the French locale, type:

```
env LANG=fr dtterm &
```

where *fr* sets the LANG environment variable for the French locale. Alternatively, you may start Terminal in the French locale directly:

```
dtterm -xnllanguage fr &
```

8.1.5 Specifying Fonts

The user usually changes fonts by using Style Manager, which in turn restarts Workspace Manager, resetting the desktop fonts. You can also customize fonts at the command line or using resource files. See Section 6.2.1, *Selecting Fonts,* on page 94 for more information about specifying fonts with the X Logical Font Description (XLFD) names.

8.1.6 Changing Fonts

You can change fonts for any application with either of the following methods:

- Specifying fonts from the command line
- Specifying fonts within a resource file

8.1.6.1 Specifying Fonts from the Command Line

To change the fonts for the menu from the command line, type:

```
dtterm -xrm '*fontList: fontset'
```

where *fontset* is a font set specification. A font set specification can be given by a full X Logical Font Description (XLFD) name list, a simple XLFD pattern, or an alias name. Note that a font set specification is filled in by the prevailing locale. Here are two examples, which work for any locale.

To use a larger font except for the menu font, type:
```
dtterm -xrm '*fontList:-dt-interface user-medium-r-normal-l*-*-*-*:'
```

To use a smaller font except for the menu font, type:
```
dtterm -xrm '*fontList:-dt-interface user-medium-r-normal-s*-*-*-*:'
```

8.1.6.2 Specifying Custom Fonts for an Application

For example, to change font selections for dtterm in a resource file:

1. **Become superuser and edit the Dtterm resource file.**

   Setting the LANG environment variable alters the search path of resource files to include /usr/dt/app-defaults/*locale*, where *locale* is the value of LANG. Edit /usr/dt/app-defaults/C/Dtterm if LANG is not set.

   In the .Xdefaults file, you could use either the class name (Dtterm) or the application name (dtterm) for a setting a resource.

2. Insert the font list you want to use at the bottom of the file.

For example, to make serif fonts available, put these lines at the bottom of the `app-defaults` file:

```
*userFontList: \
-sun-serif-medium-r-normal-serif-10-100-72-72-m-70-iso8859-1:\n\
-sun-serif-medium-r-normal-serif-11-110-72-72-m-70-iso8859-1:\n\
-sun-serif-medium-r-normal-serif-12-120-72-72-m-70-iso8859-1:\n\
-sun-serif-medium-r-normal-serif-14-140-72-72-m-80-iso8859-1:\n\
-sun-serif-medium-r-normal-serif-16-160-72-72-m-90-iso8859-1:
```

3. Save the file, and start up dtterm.

8.1.7 Choosing Your Input Method and Keyboard

Each locale has a single default input method associated with it. If the user does nothing, this default is selected. Some locales, such as Japan, might have multiple input method servers (`htt` and `ATOK8`). The sections below explain how input methods are selected on behalf of the user.

8.1.7.1 Using Input Method Modifiers

When there are multiple input methods for a locale, use the `XmNinputMethod` resource to identify the one to be used. This is done by specifying a *modifier*. The modifier must be of the following form, where *modifier* is the name used to uniquely identify the input method:

```
Dtwm*inputMethod: @im=htt
```

The *modifier* string specified in the `XmNinputMethod` resource is used to choose which input method is used.

Alternatively, set the `XMODIFIERS` environment variable. The syntax is the same as for the `XmNinputMethod` resource, but the values are different.

8.1.7.2 Specifying the Input Method Style

The input method style determines how pre-editing occurs. It is controlled by the `XmNpreeditType` resource. The syntax, possible values, and default value type of the `XmNpreeditType` resource are listed in Table 8-1:

Table 8-1   `XmNpreeditType` *Resource*

Syntax	value[,value,....]
Possible values	OverTheSpot, OffTheSpot, Root, None
Default value	OverTheSpot, OffTheSpot, Root

The string list, separated by commas, specifies the priority order for this resource. The first value supported by the input method is used.

8.1.7.3 Changing the X Keyboard Map at the Server

If the keymaps used by the X server do not match the physical keyboard on the system, you can change them manually by using the xmodmap(1) command. This is generally not necessary with SPARC type-5 keyboards or with standard PC-101 keyboards, but nonstandard keyboard layouts could cause problems, such as the wrong character appearing on the screen.

8.2 Using App Builder

App Builder is a development tool that speeds up and simplifies the design, implementation, and testing of a new user interface. App Builder gives you the freedom to create and try user interfaces without writing any code. Because you can create and modify an interface easily, you'll find that you can spend more time designing and testing, the surest route to better user interfaces.

8.2.1 Application Builder Primary Window

The Application Builder primary window, shown in Figure 8-1, is the starting point for creating a user interface.

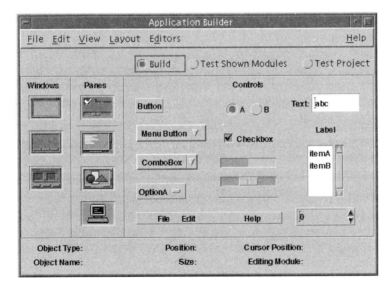

Figure 8-1   Application Builder Primary Window

The basic method for creating a user interface is to *drag and drop* objects from the App Builder window onto the workspace or onto other App Builder objects.

♦ **To start App Builder, run `dtbuilder` from the command line.**

If `dtbuilder` is in your path, App Builder will start. If it is not in your path, you will need to type the full path name (`/usr/dt/bin/dtbuilder`) or first change to the folder where `dtbuilder` is located.

♦ **To quit App Builder, choose Exit from the File menu of the main window.**

If you have not saved changes, a message box asks what you want to do.

The CDE Application Builder (App Builder) is an interactive tool for developing Motif applications. App Builder provides features that facilitate the construction of an application's graphical user interface (GUI) as well as the incorporation of many useful desktop services, such as Help, Drag and Drop, or ToolTalk®.

The *CDE Application Builder User's Guide* explains how to create an interface by selecting and moving GUI objects on a palette. It also explains how to make connections between interface objects, how to use the application framework editor to integrate desktop services, how to generate C code, how to add modules to the App Builder output, and how to produce a finished application.

8.2.2 Overview of the App Builder Process

The basic process of building and maintaining a user interface with App Builder is simple and straightforward. There are many variations on this formula, but the process is similar for any application.

1. Start App Builder. Open a new project and a new module.
2. Drag and drop windows (main windows and custom dialogs) to the workspace, creating a new module for each window, in most cases.
3. Drag and drop panes onto main windows or custom dialogs.
4. Drag and drop controls (buttons, choice objects, text fields, for example) onto control panes.
5. Create pane objects, menus, and message dialogs.
6. Create help dialogs.
7. Edit the properties of interface objects.
8. Make functional connections between objects in the user interface.
9. Go into test mode to test menus, help, and connections.
10. Start the Code Generator to generate code and create the user interface.
11. Add modules of user code to the code generated by App Builder.

12. Debug the code, make, and run the application. Repeat as necessary.

8.2.3 App Builder Internationalization

App Builder can help you create worldwide software. You can set it up to include catgets(3C) calls around all user-visible strings.

8.2.3.1 Automating App Builder Messaging

To have App Builder automatically generate message catalogs, follow these steps:

1. **Choose Application Framework from the Editors menu.**

   The Application Framework Editor window appears.

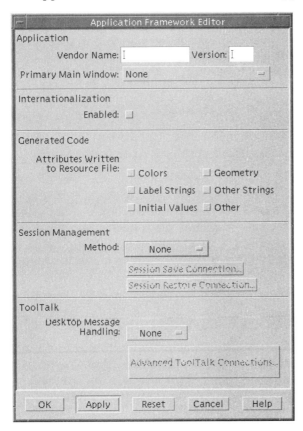

2. **In the Internationalization section, click Enabled.**

   This button enables automatic messaging.

The internationalization check box specifies whether internationalization is enabled. If checked, it turns on XPG4-compliant messaging in the generated code for this project. In the *module_ui.c* file, all labels and strings for objects generated are enclosed by `catgets()` calls. Also, `dtcodegen` automatically generates and maintains the message catalog *project.msg*, which contains strings for all the generated `catgets()` calls.

App Builder also produces a resource file that you can customize to specify object layout. Since App Builder generally uses *x,y* coordinates for object placement, localization teams often need to customize layouts by modifying the resource file.

8.3 Other CDE Applications

If you have access to a system with multiple locales installed, you might want to take a look at the `dtcalendar` program, a calendar manager, to see how CDE implements date and time for different locales.

The `dtmail` program, the CDE multimedia mail application, is interesting for the methods used to convert text between locales. Codesets are described by either MIME or OpenWindows conventions, and conversion is based on `iconv(5)`.

The `dthelp` program, CDE's desktop help facility, can display localized help files by looking for the prevailing locale under `/usr/dt/dthelp/nls`.

8.3.1 Distributed X11 Locales

Because each system's local X11 server is responsible for font display, it is not possible to run localized applications on remote machines with exotic locales installed. For example, you can't `rlogin` to a Japanese system, run an X11 program, and expect Kanji fonts to display. The X11 protocol sends text, not bitmaps, across the network.

8.4 Summary

CDE provides a standard X Windows environment with intuitive Motif interface on several different UNIX platforms. If you develop international applications using App Builder, you can easily port your applications to any system platform that provides Motif library support and X Windows runtime interfaces.

Motif Programming 9 ≡

This chapter describes how to write international Motif applications. Sample code demonstrates how Motif makes it easy to create worldwide software. If you need to dip down and program at the Xlib level or are working with another toolkit, see Chapter 10, *X11 Programming*.

The Motif toolkit, a user-interface toolkit based on the X11 window system and the Xt intrinsics, allows developers to create graphical applications easily, without having to modify their source code for each supported language. An application developed and compiled with Motif can operate in any supported locale and process data according to the rules of the prevailing language.

When internationalizing a Motif application, you should address the following issues. The remainder of this chapter discusses these issues.

- *Locale announcement* is the part of your application that sets the language or cultural environment. See *Locale Announcement* on page 131.

- *Character encoding* is the method by which a language's character set is represented digitally. Conventional applications use 7-bit ASCII encoding to represent each character. However, some languages have larger character sets that require more than the 128 character range permitted by mere 7-bit encoding. See *Character Encoding and Text Formats* on page 132.

- *Font handling* is the way an application employs system font resources to represent a language's character set. This is simple for certain languages that have a simple character set requiring only one font. However, some languages employ multiple character sets and therefore require multiple fonts, called a *font set*. See *Handling Fonts* on page 133.

- *Localized text handling.* The translator needs to take application strings (that is, menu and button text, error messages, and so forth), convert them into the target language, and have those strings printed in the language specified by a locale. The best way to handle this in Motif is by translating application resource files. See *Localized Text Handling* on page 134.

- *Input method* is the way that users enter natural language text into their computer. All languages have an input method, even if it is as simple as typing letters on a keyboard. Some languages, however, have very large character sets that may require several keystrokes to create one character. See *Input Method* on page 136.

- *Standards*. Most developers want their applications to port easily to other platforms besides Solaris. Motif and CDE help ensure that they do. To make applications portable across a wide variety of hardware platforms, it is important to use a toolkit that follows standards as much possible, such as Motif. See *Standards* on page 147.

- *Compiling and linking* is how you get an application to run on a particular system platform. See *Compiling Motif Programs* on page 139.

This chapter presents these issues in detail and discusses how Motif addresses these issues. In addition, the section *Compiling Motif Programs* on page 139 shows how to localize a sample application.

Localizing a Motif application consists primarily of changing messages, labels, and other strings in resource files, setting the default text format, and providing localized *input methods* (IM) if required. An input method is a language-specific way of entering text into system files. See *Input Methods* on page 109 and *Input Method Architecture* on page 118 for more information about input methods.

9.1 System Requirements

Originally, Solaris systems came bundled with OpenWindows, an X11 window system manager with its own look and feel. Although it was available from third-party vendors, the Motif window system manager and toolkit were not bundled with the Solaris system until late 1995. At that time, Motif libraries and headers were available as part of CDE (Common Desktop Environment) on a separate CD-ROM. Afterwards, CDE and Motif were integrated into Solaris releases.

Most commercial developers use the Motif toolkit nowadays. Motif programs can usually run under OpenWindows, so Motif offers backward compatibility.

Motif programs can be localized for several Asian languages. To do so, you need both Solaris and the *Feature Package* for the target locale. For example, obtain the Japanese Feature Package (JFP) for Japan and the Korean Feature package (KFP) for Korea. These packages consist of extensions to Solaris and numerous facilities, such as input methods, for handling local linguistic and cultural conventions. See Chapter 3, *Encoding Character Sets* for more details.

9.2 Locale Announcement

The X Toolkit Intrinsics layer, on which Motif is layered, must be initialized to handle international data. Establishing locale is the responsibility of Motif and Xlib. Your application does not need to call the setlocale(3) function directly, because Xt calls this function internally. Use the following call:

```
XtSetLanguageProc(NULL, NULL, NULL);
```

The three arguments to XtSetLanguageProc() specify application context, language procedure, and optional client data. Usually all three are NULL, indicating the application context of the current program, the standard system setlocale() routine, and no client data.

Note – Until your application calls XtAppInitialize(), the locale is not set, so do not try any locale-dependent processing until your program has called both routines. Always call XtSetLanguageProc() before XtAppInitialize().

Xt provides an application resource called XnlLanguage (class XnlLanguage) that announces the user's locale to the toolkit and to the operating system. Some currently supported values for this resource are de, es, fr, it, ja, ko, sv, zh, and zh_TW; see Appendix A, *Languages, Territories, and Locale Names* for details.

Here are the three ways to establish an application's locale:

1. Specify -xnllanguage on the command line of a Motif application. For example, to set the locale for *myapplication* to Korean, type:

```
% myapplication -xnllanguage ko
```

2. Specify *xnlLanguage: *language* in an X11 resource file. For example, to set locale to traditional Chinese, add this line to your .Xdefaults file:

```
*xnlLanguage: zh_TW
```

3. Set the LANG environment variable in the shell from which you are starting the application. For example, to set the locale to Japanese, type:

```
% setenv LANG ja
```

9

9.3 Character Encoding and Text Formats

Motif supports three character encoding types, or *text formats:*

- Single byte, representing each character with one byte
- Multibyte, representing each character with a variable number of bytes
- Wide character, representing each character with a fixed number of bytes

Treat single byte characters as multibyte characters. Avoid X11 text routines such as XDrawString(3X) and XDrawText(3X), which are not internationalized, as are XmbDrawString(3X) and XwcDrawString(3X).

For Motif programs, it is a good idea to take advantage of built-in compound string support and use XmStringCreate(3X) and XmStringDraw(3X). The lower-level X11 routines can be used if you need to deal specifically with wide or multibyte characters; see *Text Rendering Routines* on page 154.

Applications can create single byte, multibyte, or wide character Motif objects, or a combination of these. If you are writing an application intended for single byte locales only, you might want to use single byte text for the increased performance you think it provides. However, this will make it harder to internationalize your application at a later date, and performance differences could be minimal at best. See Chapter 3, *Encoding Character Sets* for more details on these trade-offs.

Motif supports the single byte text format primarily for backward compatibility.

The multibyte text format is fully compatible with ASCII. Because each different character can potentially be a different size, programming with multibyte text can sometimes be difficult. However, the multibyte format uses memory efficiently.

Wide character text format, on the other hand, is easier to program because all characters are represented with the same number of bytes. However, this format consumes more memory because it represents all characters with a fixed number of bytes (four on Solaris and many other systems). If all characters are ASCII, many of these bytes will be superfluous.

When deciding which format is best for an application, consider the following:

- Conversion between formats reduces performance
- Processing multibyte data is inherently more time consuming than processing single byte or wide character data. Objects that perform intensive data manipulation (for example, text-editing objects such as Motif's TextEdit or TextField widgets) will perform better if created as wide character objects. If an object is certain to handle only 8-bit data, the optimal solution is to create single byte objects.

You should design your application to minimize conversion between formats. For example, you may want to decide on an object-by-object basis whether textual data must be processed intensively and if so, then use wide character format.

9.4 Handling Fonts

Motif uses font lists to organize character sets. In East Asian locales, for example, the four EUC codesets often employ different fonts, each of which represents one character set. A *font* is a set of glyphs organized as a single entity to represent the characters in a given codeset (for example ISO 8859-1). A *font set* is a single font or a group of fonts needed to display text for a given language or locale. A *font list* is a collection of fonts, font sets, or both.

9.4.1 Specifying Font Lists

Motif requires a font list for text display. A Motif font list is a list of fonts, font sets, or both, each of which has a tag to identify it. If available, use a font set to ensure that all characters in a given locale can be displayed. With simple fonts, it is the user's responsibility to ensure that all characters can be displayed.

Specify a Motif font list in an X11 resource file or the application defaults file by using the following format:

```
*fontList: font-list-string:
```

Separate single fonts with a comma. Separate font set elements with a semicolon. End the Motif font list string with a colon. Here is a sample Motif font list, which contains one font, for Western European locales:

```
*fontList:\
-sun-serif-medium-r-normal-serif-14-140-72-72-m-80-iso8859-1
```

Here is a sample Motif font list specification for the Japanese locale. This Motif font list contains one font set and could be entered in the .Xdefaults file:

```
*fontList:\
-adobe-courier-bold-r-normal--16-*-*-*-p-*-iso8859-1;\
-sun-gothic-bold-r-normal--16-140-75-75-c-70-jisx0201.1976-0;\
-sun-gothic-bold-r-normal--16-140-75-75-c-140-jisx0208.1983-0:
```

When users want to run Japanese applications, they must specify these fonts in a resource file *before* starting up the application. Otherwise, there might be no fonts available to represent special Japanese characters.

Of course, it is possible for localization teams to specify a Motif font list for a particular locale. This can be done in the `app-defaults` file, which can be picked up according to the `XFILESEARCHPATH` environment (see below).

9.4.2 Localized Resource Files

The Xt resource manager and the help facility both search the directories listed by `XFILESEARCHPATH` for the requested file name. If you set the file name from within your program as an absolute path, help ignores `XFILESEARCHPATH`. If the `XFILESEARCHPATH` expansion does not find a resource or help file, the current directory is searched.

Within the `XFILESEARCHPATH` variable, any occurrence of the string `%L` is replaced with the current locale name, any occurrence of `%T` is replaced with the object type, and any occurrence of `%N` is replaced with the application class or file name; see `XtResolvePathname(3X)` for details.

Here is a sample setting for `XFILESEARCHPATH`:

```
/usr/dt/lib/nls/%T/%L/%N:/usr/openwin/lib/locale/%L/%T/%N
```

9.5 Localized Text Handling

Motif provides resources that enable you to set various text strings (messages, menu items, button labels, and so on) in an application. For information on the text string resources for a particular widget, see the reference section for that widget. When you create an internationalized application, remove all these resources from your application and keep them in locale-specific resource files. You may instead prefer to create message catalogs and use `catgets()` or `gettext()`, but this can get complicated because of compound strings.

Motif uses compound strings to display all text, except inside Text and TextField widgets, where it uses regular C-style strings. Compound strings are a way of encoding text for possible display in many locales and fonts without requiring any change to your application.

9.5.1 Compound Strings

Compound strings include one or more segments, each of which may contain a Motif font list element tag, string direction, and text component. When a compound string is displayed, the Motif font list element tag and the string direction are used to determine how to display the text. See XmString(3X) for more information about the data type that represents compound strings.

When Motif displays the text of a compound string segment, it matches the segment's Motif font list element tag with a font list element tag from the widget's font list. It then uses the associated font or font set to display the text of the segment. A special font list element tag, XmFONTLIST_DEFAULT_TAG, indicates that text is encoded in the codeset of the current locale and should be displayed with the fonts used for that locale.

If your application reads text labels, menu items, and so forth from resource files, Motif automatically converts these to compound strings. For example, suppose the label for a PushButton widget is inherited from the Label widget; the resource is XmNlabelString, which is of type XmString. This is the correct type.

By contrast, if your application reads text labels, menu items, and so forth from a message catalog by using catgets() or gettext(), you will have to convert ordinary C-style strings to compound strings. Conversion can be done with the XmStringCreateLocalized() routine, as in this example:

```
Widget button;
XmString pushButton;
...
pushButton = XmStringCreateLocalized(catgets(catd, 1, 1, "PushMe"),
    XmFONTLIST_DEFAULT_TAG);
n = 0;
XtSetArg(args[n], XmNlabelString, pushButton); n++;
button = XmCreatePushButton(toplevel, "button", args, n);
XtManageChild(button);
XmStringFrce(pushButton);
```

The inconvenience of doing this for every label, and the greater ease of user customization, are two reasons why resource files are often used instead of message catalogs. The reason for preferring message catalogs with catgets() is improved performance for very large message sets. Most of the lines above could be eliminated by this entry in the app-defaults file:

```
*toplevel.button.labelString: PushMe
```

9.5.2 Compound Strings and Compound Text

For drag and drop between windows, X11 relies on the compound text facility. The compound text format is described in the X standard and is used for the interclient communication conventions method (ICCCM).

Text and TextField widgets use regular C-style strings. When a user cuts text from one text widget and pastes it into another, Motif automatically performs the conversion to compound text and back. This allows one codeset to get translated into another during the cut and paste operation, thus preventing loss of data.

However, when a program passes text in a Text or TextField widget to or from a non-Text widget, the application must convert between compound string and compound text.

Motif offers the `XmCvtXmStringToCT()` function for converting compound strings to compound text, and the `XmCvtCTtoXmString()` function for converting compound text to compound strings.

9.6 Input Method

The input method is the algorithm by which users can enter text of a language. Input methods for each language may be different, depending on the linguistic structure and conventions of that language.

Motif follows the *X Window System Version 11, Input Method Specification*, which resulted from discussions among X Consortium members on standardizing the input handling of characters in various languages by X clients.

Motif widgets that deal with text, such as Text and TextField, provide built-in input method handling, which is mostly transparent to an application. Therefore, application programmers need not know the details of input manager handling. In general, input methods just work.

However, the DrawArea widget does not provide built-in input method handling, so application programmers who want to provide text input inside a drawing area must know how to implement an input manager. See *Using Input Methods* on page 156 for a discussion of this topic.

9.6.1 What an Input Method Does

For many languages, there isn't a one-to-one key to character mapping, regardless of how the keyboard is configured. In order to support such languages, an input method is required.

In English, users enter the desired text by typing in a sequence of letters to create a word. However, for languages based on ideographic characters, input is more complicated. We've seen Japanese can use three phonetic alphabets—Hiragana, Katakana, or Romaji—or the traditional ideographic alphabet, Kanji. In any piece of writing, all four writing systems can be mixed.

To handle languages for which there isn't a one-to-one key to character mapping, input methods may provide features such as the following:

- A control key sequence, which selects the *input mode*
- A pre-edit region, which displays characters as the user enters them but before the user *commits* them
- An optional lookup choice region, which displays ideographic characters and allows the user to choose one
- A status region, which provides information such as whether conversion is activated and the state or mode of the input method

Text input widgets, in conjunction with some input methods, can also provide advanced, language-specific, pre-editing features. The Motif TextEdit widget, for example, can detect certain conditions when it will commit any uncommitted pre-edit text without the user having to take further action. This technique is known as *implicit commit*.

Example: In a mail application the user enters a message in Japanese and presses a "send" button to dispatch the composed message. If pre-edit text has not been committed to the text buffer, and the user's intention is for that text to be part of the message, then it may be useful for the toolkit to intervene and cause a commit to occur before the application processes the buffer and sends the message. (The OpenWindows `mailtool` did this, but the CDE `dtmail` does not.)

Details of which operations trigger implicit commit semantics in Motif widgets can be discovered by experimentation.

The use of these features varies with the input method. For more information, see the documentation for the input method you are using.

Figure 9-1 shows the input method screen regions described above.

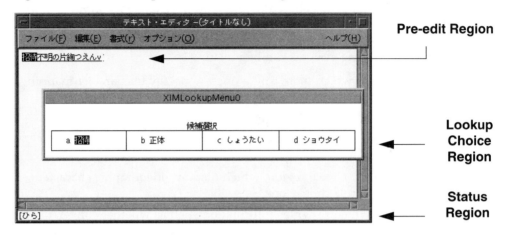

Figure 9-1   Input Method Regions for Japanese Locale

9.6.2 VendorShell Widget Class

In CDE, the VendorShell widget class provides an interface to the input method. In addition to controlling MainWindow, VendorShell also controls the layout of these two areas, when required by the input method:

- The *pre-edit area*, which shows pre-edit data as it occurs. In some Motif implementations, the pre-edit style can vary from widget to widget within a VendorShell. In other Motif implementations, multiple text widgets share a single pre-edit area for input context.

- The *status area*, which specifies where status feedback is presented. The status style, unlike the pre-edit, is an attribute of the shell and is expected to remain the same across all widgets inside the shell.

The *lookup choice area* is usually managed as a separate window, since it comes up in different sizes according to how many choices exist.

Any status area or pre-edit area is managed by VendorShell internally and is not accessible to the client. These two areas are managed as part of MainWindow.

The user can change the input method by setting the locale or by setting the XmNinputMethod resource, for example @im=alt.

Since the VendorShell class is a superclass of TopLevelShell and TransientShell, the top-level window and dialog boxes inherit resources from VendorShell.

A VendorShell widget behaves as an input manager only if one of its descendants is an XmText or XmTextField widget. VendorShell does the following:

- Manages an input method
- Enables applications to process character input and output as supported by system locales
- Sets up pre-editing in either OffTheSpot, OverTheSpot, Root, or None mode
- Provides geometry management for descendant child widgets

Typically, the child of the VendorShell widget is a container widget, such as an XmBulletinBoard or XmRowColumn widget, that itself manages multiple Text and TextField widgets. All Text widgets share the same input method.

In this way, input manager support is almost automatic in Motif. The application programmer doesn't have to plan ahead to support each locale—they come as part of the package.

9.7 Compiling Motif Programs

To compile and link a Motif application, run the following compiler command:

```
cc -I/usr/openwin/include -I/usr/dt/include \
    -L/usr/openwin/lib -L/usr/dt/lib -R/usr/dt/lib \
    application.c -o application -lXm -lXt -lX11
```

On Solaris, many X11 headers and libraries reside in /usr/openwin, so you need to include these header files and libraries with the -I and -L options. Motif headers and libraries reside mostly in /usr/dt, so you also need to include these header files and libraries with secondary -I and -L options.

The -R option tells the compiler to insert instructions for the runtime loader to resolve shared libraries by looking first in /usr/dt/lib. This helps prevent runtime linking errors and versioning problems.

At the end of the command line, you need to link with the Motif library -lXm, the Xt Intrinsics library -lXt, and finally with the X windows library -lX11.

9.7.1 Motif in a Makefile

Since the command line for compiling a Motif application is quite complicated, and to aid program development, it is generally best to create a `Makefile` to help compile your application. Here is a sample `Makefile`:

```
PROGRAMS = app1 app2
INCLUDE = -I/usr/openwin/include -I/usr/dt/include
LIBPATH = -L/usr/openwin/lib -L/usr/dt/lib -R/usr/dt/lib
LIBS    = -lXm -lXt -lX11

all: $(PROGRAMS)

app1:
     $(CC) $(INCLUDE) $(LIBPATH) app1.c -o app1 $(LIBS)
app2:
     $(CC) $(INCLUDE) $(LIBPATH) app2.c -o app2 $(LIBS)
```

9.7.2 Example of Internationalizing a Motif Application

To internationalize a simple Motif application, follow these steps:

1. Remove any resources that contain display text from the application code and put them into a resource file.

2. Call `XtSetLanguageProc()` before calling `XtAppInitialize()`.

3. Use `catgets()` or `gettext()` to encapsulate user-visible strings not already included in the resource file.

4. Specify a Motif font list in the application defaults file, or rely on the user to have the correct font set.

5. Use wide character library routines whenever it is necessary to do heavy string manipulation.

Suppose you want to write an internationalized application that displays a calendar of selected months, possibly including some wide character text in certain locales. This program should be able to traverse months forward and backward, and should also allow resetting to the current month.

Code for such a program is given below. Lines that were modified to deal with wide character text are shown in boldface. These modified lines are all contained in the `calendar()` function.

Here is sample code for a calendar program.

```
#include <Xm/Xm.h>
#include <Xm/PanedW.h>
#include <Xm/RowColumn.h>
#include <Xm/PushB.h>
#include <Xm/Text.h>
#include <locale.h>
#include <langinfo.h>
#include <time.h>
#include <wchar.h>

struct date {      /* keep track of calendar month and year */
    int month;
    int year;
} date;

void format_calendar();

char *
calendar(incr)   /* return localized month/year/days then dates */
int incr;
{
    static int abday[] = {
        ABDAY_1,ABDAY_2,ABDAY_3,ABDAY_4,ABDAY_5,ABDAY_6,ABDAY_7
    };
    time_t clock;
    struct tm *tm;
    static char buf[BUFSIZ*2];
    char buf2[BUFSIZ];
    wchar_t wday[BUFSIZ/4];
    int maxcolwidth;
    int colwidth;
    int d;
    /*
     * fill in month/year first time this function is called
     * then handle wraparound of year in January and December
     */
    if (date.month == 0) {
        clock = time((time_t *) 0);
        tm = localtime(&clock);
        date.month = tm->tm_mon + 1;
        date.year = tm->tm_year + 1900;
    }
```

```
        if (date.month == 1 && incr < 0) {
            date.month = 12;
            date.year--;
        } else if (date.month == 12 && incr > 0) {
            date.month = 1;
            date.year++;
        } else {
            date.month += incr;
        }
        sprintf(buf, "%14s %d\n\n ",
            nl_langinfo(MON_1 - 1 + date.month), date.year);
        /*
         * check to see if ABDAYs take extra display columns
         */
        maxcolwidth = 3;  /* e.g. " 31" */
        for (d = 0; d < 7; d++) {
            if (mbstowcs(wday, nl_langinfo(abday[d]), BUFSIZ/4) ==
                (size_t) -1)
                perror(nl_langinfo(abday[d]));
            colwidth = wcswidth(wday, sizeof(wday)/sizeof(wday[0]));
            if (colwidth > maxcolwidth)
                maxcolwidth = colwidth;
        }
        for (d = 0; d < 7; d++) {
            sprintf(buf2," %*s", maxcolwidth, nl_langinfo(abday[d]));
            strcat(buf, buf2);
        }
        strcat(buf,"\n");
        format_calendar(buf, maxcolwidth);
        return buf;
}

static String fallback_resources[] = {
    "*fontList: serif.r.16",
    "*background: sky blue",
    "*Text.background: white",
    "*Text.rows: 10",
    "*Text.columns: 30",
    NULL
};
```

```
Widget text;    /* global for callback routines below */
/*
 * callback routine to draw calendar for following month
 */
void nextCB(widget, client_data, call_data)
Widget widget;
XtPointer client_data, call_data;
{
    XmTextSetString(text, calendar(1));
}

/*
 * callback routine to draw calendar for previous month
 */
void lastCB(widget, client_data, call_data)
Widget widget;
XtPointer client_data, call_data;
{
    XmTextSetString(text, calendar(-1));
}

/*
 * callback routine to reset calendar
 */
void resetCB(widget, client_data, call_data)
Widget widget;
XtPointer client_data, call_data;
{
    date.month = 0;
    XmTextSetString(text, calendar(0));
}

/*
 * callback routine to quit program
 */
void exitCB(widget, client_data, call_data)
Widget widget;
XtPointer client_data, *call_data;
{
    exit(0);
}
```

```
main(argc, argv)     /* window with buttons and title area */
int argc;
char **argv;
{
    XtAppContext    app_context;
    Widget        parent, pane, row, push1, push2, push3, push4;
    Arg     args[20];
    Cardinal    n = 0;

    /*
     * Xt set locale
     */
    XtSetLanguageProc(NULL, NULL, NULL);
    /*
     * initialize the X toolkit
     */
    parent = XtAppInitialize(&app_context,
        "xcal", (XrmOptionDescList) NULL, 0,
        (Cardinal*) &argc, argv, fallback_resources, args, 0);
    /*
     * put sash between button and text panes
     */
    pane = XmCreatePanedWindow(parent,
        "pane", args, n);
    /*
     * create row of buttons left to right
     */
    row = XtVaCreateWidget("row",
        xmRowColumnWidgetClass, pane,
        XmNorientation, XmHORIZONTAL, NULL);
    /*
     * first button draws calendar for last month
     */
    push1 = XmCreatePushButton(row,
        "Last", args, n);
    XtAddCallback(push1,
        XmNactivateCallback,
        (XtCallbackProc) lastCB,
        (XtPointer) NULL);
```

```
/*
 * second button draws calendar for next month
 */
push2 = XmCreatePushButton(row,
    "Next", args, n);
XtAddCallback(push2,
    XmNactivateCallback,
    (XtCallbackProc) nextCB,
    (XtPointer) NULL);
/*
 * third button resets calendar to current month
 */
push3 = XmCreatePushButton(row,
    "Reset", args, n);
XtAddCallback(push3,
    XmNactivateCallback,
    (XtCallbackProc) resetCB,
    (XtPointer) NULL);
/*
 * fourth button quits the program
 */
push4 = XmCreatePushButton(row,
    "Quit", args, n);
XtAddCallback(push4,
    XmNactivateCallback,
    (XtCallbackProc) exitCB,
    (XtPointer) NULL);
/*
 * establish pushbuttons in row
 */
XtManageChild(push1);
XtManageChild(push2);
XtManageChild(push3);
XtManageChild(push4);
XtManageChild(row);
/*
 * create multi-line text widget
 */
XtSetArg(args[n], XmNeditMode, XmMULTI_LINE_EDIT); n++;
text = XmCreateText(pane,
    "Text", args, n);
```

```
    /*
     * establish row and text inside panes
     */
    XtManageChild(text);
    XtManageChild(pane);
    XmTextSetString(text, calendar(0));
    /*
     * create widgets in window hierarchy
     */
    XtRealizeWidget(parent);
    /*
     * loop forever waiting for user commands
     */
    XtAppMainLoop(app_context);
    return(0);
}
/*
 * put in buf a calendar with all columns columnwidth wide
 */
void
format_calendar(buf, columnwidth)
char *buf;
int columnwidth;
{
    char    s[BUFSIZ];
    FILE    *fp;
    int i;

    sprintf(s,
"cal %d %d | tail +3 | sed 's/^/ /;s/   /%*s&/g;s/ [0-9]/%*s&/g;s/^%*s//'",
        date.month, date.year, columnwidth-2,"",columnwidth-2,"",
        (columnwidth-2)/2,"");
    if ((fp = popen(s, "r")) == NULL)
        return;
    for (i = 0; i < 6; i++) {   /* six lines of days */
        if (!fgets(s, sizeof(s), fp))
            return;
        strcat(buf, " ");
        strcat(buf, s);
    }
    fclose(fp);
}
```

Figure 9-2 and Figure 9-3 show the calendar application in Spanish and Japanese.

Figure 9-2   Calendar Program in Spanish

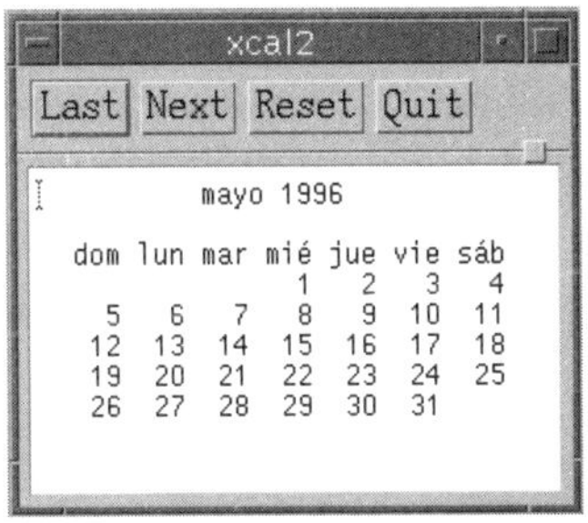

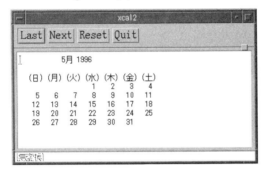

Figure 9-3   Calendar Program in Japanese

9.8 Standards

Many organizations concern themselves with international standards, including ANSI, IEEE (POSIX), IETF, ISO, and the Open Group.

Motif and CDE follow five major standards:

- X/Open standards for international UNIX
- ANSI C standard for language routines
- MIT X11R5 and X11R6 window system standards
- Open Software Foundation's Motif 1.1 and/or 1.2 specification
- Common Desktop Environment (CDE) consortium standard

9

9.9 Summary

Motif is an excellent full-featured GUI programming toolkit. In the hands of a capable programmer, it can produce superb user interfaces that perform well. Motif run-time support is available on almost every modern UNIX platform, and is widely implemented on many other operating system platforms as well.

X11 Programming

This chapter describes how to internationalize X Windows programs. If you are doing Motif programming, see Chapter 9, *Motif Programming*.

10.1 A Brief History of X11

Before release 5, X11 did not contain full support for internationalization. In X11R5, features were added to deal with multibyte East Asian locales, including support for font sets, input methods, multibyte text rendering, and text extents. Even before X11R5, Motif had its own support for multibyte locales, including the font list facility and compound string support. In X11R6, features were added to deal with bidirectional Mideastern locales.

X11 internationalization support is provided on the X client side, so the client application can deal with locale issues without relying on the X server. The benefit of this arrangement is that no server changes are necessary, and the X protocol is unchanged. This preserves backward compatibility, so new global applications can run on old servers.

In early releases of X11, there was no general support for character sets other than ISO Latin-1. Release 5 and later allow other character sets but do require the *X Portable Character Set* for all locales supported by Xlib. The portable character set comprises printable ASCII plus the newline and tab. Strings used or returned by Xlib are either in the X portable character set or in a locale-specific encoding. The Xlib man pages specify which encodings are used where.

Since X is locale independent, there are some limitations on its ability to support internationalization. The X protocol and Xlib specification, together with ANSI C and POSIX restrictions, have led to the following limitations:

- Resource names must be in the X portable character set.

- There is no built-in support for vertical text. Applications may draw strings vertically only by laying out the text manually.

- Full use of X11 internationalization means calling some new routines supplied in Xlib. While all old Xlib applications work with the new Xlib, developers must change their code in places, described in this chapter.

When internationalizing an X application, you should address the following issues. The remainder of this chapter discusses these issues.

- *Locale announcement* is the part of your application that sets the language or cultural environment. See *Locale Announcement* on page 151.

- *Character encoding* is the method by which a language's character set is represented digitally. Conventional applications use 7-bit ASCII encoding to represent each character. However, some languages have larger character sets that require more than the 128 character range permitted by mere 7-bit encoding. See *Character Encoding and Text Formats* on page 151.

- *Font handling* is the way an application employs system font resources to represent a language's character set. This is simple for certain languages that have a simple character set requiring only one font. However, some languages employ multiple character sets and therefore require multiple fonts, called a *font set*. See *Handling Font Sets* on page 152.

- *Localized text handling.* The translator needs to take application strings (that is, menu and button text, error messages, and so forth), convert them into the target language, and have those strings printed in the language specified by a locale. The best way to handle this is with message catalogs. See *Localized Text Handling* on page 153.

- *Input method* is the way that users enter natural language text into their computer. All languages have an input method, even if it is as simple as typing letters on a keyboard. Some languages, however, have very large character sets that may require several keystrokes to create one character. See *Input Method* on page 155.

- *Standards.* Most developers want their applications to port easily to other platforms besides Solaris. To make applications portable across a wide variety of hardware platforms, it is important to use a toolkit that follows standards as much possible. See *Standards* on page 147.

- *Compiling and linking* is how you get an application to run on a particular system platform. See *Compiling X11 Programs* on page 167.

This chapter presents these issues in detail and discusses how X11 addresses these issues.

10.2 Locale Announcement

To initialize locale within Xlib, programs must call the `setlocale`(3) function directly. Use code something like this to check for errors:

```
if (setlocale(LC_ALL, "") == NULL)
    fprintf(stderr, "System cannot set locale\n");
if (! XSupportsLocale())
    fprintf(stderr, "X does not support locale\n");
if (XSetLocaleModifiers("") == NULL)
    fprintf(stderr, "Cannot set input modifiers\n");
```

Instead of just printing an error message, you might want your application to exit. This is a case-by-case decision.

Some currently supported values for this resource are: de, es, fr, it, ja, ko, sv, zh, and zh_TW; see Appendix A, *Languages, Territories, and Locale Names* for more information about locale names.

The two ways to establish the locale are listed below:

1. Set the locale for the window system session. In CDE for example, choose the locale on the `dtlogin` screen. In OpenWindows, set the locale with the Localization Properties dialog box.

2. Set the LANG environment variable in the shell from which you are starting the application. For example, to set the locale to Japanese, type:

```
% setenv LANG ja
```

10.3 Character Encoding and Text Formats

In X11R5 and after, a string may contain characters from more than one codeset. There are several methods for determining which codeset a given character is in; the method depends on the locale and the encoding used.

A *font* is a group of glyphs that represent the characters in a given codeset, for example ISO 8859-1. A *font set* is a group of fonts that are all needed to display text for a given language or locale.

10.3.1 Handling Font Sets

Multi-codeset strings generally cannot be rendered with a single font. A *font set* is a collection of fonts suitable for rendering all codesets represented in a locale's encoding. A font set includes information that indicates in which locale it was created. Applications create font sets for their own use; when a program creates a font set, it is informed which requested fonts are unavailable.

To render strings encoded in Japanese EUC, an application needs fonts encoded in ASCII (or its superset 8859), JIS X0208 and JIS X0212 (for Kanji), and JIS X0201 (for half-width Katakana). The application need not know which characters in a string go with which font. It simply creates a font set made from a list of user-specified fonts, assuming that a locale makes these available. Rendering is done with that font set. A locale-aware rendering system chooses the appropriate font for each character being rendered.

To represent data consisting of multiple character sets, X11R5 and later releases provide XFontSet, an X11 data structure to support font sets. From the user's perspective, an XFontSet represents a list of X Logical Font Description (XLFD) fonts that allows the application to fully represent characters used in a particular locale. For full details on XLFD and font sets, refer to the X11 documentation.

A font set specification is just a string enumerating the XLFD names of fonts. This string can include wild card characters. For example, a specification of 14-point "fixed" fonts might be as follows:

```
char *fontSet = "*fixed-*-r-*140*";
```

Based on the fonts available, a particular Xlib server might expand this to a string such as:

```
-sun-fixed-medium-r-normal-serif-14-140-72-72-m-80-iso8859-1
-adobe-fixed-medium-r-normal--14-140-72-72-c-80-jisx0208.1983-0
-adobe-fixed-medium-r-normal--14-140-72-72-c-80-jisx0201.1976-0
```

Specifying the font set by simply enumerating the fonts is perfectly acceptable, though not the best practice for international applications:

```
    char *fontSet =
 "-sun-serif-medium-r-normal-serif-14-140-72-72-m-80-iso8859-1,\
 -adobe-fixed-medium-r-normal--14-140-72-72-c-80-jisx0208.1983-0,\
 -adobe-fixed-medium-r-normal--14-140-72-72-c-80-jisx0201.1976-0";
```

A German locale would work with only the ISO 8859-1 font; a Japanese locale might use all three; a Chinese locale would not work with this font set.

Note – Using font family names such as Times and Helvetica is not good practice for international applications, since such fonts are unavailable in many locales. Also, italic fonts are generally not available in Asian locales.

The developer should specify a default font set suitable for the default locale, so users can set the correct font set in their preferred locale. Furthermore, developers should ensure that the application accepts localized font set specifications by means of resources or command-line options. Localization teams are responsible for providing default font set specifications suitable for their locales.

10.3.1.1 Creating a Font Set

Creating font sets in X is simply a matter of providing a string that names the fonts, as described above.

```
XFontSet fontset;
char *base_name, **missingCharsetList;
int missingCharsetCount;
char *defaultStringForMissingCharsets;

base_name = "*serif-*-r-*140*"; /* should really use resources! */
fontset = XCreateFontSet(display, base_name,
            &missingCharsetList,
            &missingCharsetCount,
            &defaultStringForMissingCharsets);
```

The locale in effect when this code is executed will be bound to the font set. Font sets may be freed with `XFreefontset()`.

Font sets are used when rendering text with the `Xmb*` or `Xwc*` text rendering routines, which are described below.

10.4 Localized Text Handling

Xt provides a resource mechanism, described in the previous chapter, which is not available from Xlib. The best way to deal with translated messages in Xlib is to create message catalogs and use `catgets()` or `gettext()`.

10.4.1 Text Rendering Routines

X11R5 and X11R6 include text rendering routines intended for multibyte and wide character strings. These routines are similar to the X11R4 text rendering routines XDrawText(), XDrawString(), and XDrawImageString(), which still work as they did but cannot deal with font sets or multibyte characters.

- XmbDrawText(3X) and XwcDrawText(3X) take lists of TextItems, each of which contains (among other things) a string. Strings are rendered by use of font sets. These routines allow complex spacing and font set shifts between strings.

- XmbDrawString(3X) and XwcDrawString(3X) render a string by using a font set. These routines render in the foreground only and use the raster operation from the current graphics context.

- XmbDrawImageString(3X) and XwcDrawImageString(3X) also render a string by using a font set. These routines fill the background rectangle of the entire string with the background, then render the string in the foreground color, ignoring the currently active raster operation.

For multibyte characters, declare strings as arrays of char and use the Xmb*() routines. For wide character encoding, declare characters wchar_t and use the Xwc*() routines. To convert multibyte to wide characters, use mbtowc(3C). For strings, use mbstowcs(3C). To convert in the other direction, use wctomb(3C) and wcstombs(3C).

Refer to the appropriate reference manual pages for details about these routines.

10.4.2 Text Extents Functions

X11 provides multibyte and wide character versions of width and extents interrogation routines, which supply the maximum amount of space required to draw any character in a given font set. These routines depend on font sets to interpret strings and use locale-specific data.

The XFontSetExtents structure contains the two kinds of extents that a string can have:

```
typedef struct {
    XRectangle max_ink_extent;
    XRectangle max_logical_extent;
} XFontSetExtents;
```

Xrectangle `max_ink_extent` gives the maximum boundaries needed to render the drawable characters of a font set. It considers only the parts of glyphs that would be drawn and gives distances relative to a constant origin.

Xrectangle `max_logical_extent` gives the maximum extent of the *occupied space* of drawable characters of a font set. The occupied space of a character is a rectangle specifying the minimum distance from other graphical features; other graphics generated by a client should not intersect this rectangle. The structure `max_logical_extent` is used to compute interline spacing and the minimum amount of space needed for a given number of characters.

Here are descriptions of a few of the new extents-related functions (consult the appropriate reference pages for details):

- `XExtentsOfFontSet()` returns an `XFontSetExtents` structure for a font set.

- `XmbTextEscapement()` and `XwcTextEscapement()` take a string and return the distance in pixels (in the current drawing direction) to the origin of the next character after the string, if the string was drawn. Escapement is always positive, regardless of direction.

- `XmbTextExtents()` and `XwcTextExtents()` take a string and return information detailing the overall rectangle bounding the string's image and the space the string occupies (for spacing purposes).

- `XmbTextPerCharExtents()` and `XwcTextPerCharExtents()` take a string and return ink and logical extents for each character in the string. Use this for redrawing portions of strings or for word justification. If the font set might include context-dependent drawing, the client cannot assume that it can redraw individual characters and get the same rendering.

- `XContextDependentDrawing()` returns a Boolean telling whether a font set might include context-dependent drawing.

Refer to the appropriate reference manual pages for details about these routines.

10.5 Input Method

The input method (IM) is the algorithm by which users enter the text of a language. The input method for each language may be different, depending on the linguistic structure and conventions of that language. For a general discussion of input methods, see *What an Input Method Does* on page 136.

The following section is provided as background for the Motif implementation of input methods and for programmers who are implementing an input method in some other toolkit, or directly in Xlib.

10.5.1 Using Input Methods

Input methods are ways to translate keyboard input events into text strings. Typing on a regular US English keyboard constitutes one input method. Typing Chinese characters on the same keyboard would constitute another, much more complex, input method. A Chinese input method is needed because it would be too difficult or costly to build keyboards suitable for direct input of the tens of thousands of distinct Chinese characters.

Two types of input methods exist: *front-end* and *back-end*. Both types have identical application programming interfaces, so you lose no generality by using back-end methods, which are simpler.

To use an input method, follow these steps:

1. Open the input method and determine what the input method can do.
2. Decide which capabilities to use.
3. Create input contexts with preferences and window specified (see *Using Input Contexts* on page 162).
4. Set the input context focus.
5. Process events.

Although all applications go through the same setup when establishing input methods, the results can vary widely. In a Japanese locale, you might end up with networked communications with an input method server and a Kanji translation server, with circuitous paths for Key events. But in a Swiss locale, it is likely that nothing would occur besides a flag or two being set in Xlib. Since operating in non-Asian locales ends up bypassing almost all of the things that might make input methods expensive, Western users are not noticeably penalized for using Asia-ready applications.

10.5.1.1 Opening an Input Method

The XOpenIM() routine opens an input method appropriate for the locale and modifiers in effect when it is called (see the XOpenIM(3X) manual page for details). The locale is bound to that input method and cannot be changed. (But you can open another input method if you want to switch later.)

To close an input method, call XCloseIM().

Most of the complexity associated with input method use comes from configuring an input context to work with the input method. Input contexts are discussed in *Using Input Contexts* on page 162.

Strings returned by XmbLookupString() and XwcLookupString() are encoded in the prevailing locale when the input method was opened, no matter what the current input context. The syntax for XOpenIM() is:

```
XIM
XOpenIM(Display *display, XrmDataBase db, char *resName, char *resClass);
```

Variable *resName* is the resource name of the application, *resClass* is the resource class, and *db* is the resource database that the input method should use for looking up resources private to itself. Any of these can be NULL. The following code fragment shows how easy it is to open an input method:

```
XIM im;
if ((im = XOpenIM(dpy, NULL, NULL, NULL)) == NULL);
    exit_with_error();
```

XOpenIM() finds the IM appropriate for the current locale. If XOpenIM() fails but XSupportsLocale() returns TRUE (see the XSupportsLocale(3X) manual page), it probably indicates that system locales are not properly set up.

The XSetLocaleModifiers() function sets X modifiers for the current locale. The locale host X modifiers announcer (the XMODIFIERS environment variable) is appended to the modifier list to provide default values on the locale host. The modifier list argument is a null-terminated string containing zero or more concatenated expressions of the form: *@category=value*.

For example, if you want to connect Input Method server *xwnmo*, set modifiers _XWNMO for category @im as follows:

```
XSetLocaleModifiers("@im=_XWNMO");
```

It is not good practice to hardcode such strings into international applications.

It would be preferable to have users set the environment variable XMODIFIERS to the string @im=_XWNMO and pass a null string to the function:

```
XSetLocaleModifiers("");
```

The XSetLocaleModifiers() function must be called before the XOpenIM() function. Note that if XSetLocaleModifiers() is called with a missing input method or other locale modifiers, XOpenIM() will fail.

10.5.2 Input Method Styles

If the application requests it, an input method can often supply status information about itself. For example, a Japanese IM may be able to indicate whether it is in Japanese input mode or Romaji input mode. An input method can also supply pre-edit information, partial feedback about characters in the process of being composed. The way an IM deals with status and pre-edit information is referred to as an IM style. This section describes styles and their naming.

10.5.2.1 Root Window

The *Root Window* style has a pre-edit area and a status area in a window owned by the IM as a descendant of the root. The application does not manage the pre-edit data, the pre-edit area, the status data, or the status area. Everything is left to the input method to do in its own window, as illustrated in Figure 10-1.

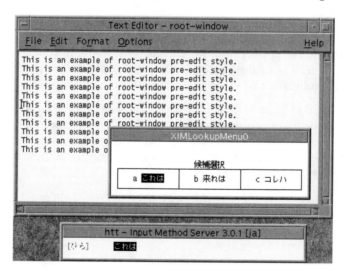

Figure 10-1   Root Window Input Method

10.5.2.2 Off-the-Spot

The *Off-the-Spot* style places a pre-edit area and a status area in the current window, usually in reserved space away from the place where input appears. The application manages the pre-edit area and status area, but allows the IM to update the data there. (The application provides information about foreground and background colors, fonts, and so on.)

A window using Off-the-Spot input might look like that shown in Figure 10-2.

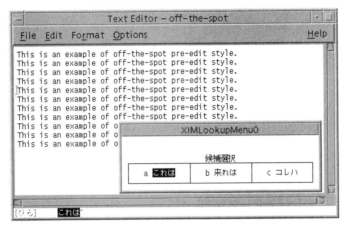

Figure 10-2   Off-the-Spot Input Method

10.5.2.3 Over-the-Spot

The *Over-the-Spot* style involves the IM creating a small, pre-edit window over the point of insertion. The window is owned and managed by the IM as a descendant of the client window, but gives users the impression that input is being entered in the right place. In fact, the pre-edit window often has no borders and is invisible to the user, giving the same appearance as On-the-Spot input. The application manages the status area as in Off-the-Spot but specifies the location of the editing so that the IM can place pre-edit data over that spot.

A window using Over-the-Spot input might look like that shown in Figure 10-3.

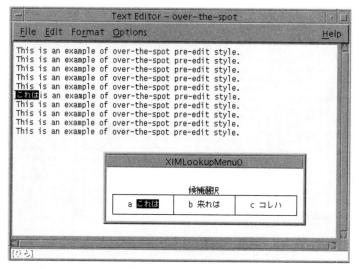

Figure 10-3   Over-the-Spot Input Method

10.5.2.4 On-the-Spot

On-the-Spot input is by far the most complex for the application developer. The IM delivers all pre-edit data through callbacks to the application, which must perform in-place editing—complete with insertion and deletion and so on. This approach usually involves a great deal of string and text rendering support at the input generation level, above and beyond the effort required for completed input. Since this might mean a lot of updating of surrounding data or other display management, everything is left to the application. There is little chance an IM could ever know enough about the application to be able to help it provide user feedback. The IM therefore provides status and edit information by callbacks. This style can often be the most intuitive one for a user.

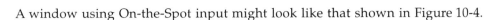

A window using On-the-Spot input might look like that shown in Figure 10-4.

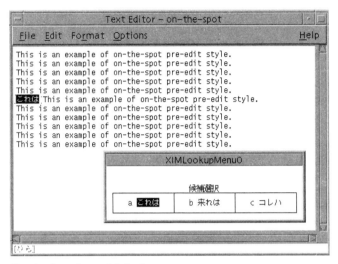

Figure 10-4   On-the-Spot Input Method

10.5.2.5 Setting the IM Style

A style describes how an IM presents its pre-edit and status information to the user. An IM supplies information detailing its presentation capabilities. The information comes in the form of flags combined with OR. The flags to use with each style are defined in <X11/Xlib.h> and are as follows:

Root Window	XIMPreeditNothing | XIMStatusNothing
Off-the-Spot	XIMPreeditArea | XIMStatusArea
Over-the-Spot	XIMPreeditPosition | XIMStatusArea
On-the-Spot	XIMPreeditCallbacks | XIMStatusCallbacks

CDE 1.x provides the following input manager styles: Root Window, Off-the-Spot, and Over-the-Spot. CDE 2.x provides On-the-Spot as well.

For example, if you wanted a style variable to match an Over-the-Spot IM style, you could write:

```
XIMStyle over = XIMPreeditPosition | XIMStatusArea;
```

If an IM returns `XIMStatusNone` (not to be confused with `XIMStatusNothing`), it means the IM will not supply status information.

An input method supports one or more styles. It's up to the application to find a style that is supported by both the IM and the application. If several exist, the application must choose. If none exist, the application is out of luck.

10.5.3 Using Input Contexts

An input method may serve multiple clients, one client with multiple windows, or one client with multiple input styles in one window. Specification of style and client/IM communication is done with *input contexts* (ICs). An input context is simply a collection of parameters that describe how to go about receiving and examining input under a given set of circumstances.

To set up and use an input context:

1. Decide what styles your application can support.
2. Query the IM to find out what styles it supports.
3. Find a match.
4. Determine what information the IC needs to work with your application.
5. Create the IC.
6. Employ the IC.

10.5.3.1 Find an IM Style

The IM may be able to support multiple styles—for example, both Off-the-Spot and Root Window. The application may be able to do, in order of preference, Over-the-Spot, Off-the-Spot, and Root Window. Thus, the application determines that the best match in this case is Off-the-Spot.

First, discover what the IM can do, then set up a variable describing what the application can do, as shown in this example:

```
XIMStyles *IMcanDo;
XIMStyle  clientCanDo; /* note type difference */
XIMStyle  styleWeWillUse = NULL;
XGetIMValues(im, XNQueryInputStyle, &IMcanDo, NULL);
clientCanDo =
/*none*/ XIMPreeditNone | XIMStatusNone |
/*over*/ XIMPreeditPosition | XIMStatusPosition |
/*off*/  XIMPreeditArea | XIMStatusArea |
/*root*/ XIMPreeditNothing | XIMStatusNothing;
```

A client should always be able to handle XIMPreeditNone|XIMStatusNone, which is likely to occur in a Western locale. For an application, this is not very different from the *RootWindow* style, but it comes with less overhead.

Once you know what the application can handle, look through the IM styles for a match, as shown in this example:

```
if (IMcanDo != (XIMStyle *) NULL) {
    for(i=0; i < IMcanDo->count_styles; i++) {
        XIMStyle tmpStyle;
        tmpStyle = IMcanDo->support_styles[i];
        if ( ((tmpStyle & clientCanDo) == tmpStyle) ) {
            styleWeWillUse = tmpStyle;
            break;
        }
    }
}
if (styleWeWillUse = NULL)
    exit_with_error();
XFree(IMcanDo);
/* styleWeWillUse is set, which is what we were after */
```

10.5.3.2 Input Context Values

There are several pieces of information an input method may require, depending on the input context and style chosen by the application. The input method can acquire any such information it needs from the input context, ignoring any information that does not affect the style or IM.

A full description of every item of information available to the IM is supplied in *X Window System, Third Edition*. Table 10-1 shows a brief list:

Table 10-1   Input Context Information

XNClientWindow	Specifies to the IM in which client window it can display data or create child windows; set once and cannot be changed
XNFilterEvents	An additional event mask for event selection on the client window
XNFocusWindow	The window to receive processed (composed) Key symbol events
XNGeometryCallback	A geometry handler that is called if the client allows an IM to change window geometry

Table 10-1   Input Context Information

XNInputStyle	Specifies the style for this IC
XNResourceClass XNResourceName	The resource class and name to use when the IM looks up resources that vary by IC
XNStatusAttributes XNPreeditAttributes	The attributes to be used for any status and pre-edit areas (nested, variable-length lists)

10.5.3.3 Pre-Edit and Status Attributes

When an IM is going to provide state, it needs some simple X information with which to do its work. For example, if an IM is going to draw status information in a client window in an Off-the-Spot style, it needs to know where the area is, what color and font to render text in, and so on. The application gives this data to the IC for use by the IM.

Table 10-2 shows a brief list of pre-edit and status information. As with the table above, details are available in *X Window System, Third Edition*.

Table 10-2   Pre-Edit and Status Information

XNArea	A rectangle to be used as a status or pre-edit area
XNAreaNeeded	The rectangle desired by the attribute writer; either the application or the IM can provide this information, depending on circumstances
XNBackgroundPixmap	A pixmap to be used for the background of windows the IM creates
XNColormap	The colormap to use
XNCursor	The cursor to use
XNFontSet	The font set to use for rendering text
XNForeground XNBackground	The foreground and background colors to use for rendering
XNLineSpacing	The line spacing to be used in the pre-edit window if more than one line is needed
XNSpotLocation	Specifies where the next insertion point is located, for use by XIMPreeditPosition styles
XNStdColormap	Specifies the IM should use XGetRGBColormaps() with the supplied property (passed as an Atom) to determine which colormap to use

10.5.3.4 Creating an Input Context

Creating an input context is a simple matter of calling XCreateIC() with a variable-length list of parameters specifying IC values. The following is a simple example:

```
XVaNestedList arglist;
XIC ic;
arglist = XVaCreateNestedList(0, XNFontSet, fontset,
                              XNForeground,
                              WhitePixel(dpy, screen),
                              XNBackground,
                              BlackPixel(dpy, screen),
                              0);
ic = XCreateIC(im, XNInputStyle, styleWeWillUse,
               XNClientWindow, window, XNFocusWindow, window,
               XNStatusAttributes, arglist,
               XNPreeditAttributes, arglist, NULL);
XFree(arglist);
if (ic == NULL)
    exit_with_error();
```

10.5.3.5 Using the Input Context

A multiwindow application may choose to use several input contexts. But for simplicity, assume that the application just wants to get to the internationalized input, using one method in one window.

Using the IC is a matter of making sure you check events the IC wants and of setting IC focus. If you are setting up a window for the first time, you know the event mask you want, and you can use it directly. If you are attaching an IC to a previously configured window, you should query the window and add in the new event mask.

Here is an example of checking and setting the event mask:

```
unsigned long imEventMask;
XGetWindowAttributes(dpy, win, &winAtts);
XGetICValues(ic, XNFilterEvents, &imEventMask, NULL);
imEventMask |= winAtts.your_event_mask;
XSelectInput(dpy, window, imEventMask);
XSetICFocus(ic);
```

At this point, the window is ready for use.

10.5.4 Events Under IM Control

Processing events under input method control is almost the same in X11R5 and X11R6 (or X11R6.1) as it was under previous releases. There are two essential differences: the XFilterEvent() and X*LookupString() routines.

10.5.4.1 Filtering X Events

Every event received by your application should be fed to the input method with XFilterEvent(), which returns a value telling you whether or not to disregard the event. IMs asks you to disregard the event if they have extracted the data and plan on giving it to you later, possibly in some other form. All events (not just KeyPress and KeyRelease events) go to XFilterEvent().

If you compacted the event processing into a single routine, a typical event loop would look something like the code in this example:

```
Xevent event;
while (TRUE) {
    XNextEvent(dpy, &event);
    if (XFilterEvent(&event, None))
        continue;
    DealWithEvent(&event);
}
```

10.5.4.2 Using **X*LookupString**

When using an input method, you should replace any calls to XLookupString() with calls to XmbLookupString() or XwcLookupString(), depending on whether the code uses multibyte or wide characters. The multibyte and wide character versions have very similar interfaces.

The explanation below uses XmbLookupString() but applies to both versions.

There are two new situations to deal with:

1. The string returned might be long.
2. There might be an interesting keysym returned, an interesting set of characters returned, both, or neither.

Dealing with the former is a matter of maintaining a sufficiently long string area using realloc().

To tell the application what to look for in a given event, XmbLookupString() returns a status value in a passed parameter, equal to one of the values shown in Table 10-3.

Table 10-3   Lookup Event Values

`XLookupKeysym`	Indicates that the keysym should be checked
`XLookupChars`	Indicates that a string has been typed or composed
`XLookupBoth`	Means both of the above
`XLookupNone`	Indicates that neither is ready for processing
`XBufferOverflow`	Indicates that the supplied buffer is too small— call `XmbLookupString()` again with a bigger buffer

`XmbLookupString()` also returns the length of the string in question. Note that `XmbLookupString()` returns string length in bytes, while `XwcLookupString()` returns string length in characters.

10.6 Compiling X11 Programs

To compile and link an X11 application, run the following compiler command:

```
cc -I/usr/openwin/include -L/usr/openwin/lib \
    application.c -o application -lX11
```

On Solaris, many X11 headers and libraries reside in `/usr/openwin`, so you need to include these header files and libraries with the `-I` and `-L` options. At the end of the command line, you need to link with the X windows library `-lX11`.

Note – The application must link dynamically with the X11 library, so do not have the static flag in effect before the `-lX11` flag.

To compile and link an Athena widgets application, run this compiler command:

```
cc -I/usr/openwin/include -L/usr/openwin/lib -R/usr/openwin/lib \
    application.c -o application -lXaw -lXmu -lXt -lX11
```

The Athena widgets library `-lXaw` is built on top of `-lXmu`, which in turn is built on top of the X intrinsics `-lXt`.

The `-R` option tells the compiler to insert instructions for the runtime loader to resolve shared libraries by looking first in `/usr/openwin/lib`. This helps prevent runtime linking errors and versioning problems.

10

10.7 Summary

Most programmers do not need to code using Xlib routines, since higher level toolkits (such as Motif) are available, and provide internationalized routines and interfaces. The material in this chapter is provided mostly for toolkit developers, and for programmers working at a lower level than Motif.

Communicating
Network Data 11 ≡

This chapter discusses network programming considerations for international applications, and is divided into two parts:

- *Programming for networks* is a short discussion of what you need to think about when creating international network applications.

- *OSI network layers* shows the OSI (Open Systems Interconnection) model for international applications. See *OSI Network Layers* on page 170.

11.1 Programming for Networks

What is new or different about internationalizing network applications? There are many good existing standards, although the multiplicity of possible locales makes your task seem overwhelming.

11.1.1 Delivering Network Data

Any network transport protocol, such as TCP, delivers a stream of octets (8-bit bytes) to a system. Applications must properly interpret that octet stream using the proper character set encoding. Transport protocols simply deliver a stream of octets without regard to the content or encoding of the data.

11.1.2 Interpreting Network Character Data

Applications can use existing session mechanisms, such as the Web-based HTTP (HyperText Transport Protocol), to advertise and discover the encoding method for transmitted data. Applications can also use existing presentation mechanisms, such as the e-mail convention MIME (Multipurpose Internet Mail Extensions), to label included data. Here is a sample MIME header for European e-mail, and an HTTP header for a Japanese Web page:

```
Content-Type: text/html; charset=ISO-2022-JP
Content-Type: text/plain ; name="iso" ; charset=iso-8859-1
```

11

Text from different locales is not guaranteed to be mutually intelligible, unless those locales employ a common codeset, such as `iso-8859-1`.

See *HTTP—HyperText Transport Protocol* on page 174, and *Mail with Multipurpose Internet Mail Extensions (MIME)* on page 176 for more details.

11.2 OSI Network Layers

The remainder of this chapter is organized according to the OSI (Open Systems Interconnection) network layer model, as shown in Table 11-1.

Table 11-1   Seven Layers of OSI Architecture

OSI Layer	Examples	Responsibilities of the OSI Layer
1. Physical layer	twisted pair, fiber	Transmission of binary data on a medium
2. Data Link layer	10baseT, ATM	Information transfer, framing, error checking
3. Network layer	IP	Routing and delivery of information packets
4. Transport layer	TCP, UDP	End-to-end delivery, reliable and unreliable
5. Session layer	X11, HTTP, PPP	Establishment and maintenance of sessions
6. Presentation	HTML, MIME, PGP	Data formatting and encryption
7. Applications	ftp, telnet, Netscape	File transfer, terminal emulation, etc.

11.2.1 Physical Layer

At the hardware level, the transmission layer doesn't care about character sets or encodings. Everything is just bits.

A bandwidth shortage exists everywhere, partly because of the huge expense of upgrading copper wire to fiber-optic cable, and partly because governments and telephone companies still control long-distance transmission; the latter are more concerned with charging for connections than with increasing overall throughput.

Hardware manufacturers must consider the ease of installation and maintenance for sites around the world. Cabinet enclosures are best marked with universal symbols indicating port usage and connection type. Just as AC power plugs vary around the world, so can connector types. The twisted pair J45 connector used for digital phones (ISDN) has become popular for connecting workstations to local area networks everywhere.

11.2.2 Data Link Layer

At the transfer level, character sets and encodings are not an issue.

Most local area networks use Ethernet (10baseT or the newer 100baseT, ten times as fast at 100 megabits per second), although some use token-ring protocols. Most wide area networks use ATM on digital lines leased from a telephone company, although some employ point-to-point microwave transmission.

Individuals may connect to networks by using analog phone modems (currently rated at 28.8 kilobits per second with 56 coming soon), or pay extra for ISDN connections (64 or 128 kilobits per second). There is every indication that ISDN will soon be superseded by much faster ADSL (Asymmetric Digital Subscriber Line) or by cable transmission. When writing network software, pay attention to how well your application performs over slow transmission lines.

11.2.3 Network Layer

At the routing level, character sets and encodings are still not an issue.

The Internet Protocol (IP), first implemented in Berkeley UNIX 4.2, has almost completed its imperialistic domination of the world. Other once-contending protocols such as XNS (Xerox® Network Systems) were never implemented by Berkeley UNIX, so they were never widely implemented anywhere else. In Europe, the slower X.25 protocol has sometimes been mandated by governments, but the faster X.400 and X.500 protocols have been all but abandoned.

The `socket`(2) system call provides access to the Internet Protocol family through the `PF_INET` domain format.

11.2.4 Transport Layer

At the delivery level, character sets and encodings start to become an issue.

TCP (Transmission Control Protocol) and UDP (User Datagram Protocol) are two transport protocols above the IP layer. TCP provides reliable, flow-controlled, connection-oriented, two-way data transmission. TCP locates endpoints using standard Internet address format, and also provides a per-host collection of port addresses for different uses.

UDP is a simple, unreliable datagram protocol, and is generally connectionless. Datagrams are messages of fixed length, typically 8 kilobytes.

TCP and UDP are called byte oriented, although they are really octet oriented, since they operate on bytes that are 8 bits long. As such, they are still below the level of character sets and encodings.

The `socket`(2) system call provides access to TCP through the `SOCK_STREAM` protocol type, and to UDP through the `SOCK_DGRAM` protocol type.

Here are examples of TCP and UDP socket creation:

```
#include <sys/socket.h>
#include <netinet/in.h>
int sT, sU;


sT = socket(PF_INET, SOCK_STREAM, 0);
sU = socket(PF_INET, SOCK_DGRAM, 0);
```

11.2.4.1 RPC—Remote Procedure Call

The Remote Procedure Call (RPC) is layered on top of either UDP or TCP (usually UDP) but does not fit neatly into the seven-layer OSI model. It is a cross between a transport and a session mechanism.

RPC routines allow programs to make procedure calls on machines across the network. First, the client calls a procedure to send a data packet to the server. Upon receipt of the packet, the server calls a dispatch routine to perform the requested service, and then sends back a reply. Finally, the procedure call returns to the client. See the rpc(3N) manual page for details about RPC routines.

The RPC mechanism required no modification to support European or East Asian languages. The encapsulation mechanism, eXternal Data Representation (XDR), ensures canonical byte order; programmers need not worry about byte swapping on different hardware architectures or about different floating-point formats. As long as users' locales are set correctly, they can access data equally well on any machine architecture or file system type (even using wide characters).

Applications that read or write binary data across the network may use XDR to encapsulate data and use RPC to transmit. In cases where applications read or write plain text files, files can reside either on a local file system or across the network. See the *Solaris Network Interfaces Programmer's Guide* for details.

11.2.4.2 NFS—Network File System

Since its inception in 1985, Sun's Network File System (NFS) has been 8-bit clean and multibyte capable because it was built on top of RPC and XDR. Recently, WebNFS promises to bring this capability to the Internet.

System administrators can choose which file systems to make available across the network; this is called exporting or sharing. Users with superuser permission can then remote mount these shared file systems, as if they were local.

To share a previously unshared file system, add a line to /etc/exports or /etc/dfs/dfstab (instructions are given in this file) and reboot. See the exports(4) or share_nfs(1M) manual page for details. To remote mount a shared file system, use the mount(1M) command.

The automounter can make an entire network appear to be a unified file system. It provides access under a /net or /hosts directory to all shared file systems on the network. One advantage of the automounter is that it runs as a daemon, so users do not need superuser privilege to mount file systems. Another advantage is that mounts disappear when not used. See the automount(1M) or autofs(1M) manual page for more details. For intelligibility across locales with incompatible codesets, mount points should be limited to ASCII, but this is not required.

11.2.4.3 Byte Order Issues for Multibyte Codesets

In most cases, you do not need to worry about byte order issues.

Locales in East Asia, and possibly other areas, require multibyte codesets because of their vast character repertoires. As long as locales employ a byte (octet) stream encoding method, such as EUC or UTF-8, files created and read in the same locale are readable across the network, on either SPARC or x86 machines. Avoid writing wide characters of type wchar_t (also called process code) to a file. Since wide characters are a binary data representation, they would need to be byte-swapped between SPARC and x86 machines, probably using XDR. Instead, convert wide characters to multibyte characters using wctomb(), or wcstombs() for strings, before writing anything out to a file. See Section 3.2, *Multiple Byte Codesets*, on page 36 for more information on this issue.

Files of different locales are not guaranteed to be mutually intelligible. If different locales employ a common codeset, then files really are mutually intelligible. For example, French and German both use ISO Latin-1, so French files are readable in the German locale, and vice versa. By contrast, Japanese uses various JIS encodings, while Korean uses KSC encodings. So a Japanese file is not readable in the Korean locale, and a Korean file is not readable in the Japanese locale. Unicode was designed to solve this problem.

11.2.5 Session Layer

It is often the session level that interprets different character sets and encodings.

PPP (Point to Point Protocol) is a standard method for transmitting network data using synchronous modems, asynchronous modems, or ISDN. It can transfer data between applications that are employing either TCP connections or UDP packets. Internationalization issues are mostly transparent, since PPP establishes sessions for individual users but isn't involved in character interpretation or display.

≡ 11

The X11 protocol is another example of a session layer. Because X11 handles character display, it must deal intimately with locale management. Chapters 8, 9, and 10 discuss internationalization issues for CDE, Motif, and Xlib.

It is a big problem when two sessions claim to have the same locale, but employ different codesets. This can happen in the Japanese locale, where either EUC or Shift-JIS (PC Kanji) is supported. Client and server must negotiate both the language and the encoding before continuing a session.

11.2.5.1 HTTP—HyperText Transport Protocol

HTTP (HyperText Transport Protocol), based on RFC 1945, is a third example of a session layer. HTTP allows World Wide Web clients, such as Web browsers, to access HTTP, Gopher, and FTP servers. Most Web traffic travels across networks between heterogenous machines using the TCP protocol—HTTP is usually built on top of TCP connections, although this is not required by the protocol.

The protocol requires the HTTP server to announce the content type of requested files, and possibly the codeset (`charset`). HTTP headers must be in US-ASCII. Here are some sample HTTP headers. In the first case, the codeset of transmitted data defaults to ISO-8859-1. The second case indicates Japanese with JIS encoding, represented in ISO 2022, conforming to RFC 1468:

```
Content-Type: text/html;
Content-Type: text/html; charset=ISO-2022-JP
```

11.2.6 Presentation Layer

The OSI model gets a bit confused at the presentation level. In fact, X11 handles both the session layer and the presentation layer. Its session handling involves network protocols, while its presentation layer involves font display.

If you run an X application remotely, setting the `DISPLAY` environment variable back to your local *hostname*:0 console, your fonts come from the local machine, not from the remote machine, as you might expect. This makes the use of distributed locales less than convenient, since you must install fonts for each locale that you might want to employ from a remote machine.

HTML (HyperText Markup Language) is the presentation layer counterpart of HTTP. Currently, the default encoding for HTML files is ISO 8859-1, although alternate encodings can be specified as shown above. A relatively new IETF standard, RFC 1866, describes how HTML should be extended for use with the Unicode `charset`, and how to implement bidirectional text and complex text languages in HTML browsers.

MIME is another example of the presentation layer. See *Mail with Multipurpose Internet Mail Extensions (MIME)* on page 176 for details.

11.2.7 Network Application Layer

This section discusses some common network applications that already handle codeset recognition issues.

11.2.7.1 File Transfer Protocol

The `ftp` command provides a file transfer protocol for sending and receiving files across the Internet. On Solaris, `ftp`(1) file transfer defaults to `ascii`. Before sending international files, set the transmission type to `binary` instead.

11.2.7.2 Remote Login

Sometimes permission problems or network bandwidth limitations make it impossible to access data through NFS. For such cases, the `rlogin`(1) command provides a socket connected to a shell on a remote machine. If you find that your `rlogin` shell is not 8-bit clean, even after typing `stty cs8 -istrip`, then try `rlogin -8`, which means to transmit all 8 bits. This is not always the default. Some characters are special to `rlogin`, such as ~ at beginning of line. If this is a problem, try using `telnet`(1) instead. There is no standard way to negotiate encodings before establishing a `telnet` or `rlogin` connection.

11.2.7.3 Internet Mail

According to RFC 822 (SMTP), issued in 1982, mail messages sent across the Internet should contain nothing more than lines of ASCII, that is, 7-bit characters. This limitation became problematical in Europe after ISO passed the initial 8859 codeset standards for 8-bit characters in 1987. Internet RFC 1154, issued in 1990, specified that the text portion of mail messages could be in ISO 8859, whenever transport mechanisms allowed. However, headers are still limited to ASCII. This implies that login names, machine names, and company names are limited to ASCII characters, if employees want to transmit Internet mail.

Internet RFC 1154 (ESMTP) has not been universally accepted, but is becoming more widespread, especially in Europe. In Japan, mail is exchanged based on RFC 1468. Sun made its electronic mail system 8-bit clean between SunOS 4.0 and 4.1, but later releases of Solaris do not default to 8-bit clean mail transmission. The same is true of other UNIX systems. Some vendors have implemented RFC 1154, while others are implementing MIME (Multipurpose Internet Mail Extensions). Overall, it is best not to rely on 8-bit clean mail transmission.

In East Asia, mail messages usually employ the high bit to indicate the codeset or a specific character. As a consequence, Asian messages require either 8-bit clean mail, or encapsulation with ISO 2022, a codeset switching and 7-bit representation method. The Japanese Internet community uses RFC 1468, also called ISO-2022-JP, for exchanging mail and news. ISO 8859 mail messages often produce odd results when displayed on East Asian mail systems, and vice versa.

11.2.7.4 Mail with Multipurpose Internet Mail Extensions (MIME)

Internet RFC 1521/1522 specifies MIME, which redefines the format of message bodies to allow multipart textual and nontextual data to be represented and exchanged without loss of information. Thus, a mail message can contain multiple objects, such as graphic images, rich text, audio or video files, executable programs, and of course, text in different codesets. The normative codesets are expected to be ISO 8859-1 (Latin-1) and eventually ISO 10646 (Unicode).

Here are the mail header extensions that the MIME standard specifies:

- A `MIME-Version` header field, which uses a version number to declare a message to be conformant with this specification. This field allows mail processing agents to distinguish between MIME messages and messages generated by older or nonconformant software.

- A `Content-Type` header field, which specifies the type of data in the message body and the native encoding of data. Here are some types:

  - `text`, for representing textual information in a number of character sets and formatted text description languages in a standardized manner

  - `multipart`, for combining several body parts, possibly of differing types of data, into a single message

  - `application`, for transmitting application data or binary data and implementing an electronic mail file transfer service

  - `message`, for encapsulating a mail message

  - `image`, for transmitting still image (picture) data

  - `audio`, for transmitting audio or voice data

  - `video`, for transmitting moving image data, possibly with audio

- A `Content-Transfer-Encoding` header field, which specifies an auxiliary encoding that was applied to the data in order to allow it to pass through 7-bit mail transport mechanisms. The `base64` encoding method is perhaps the most widespread way of doing this.

- Two optional header fields that can further describe the data in a message body, the `Content-ID` and `Content-Description` header fields.

MIME is extensible, so the set of `Content-Type` subtypes will grow over time. A registration process exists for public disclosure of new content types. In the initial standard, the `text` type could be either `rich` or `plain`, and the text `charset` could be either `US-ASCII` or `ISO-8859-n`, where *n* is any number in the ISO 8859 set. Unicode 1.1 is specified as `ISO-10646-1:1993`, but this has changed to `ISO-10646-UCS-2` with the Unicode 2.0 standard.

Full support for MIME will gradually be phased in over a sequence of Solaris releases. The OpenWindows `mailtool` program provides `Content-Type` labelling and multipart messages, but does not provide complete MIME support. The CDE `dtmail` program does provide full MIME support.

11.2.7.5 Web Browsers and HTML

In just a few years, most people's primary interface to the Internet has become the World Wide Web. Although it took a browser named Mosaic from the University of Illinois to really popularize the Web, much of the work piecing together the Web was done at CERN, the Conseil Européen pour la Récherche Nucléaire, in Switzerland. In a country where most citizens speak three or four languages, it makes sense that their products would be capable of supporting different locales.

The World Wide Web is 8-bit clean and supports a variety of codesets. HTML was designed with built-in support for Latin-1 characters (ISO 8859-1). In Europe, much of the traffic takes place in local languages, and Web sites often allow visitors to choose one of several languages. In Japan, Web sites usually support Shift-JIS (PC Kanji) encoding, rather than EUC or Unicode.

The original Mosaic from the National Center for Supercomputing Applications (NCSA) supports Latin-1 characters on all platforms, even those that were not originally designed with Latin-1 in mind, such as Microsoft® Windows™ and the Apple Macintosh®. NCSA Mosaic does not support JIS or EUC.

Newer browsers, such as Netscape Navigator™ from Netscape Communications, have been translated into several languages, including French, German, and Japanese. Figure 11-1 shows the French version of Netscape. Netscape supports Latin-1, Latin-2, Japanese EUC-JP, Japanese Shift-JIS, Korean ISO-2022-KR, Korean EUC-KR, Chinese GB, Chinese EUC-TW, and Chinese Big5—all selectable by choosing Document Encoding from the Options menu.

Note that FTP transfers take place by default in ASCII mode. When you use the command-line `ftp` interface, you switch to `binary` mode if you want to transfer material that requires 8-bit clean transmission or that contains nontextual data (the FTP `ascii` option maps newlines into carriage return and linefeed). Web browsers such as Mosaic and Netscape automatically set `binary` mode when you use them to retrieve files from an `ftp`-based Web site.

11.2.7.6 Designing a Web Page

When you create a Web page in HTML, you might think about providing buttons so visitors can access a translation in their preferred language. Of course, this requires additional investment and creates the maintenance problem of keeping many translated pages current and synchronized with one another.

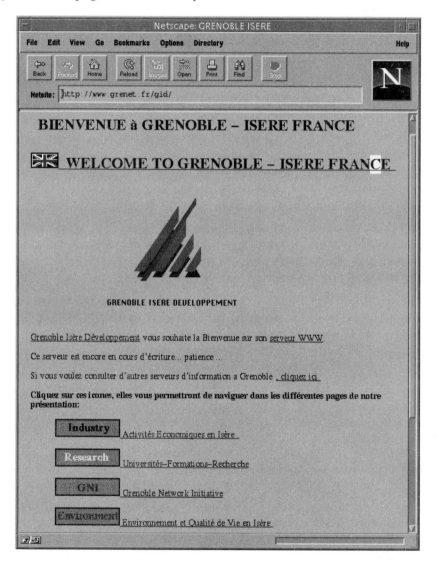

Figure 11-1   French Version of Netscape

11.2.7.7 Java Language

The Java™ language provides a means of writing operating-system-independent applications for the Web, and might radically change the software industry.

The Java language uses Unicode as its native char data type, but also provides the byte data type, which is equivalent to the C language char. The Hot Java™ browser, written in Java, also supports Unicode.

Java release 1.1 provides significant features for writing international software. The class java.util.Locale is similar to the C locale, specifying language and territory. The class java.text encapsulates methods for character encodings, numeric formats, date and time formats, time zones, arbitrary pattern templates, collation, and text boundaries (character, word, line, sentence). Event handling is sensitive to keyboard mappings and allows integration of input methods.

For up-to-the-minute information, visit the Web site http://java.sun.com/Series.

11.2.8 Distributed Locales

The original locale concept was predicated on a single user using a single machine, but the model starts to break down with distributed computing, and also with multithreaded programming.

For example, if a network server receives requests from three users in three different locales, which locale should it use when replying? The most obvious answer, the locale of the client, makes implementation very difficult. How can a server know the details of all possible locales? Moreover, the locale model is a heavyweight technique, and provides no mechanism for switching the server from one locale to another.

A better answer might be for each client to translate universal messages issued by the server into its own locale. This scheme might be workable if there were commonly agreed-upon universal formats and messages. There are not.

If distributed locales are to succeed, it is critical that the locale namespace be identical across the network. This discipline is absolutely essential if servers are to recognize client locales, and vice versa. The locale names in Appendix A, based on the ISO 639 and 3166 standards, are a good starting place.

One possible solution is to have a server fork one process per client and ask the client which locale it should use. This is similar to the way users pick a language in a Web browser. This isn't a very general or efficient solution, and cannot be multithreaded, but might work in some cases. Another possible solution is to use a multilocale programming interface, although none has yet been standardized. The section below discusses one proposed interface.

11.2.8.1 Multilocale Handling with M-star

The POSIX locale mechanism was not designed with distributed computing in mind. Not only are locales generally a heavyweight mechanism, making it costly for applications to switch from one to another, but only one locale can be active at a time. Switching locales is something a window system server, or an object service, performs regularly. Moreover, multithreaded applications often must operate in more than one locale simultaneously.

Current technology does not allow processing of data in more than one locale, because locales are tied to a process. To address this problem, the X/Open Internationalization Working Group devised a new API, called "m-star," to support multilocale computing.

Applications that handle multiple locales would no longer need to switch locales. Instead, they could call any of a set of multilocale routines, passing the attribute handle for the locale in question. Table 11-2 is a list of proposed (but not formally implemented) m-star functions. All these should be handed an attribute handle, followed by the normal parameters of their associated library routine.

Table 11-2   List of M-star Routines

m__tolower()	m_gettext()	m_localeconv()	m_towlower()
m__toupper()	m_getwc()	m_mblen()	m_towupper()
m_catopen()	m_getwchar()	m_mblen()	m_ungetwc()
m_csetcol()	m_getwidth()	m_mbstowcs()	m_vfprintf()
m_csetlen()	m_isalnum()	m_mbtowc()	m_vprintf()
m_dgettext()	m_isalpha()	m_mbtowc()	m_vsprintf()
m_doprnt()	m_iscntrl()	m_nl_langinfo()	m_wcstombs()
m_doscan()	m_isdigit()	m_printf()	m_wcstombs()
m_euccol()	m_isgraph()	m_regexp()	m_wctomb()
m_euclen()	m_islower()	m_scanf()	m_wctomb()
m_eucscol()	m_isprint()	m_setlocale()	m_wscasecmp()
m_fgetwc()	m_ispunct()	m_sprintf()	m_wscol()
m_fgetws()	m_isspace()	m_sscanf()	m_wscoll()
m_fprintf()	m_isupper()	m_strcoll()	m_wsncasecmp()
m_fscanf()	m_isw*()	m_strftime()	m_wsxfrm()
m_getdate()	m_isxdigit()	m_strxfrm()	

M-star is based on the attribute handle, which is a pointer to an object containing locale data. The attribute handle is flexible and may point to other objects (security or real-time information, for instance). Locale objects are created with m_create_handle() and initialized to the C locale. They contain character type, numeric, collation, time, and monetary data. The locale object can be populated with data from any valid locale by passing an attribute handle as a parameter to the m_setlocale() function.

As an example, here is a function that prints out the date and time, using m_strftime(), in two locale formats:

Code Example 11-1   Multilocale Date and Time Function

```
#include <locale.h>
#include <time.h>

local_date(char *locale1, char *locale2);
{
    m_handle handle[2];
    time_t clock;
    struct tm *tm;
    char buf[BUFSIZ];

    if ((handle[0] = m_create_handle()) == NULL ||
                m_setlocale(handle[0], LC_ALL, locale1) == NULL)
        locale_error(locale1);
    if ((handle[1] = m_create_handle()) != NULL ||
                m_setlocale(handle[1], LC_ALL, locale2) == NULL)
        locale_error(locale2);
    clock = time((time_t *)0);
    tm = localtime(&clock);
    m_strftime(handle[0], buf, sizeof(buf), "%c", tm);
    printf("%s\n", buf);
    m_strftime(handle[1], buf, sizeof(buf), "%c", tm);
    printf("%s\n", buf);
}

locale_error(char *locale);
{
    fprintf(stderr, "No locale %s\n", locale);
    exit(1);
}
```

In early 1997, a similar multilocale interface called o-star became a DIS (Draft International Standard), number unknown. The *m* prefix was replaced with an *o*, hence the name o-star.

11

11.3 Summary

For delivering data across a network, use standard network transport protocols such as TCP or UDP, which transmit an octet stream over a physical network.

For interpreting textual data, applications can use existing session or presentation mechanisms to advertise and discover appropriate encoding methods. Whether an application can deal with most commonly encountered encoding methods is an open issue.

At present, Web masters seem satisfied with allowing users to select the language they prefer for browsing a Web site. Of course this is a maintenance chore, and users might not find the language they hoped for. Graphical content can often substitute for detailed language translations.

Runtime environments such as Java, and encoding methods such as Unicode, promise to make the World Wide Web even more global and accessible.

The information in this chapter changes fast, and could soon be out-of-date.

Writing International Documentation

This chapter provides guidelines for writing documentation that can be easily translated into other languages and delivered to audiences in other countries. These guidelines also apply to good technical writing in general. When they are not adhered to, the results are confusing, not only to native English speakers, but even more so to audiences who speak other languages.

Keep in mind as you read these guidelines that people from all over the world may read your documentation—translated or not.

Before you set up translation departments or hire translation vendors in other countries, make sure you have standardized documentation tools and templates that can be used everywhere. The consistency that these tools provide is an important prerequisite for creating uniform documentation that can be quickly and easily translated.

12.1 Gaining Cultural and Geographic Sensitivity

Many times, things often taken for granted in one country are done differently, or not at all, elsewhere. Calendar dates, for example, are displayed differently in various parts of the world. In the U.S. the order generally used is month/date/year, but in Germany it is day/month/year. Of course, a writer can't put all possible cases into a document, but should cultivate a global awareness in order to make the best choice in a given situation.

Here are some guidelines to help in writing for an international audience:

- Develop a vocabulary list (or glossary) and write using terms from this list. With a vocabulary list, translators can develop standard translations to ensure that they are conveying the correct meanings and information.

- Be sensitive to potential troubles with political or religious content. It might be best to avoid these references altogether. Use your imagination, and you should be able to use other techniques to enliven your writing.

- Always define new terms and use them consistently.

- Avoid using examples that are culturally bound, such as names of places or things that people living in other countries do not recognize.

- If you do use examples that are culturally bound, use examples from a variety of cultures and ethnic backgrounds—emphasize diversity. For geographic examples, use place names that are instantly recognizable without the state or country, such as San Francisco, Tokyo, or Paris.

- Recognize that humor varies by taste and by culture, so a joke you think is hilarious might be incomprehensible elsewhere. What is funny in English, whether an illustration or written text, might be obscene or disrespectful in another language. Humor is largely cultural and cannot easily be translated from one language to another. Puns are impossible to translate.

- Avoid idioms, slang, jargon, and adages—they might be misunderstood or mistranslated. An UNIX manual page once contained the word "grok." Unfortunately, people who had not read Robert Heinlein's science fiction books didn't understand that "grok" means "completely understand."

- Avoid irony—even native speakers of English sometimes have difficulty discerning irony in writing.

- Be aware that dates are displayed differently in various locales.
  - month/day/year—used mainly in the U.S.
  - day/month/year—used in Europe and elsewhere
  - year/month/day—ISO standard for numeric representation of dates

  For clarity, write dates out in text (for example, December 10, 1995). If you don't have enough room, use an appropriate abbreviation, and use this format consistently throughout a document.

- Always include complete information for the country given in an address. In documents that are likely to be distributed internationally, include the area code with country code when showing phone numbers, and designate hours to call within a time zone. Consider the applicability of contact information: is a reader in another country likely to write, FAX, call, or e-mail? Remember, 800 numbers are available only within the U.S.

- Don't refer to specific holidays, which can vary tremendously by culture.

- Avoid an informal tone, and strive for brevity. Many cultures value formality in writing style. Brevity usually simplifies translation, and can be easily transformed into a formal style.

- Above all, be clear. An obfuscating passage is not only difficult to translate correctly, but will probably remain unclear even after translation.

12.2 Using Illustrations and Screen Examples

A picture is worth nine hundred ninety-nine words. Moreover, readers who speak little English may be able to follow illustrations more easily than your text. Follow these guidelines to maximize international appeal and comprehensibility of illustrations and screen examples.

- Whenever possible, employ graphics instead of text to illustrate a complex concept. Well-designed graphics can lower translation costs in each of your target languages. Allow for editing and expansion of text inside graphics.

- Write text so that it complements the message conveyed by an illustration.

- Remember that not everybody reads from left to right, so the sequence of graphic images should be indicated when important.

- Use charts and tables to classify essential information. Readers everywhere are drawn to them, recognizing that they contain important material.

- Use graphics that are internationally acceptable.

- Create intuitive symbols; avoid using text as an essential part of a graphic.

- Use graphics that an international audience can easily understand. For example, almost every country has its own type of power plug. Instead of illustrating each type of plug, illustrate a generic plug and receptacle, as shown in Figure 12-1.

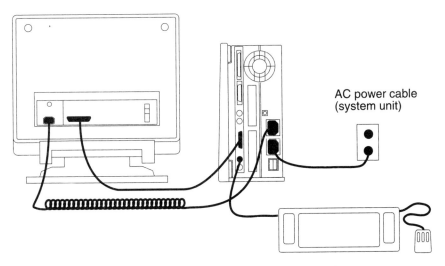

AC power cable
(system unit)

Figure 12-1   An Illustration Showing a Generic Plug and Receptacle

However, when describing various types of plugs and receptacles, illustrate and label the type used in each country, as shown in Figure 12-2.

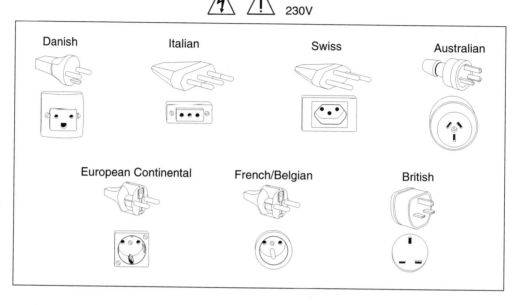

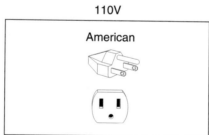

Figure 12-2   International Plugs and Receptacles

- Leave ample space for callout text in graphics, since translated text might require more space than English text.

- Make certain that callouts correlate to the paragraph text. Use callouts instead of text if a concept can be best understood graphically and requires little explanation.

- Format callouts so that you can edit them and so that they can be translated independently of the graphic.

- Do not use a human hand in a *symbolic* gesture. Just about any position the hand can be shown in is considered an obscene gesture in some foreign country (see Figure 12-3). Even the pointing index finger, common in some documentation, is considered obscene in some locales.

Figure 12-3   Examples of Gestures That Could Be Obscene in Some Cultures

- When you are showing screen snapshots or screen examples, use generic machine names, login names, and system names, such as *machine_name*, *login_name*, and *system_name*. Specific names, when translated, could possibly be offensive in other languages. For example, do not write:

```
purgatory%
```

Use a generic machine name instead:

```
hostname%
```

- Avoid using road signs in graphics, as they differ from country to country.
- Avoid references to alcohol or related material, as this could be offensive. For example, don't use graphics of wine bottles or champagne glasses to indicate celebration.
- Be careful when using everyday objects in examples. Make sure that the object exists in most countries, and keep in mind that it may be interpreted differently in different parts of the world. For example, a light bulb may be used to indicate light, but not the concept of an idea.
- Avoid using trendy objects, historical references, or film, cartoon, or other video characters.
- Avoid using animals, as they may carry symbolic significance.
- Consider the aesthetics of color and typography for different cultures.

12

12.3 Defining and Using Terms

Follow these guidelines to avoid common pitfalls that make translators (and readers) uncertain of your intended meaning.

- Use general or nontechnical terms consistently. Always provide translators with a glossary and a style sheet. Use terminology that is consistent with definitions found in your company's standard vocabulary list, or if your company doesn't have one, the *Sun Publications Glossary*.

- Define new terms and technical terms that do not appear in a regular dictionary the first time they appear in text. Italicize terms when first defining them. Also include these terms in a glossary.

- Avoid jargon or slang. If a word does not appear in a standard dictionary or a technical source book, such as the *IEEE Standard Dictionary of Electrical and Electronics Terms*, try not to use it. If the translators cannot look up a word they do not know, they will have no idea what the word means.

- Use all terms consistently throughout a document. When you use a different word to mean the same thing interchangeably throughout your document, it can become a translator's nightmare. Although to you "show," "display," and "appear" may seem similar enough in meaning to use interchangeably, a translator will think you used different words because you intended different meanings and may interpret your document incorrectly.

- Avoid the use of abbreviations (such as cont., incl., etc.) whenever possible, unless you are pressed for room, as in a table. Many languages do not have abbreviations and cannot accommodate them. Also avoid the use of Latin abbreviations and terms. Here are some sample replacements:

i.e.	that is
e.g.	for example
etc.	and so on *or* and so forth

- Avoid using general modifiers that could be interpreted in any number of different ways. For example, there is no Japanese equivalent for the word "nice." So a Japanese translator has to choose which Japanese word gives the closest meaning to what the writer intended "nice" to mean. Choices include "smart," "pretty," "cute," "good," and "useful."

- Define all abbreviations and acronyms the first time you use them in text; provide a list of them at the end of the book as part of the glossary or index. When you define the term, give the spelled-out version first, followed by the acronym or abbreviation in parentheses. For example:

  The encoder uses Data Encryption Standard (DES) hardware.

12.4 Grammar and Word Usage

Follow these guidelines when tackling issues of grammar and word usage. You want to ensure easy translatability of your documentation.

- Try to keep your sentences clear and short (under 25 words or so). A long, complicated sentence that contains several ideas or concepts is difficult to translate and understand.

- Make sure your spelling and usage are correct. Use spell checkers and employ copy editors whenever possible.

- Avoid using the same word in multiple grammatical categories such as verb, noun, and adjective.

> Instead of   File the file in a file folder.
>
> Write   Store the file in a folder.

When "file" is used as both a verb and a noun, it is confusing to the translator, who may have to use a different word for each case.

- Avoid ambiguous phrases. For example, "first-come, first-served" is ambiguous. If possible, rewrite as "in the order received" or "in the order in which they are received."

- Be precise about using the terms "when" and "if." Use "when" only if the event is virtually inevitable in the circumstances described. Use "if" when the event depends on some other event. For example, the statement:

> *When* the prompt appears...

implies that the prompt will inevitably appear, whereas the statement

> *If* the error message appears...

implies that the event may or may not occur.

- Don't leave out definite and indefinite articles as a form of shorthand.

> Instead of   Place screwdriver in groove.
>
> Write   Place a screwdriver in the groove.

- Avoid vague and uncertain references between a pronoun and its antecedent. Make sure that the noun to which a pronoun refers is clear.

> Unclear: When the results were announced by the researchers, they were questioned by the other experts in the field.

Does "they" refer to the results or to the researchers? For clarity, rewriting the sentence is often necessary (especially to avoid repeating the noun).

Awkward: When the results were announced by the researchers, the results were questioned by other experts in the field.

Better: Other experts in the field questioned the results announced by the researchers.

- Take special care to distinguish between restrictive and nonrestrictive clauses. Consider the differences in meaning of the following two sentences:

  Note the ready light that appears on the front panel. (restrictive)

  Note the ready light, which appears on the front panel. (nonrestrictive)

In the first sentence, the reader is told to note the ready light on the front panel—not the one on the side panel or back panel, but the one specifically on the front panel. In the second sentence, the reader is merely told to note the ready light; the sentence also states that the ready light happens to be on the front panel, implying that there is no other ready light to be found anywhere else. The difference in meaning is small (and may not confuse the English reader), but the difference nevertheless does exist and can cause confusion for the translator.

12.5 Expressing Numbers and Symbols

Most of the world uses the metric system of measurement, not the imperial system. As a courtesy to readers everywhere, writers should observe the following conventions:

- When providing a measurement, use the metric system by preference, and include the other measurement afterwards in parentheses. The exception is when you are writing about nonmetric products (such as floppy disks).

- Avoid using the sharp (#) symbol to indicate "pound," a single quote (') to indicate "foot," and a double quote (") to indicate "inch." These symbols are recognized in the U.S. but not in most other countries. Each measurement should always include its metric system equivalent.

- If you use the word "billion" or "trillion," use the following text in a footnote so that the exact value will be known to readers in all countries:

  One billion equals 10^9.
  or
  One trillion equals 10^{12}.

Such a footnote is necessary because the words "billion" and "trillion" (and larger denominations) have different meanings in different countries. In the United States, 1 billion means 1,000,000,000 [10^9]; in some other countries, for example Britain, it means 1,000,000,000,000 [10^{12}]. For more information on numbers large and small, refer to the "Table of Numbers" in *Webster's New Collegiate Dictionary, Tenth Edition.*

- Avoid using symbols such as "/" and "&" in regular text. Many symbols have various meanings, and a translator may have difficulty deciding what you intended. For example, the "/" symbol can mean:

  - and
  - or
  - and/or
  - with
  - divide by
  - root
  - path name divider

- Be aware that numbers may carry certain connotations. For example, in some Asian countries "4" indicates death and "9" signifies suffering. You probably already know that the numbers "13" and "666" are considered unlucky or evil in Christian cultures.

12.6 Finding a Translator

The best approach to finding a translator is to get recommendations from sales offices or partners in the target locale. Ask around, then get references and sample translations. Translation companies or translators who live in a country and are native speakers of the target language can generally do the best job of translation, since they are fluent and know all the current computer terminology.

Because translation work is both irregular and intensive, independent translation vendors usually offer the best business arrangements. Translation companies often provide other services, such as testing and limited software programming. If your company has a regular and predictable need for translation, consider hiring translators as employees to reduce costs.

Translation vendors exist in the United States and often produce superlative results. However, local content rules imposed by governments abroad may make it more favorable for you to do business with translation vendors in that country. Also, translators who have lived in the United States for many years may not be up-to-date on the latest computer terminology.

If time and money are tight, you may be tempted to find a native speaker of the target language who works at your company to do the translation work. If such people have recently visited or lived in the country in question, they may be good candidates. However, you need to also insure they have the appropriate language and translation skills to do a high quality translation. If they don't possess the requisite skills, you aren't going to save any time or money. Such employees can however, be adequate reviewers.

12.7 Working with a Translator

Once you have found a translator, the most important step is to provide a vocabulary list and work with your translator to find mutually agreeable translations for all terms in the vocabulary list. Your sales offices or partners can assist in developing the translated vocabulary list and in all cases should review and approve it. A vocabulary list not only saves time in the long run, but also results in high-quality translations. The same vocabulary list can be used for translations into all languages.

A major problem of working with translators is this: although you often want translated manuals when the product ships, you don't finish the English manuals until shortly before that date. To begin the translation job early, you are forced to provide beta-quality manuals to the translator. Later, you must indicate changes for the translator and wait for these changes to be reflected in the translation. The version control problems are daunting. It is critical to have good project managers to deal with these issues, and to administer release components during the entire product release cycle.

Preferred tone and dialect vary by target market, and according to product, but can easily be adjusted during translation.

For large projects, ask for incremental delivery of the translation—particularly when working with a new agency. Ask your sales offices or partners in the target market to review the partial translation in time to incorporate their review comments into the final product. If you don't have staff or partners in the target market, hire a competent third party to review any major translation project before it goes to press.

12.8 Summary

Translating documentation is often the most labor-intensive part of producing international products. Prepare early and prepare often!

Product Localization 13

This chapter discusses localization issues for both software and documentation.

- *Market-Driven Localization* outlines a flexible approach to determining the appropriate level of investment for various markets.

- *A Localization Overview* on page 196 gives a process overview and schedule for the typical localization project.

- *Creating a Locale Definition* on page 198 details how locales are defined. This section is of interest only to the curious, or to system localization teams.

For information on localizing visible messages in an application, see Chapter 5, *Messaging for Program Translation*.

13.1 Market-Driven Localization

It is often difficult to make decisions regarding what software products require localization, which languages and locales to offer, and the extent of localization for each locale. There are numerous criteria to address and many perspectives to consider. Developing a localization product roadmap is largely a process of identifying all of the relevant criteria and then weighing the relative importance of each. The challenge is in trying to determine a rational approach that works for a wide variety of products and markets.

The key to unraveling this puzzle is to keep things simple and focused. Here we provide a three-step planning approach.

1. Develop a set of localization priorities based on market requirements that incorporate the following factors:

   - Revenue opportunity
   - Pervasiveness of English
   - Strategic importance
   - Government requirements
   - Legal localization requirements

- Competitive environment

The output of this exercise should be a ranking of geographical markets, in order of implementation priority.

2. Determine localization content.

   It is important to recognize that the localization requirements for each geographical market will vary significantly, depending on whether it is an emerging, developing, or mature market.

   For many companies, localization has been a very binary decision. Either the entire product is fully localized, or it is not localized at all. The downside to this approach is that it places an artificially high hurdle on product localization costs, which can result in fewer localized products and thinner market coverage.

   In reality, a number of options are available that may provide a better match of localization investment with the needs of the market. A more prudent approach might be to start with minimal localization support and then increase investment as it is warranted by growth in the market or changes in the competitive environment. This incremental investment approach provides some significant benefits:

   - Results in more efficient use of localization funds and broader market coverage

   - Ensures consistent localization content for "like markets"

   - Provides a market development framework for localization planning

   An example of a phased localization investment model is outlined below. Each market should be identified as fitting into one of these stages of localization development:

   a. "Market Entry" Localization—this localization strategy is targeted for undeveloped and/or very small markets and actually requires very little localization investment. It does require full software internationalization which enables input, display, and printing of all languages. This allows a product that is basically English to be sold into most international markets, with little localization of software or documentation required.

      This proposed market entry strategy is more commonly known as "International English" and is being practiced by a growing number of major software companies today. Examples of markets for which this localization investment might be appropriate are many of the smaller Asian, Eastern European, and Baltic countries.

b. "Developing Market" Localization—the next level of investment beyond basic character handling is the localization of all additional software components. This would include things like installation and the graphical user interfaces, but would exclude hard-copy documentation, on-line help, and on-line documentation.

This level of localization is still inexpensive, since it does not require translation of hard-copy documentation. Examples of markets for which this localization investment might be appropriate are Korea, China, Eastern Europe, and Russia.

c. "Mature Market" Localization—this final level of investment entails full localization of the product, including all user interfaces, on-line help, hard-copy and on-line documentation, and product packaging.

This level of investment may be warranted for mature markets, where product volumes are significant enough to amortize the high expense associated with a full localization. Examples of markets for which this investment might be appropriate are Japan, Germany, and France.

Application of a market-based localization model will result in a generic baseline set of requirements for localization content. The 80/20 rule applies with this approach, which means that although localization requirements for most markets will be covered, there will need to be some adjustments made to the baseline plan to reflect localization requirements for specific products that do not fit the generic model.

3. Refine the localization plan.

Now that a prioritized list of geographical markets and the required level of localization appropriate for each market have been determined according to market requirements, you need to go back and adjust the localization plan to reflect specific product requirements that don't fit the generic model. Some of the factors to consider are:

- Specific vertical market needs
- Specific target user needs
- Multiplatform requirements
- Competitive localization issues

Remember also that investments in localization are being traded off against other potential uses of capital and need to offer a reasonable return on investment. A financial analysis that considers the direct costs and anticipated revenues of the localized product should be a standard component of any business case.

13.2 A Localization Overview

After you make a marketing decision for the localization of a product, you must understand and plan the localization process. The following sections provide an overview of the processes involved in product localization.

13.2.1 Planning Phase

Localization planning takes a phased approach. First, consider the criteria outlined previously to determine market priorities and identify products that are most likely to require localization. Then, decide what degree of localization is required. In other words, how much must we really invest in localization of this product to make it successful?

13.2.2 Development Process

For the developer it should not make a difference which locales the product is chosen to be marketed in. If a developer has written properly internationalized code, little more should be required.

Realistically however, internationalization quality assurance testing is done in conjunction with localization testing, which usually uncovers software problems that were not evident in the English language version. Developers need to test their application to ensure that it can handle different types of locales.

13.2.3 Project Management

Localization often involves coordination of many people in different places. Software developers, technical writers, translators, and locale testers, all work together to produce a unified localized product. Project managers are the glue.

13.2.4 Translation Process

The bulk of localization work involves translating software messages, hard-copy documentation, and on-line help. Software usually contains fewer words than documentation and help but may require more technical knowledge to translate.

When choosing a translator, consider the following:

- Translators should always be native speakers of the target language.
- Translators must also be familiar with the originating language.
- When translating software messages, it is essential to find a translator with basic computer literacy who can understand computer jargon and the commonly accepted equivalent in their local language.

- If your translator is not computer literate, you may need to provide a glossary to help them in understanding the context and meaning of messages that will be translated.

- Proofreaders and testers should be native speakers of the target language.

- Providing a glossary (a vocabulary list) helps ensure consistent terminology throughout the product.

- If possible, hire testers who are native speakers of the target language and who are familiar with the originating language.

- Each translated document or help file should be proofread, and every piece of localized software should be acceptance-tested by a native speaker.

Translators can be hired through an independent translation vendor. If there is a steady volume of work, you may want to hire in-house translators.

Testing specialists may be recruited through a translation vendor. Recruiting from a company's field offices in different countries or territories can sometimes prove beneficial because of the high level of language and technical expertise. Such people might be able to spot problems that other testers might not notice.

If your translators have limited software expertise, their progress can be delayed if they must set up, run, or test the localized software. Localization engineers may be able to help solve problems, report and fix bugs, and answer any technical questions that translation vendors might have.

If your product documentation includes many screen images showing portions of applications that will be translated, a production specialist might be helpful. Often translation vendors are unable or unwilling to run localized software and recapture these illustrations for a new locale. Moreover, localized software is often not ready during the translation phase.

Production specialists might need to run localized software and recapture the (translated) screen snapshots in the same manner as the writer did originally. These screen captures must be inserted into translated documentation before printing or conversion to on-line format.

13.2.5 Sample Localization Schedule

There are two methods for timing a localization schedule: simultaneous ship and separate ship. Simultaneous ship means that you deliver a localization at the same time as, or shortly after, the English or "base" product. Separate ship means that you deliver a localization long after the base product becomes available.

Here are the phases of a typical localization schedule:

- Product planning
  - Marketing research
  - Engineering design and specifications
  - Localization planning
- Product development
  - Software prototyping and alpha testing
  - Qualification and hiring of translation vendors
  - Development of glossary (a vocabulary list for translators)
  - Creation of locale-specific files
- Product testing
  - Software and documentation beta testing
  - Translation of on-line help and documentation
  - Testing of localized software
- Product packaging
  - Software and documentation release to customers
  - Retesting of localized software
  - Recapturing screen images (if localized)
  - Proofreading translated documentation
  - Translation of packaging and promotional materials

Now that you have information about localization marketing decisions and understand the localization process, let's look at how a locale is created.

13.3 Creating a Locale Definition

By now you might be wondering how system localizers go about defining the characteristics of a locale and where this locale-specific data resides. Most major software vendors that sell localized products provide you with locale definitions. For instance, Sun Microsystems creates localized products containing localized software packages.

To give you an understanding of what's involved in creating a locale definition, the sections below discuss some of the standard (XPG4) conventions and utilities used to create system locale definitions. Application programmers seldom have a need to run these utilities.

1. Select a locale name. Sun follows the X/Open locale naming convention. See Appendix A for more details on locale naming. On XPG4-compliant systems you can determine which locales are installed by running `locale -a`.

2. Set up codeset information by creating a `charmap` file for `localedef`(1). (The `localedef` utility converts source definitions for locale categories into a database usable by the function and utilities whose operational behavior is determined by the setting of locale environment variables.)

3. Set up character type, numeric, time and date, and monetary information for use in `LC_*` categories by creating a locale definition file for `localedef`(1).

4. Run the `localedef` command, which creates a locale definition from a `charmap` file (step #2) and a locale definition source file (step #3).

5. Decide which message files, help files, on-line documentation, and HTML files need translating, and have them translated.

6. Create translated message file objects. For `gettext()` and `catgets()`, you need to convert the translated message file source into a message file object with the `msgfmt`(1) or `gencat`(1) commands. Help files and on-line documentation must be installed in the correct location. (For existing locales, steps 4 and 5 might be the only ones required.)

13.3.1 Select the Correct Locale Name

A locale name should not be purely arbitrary, since distributed locales require a stable namespace. Furthermore, language names are standardized in ISO 639, and territory names are standardized in ISO 3166. Follow the standards.

Appendix A contains a list of standard and accepted Solaris locale names.

Of course, you are at liberty to create a private locale name. This might be especially useful for custom collation ordering, as for a telephone book. But be aware that your private locale may not be recognized elsewhere.

13.3.2 Create a `charmap` File for `localedef`

POSIX.2 defines a format for the most common locale data, such as character maps, which map symbolic character to an encoded value. Angle brackets enclose symbolic names. The following file is a `charmap` file for ISO 8859-1:

```
<code_set_name> ISO_8859-1:1987
<comment_char> %
<escape_char> /

% alias ISO_8859-1
```

```
% alias ISO-8859-1
% alias LATIN1
CHARMAP
<NU>                    /x00    <U0000> NULL (NUL)
<SH>                    /x01    <U0001> START OF HEADING (SOH)
<SX>                    /x02    <U0002> START OF TEXT (STX)
<EX>                    /x03    <U0003> END OF TEXT (ETX)
<ET>                    /x04    <U0004> END OF TRANSMISSION (EOT)
<EQ>                    /x05    <U0005> ENQUIRY (ENQ)
<AK>                    /x06    <U0006> ACKNOWLEDGE (ACK)
<BL>                    /x07    <U0007> BELL (BEL)
<BS>                    /x08    <U0008> BACKSPACE (BS)
<HT>                    /x09    <U0009> CHARACTER TABULATION (HT)
<LF>                    /x0A    <U000A> LINE FEED (LF)
<VT>                    /x0B    <U000B> LINE TABULATION (VT)
<FF>                    /x0C    <U000C> FORM FEED (FF)
<CR>                    /x0D    <U000D> CARRIAGE RETURN (CR)
<SO>                    /x0E    <U000E> SHIFT OUT (SO)
<SI>                    /x0F    <U000F> SHIFT IN (SI)
<DL>                    /x10    <U0010> DATALINK ESCAPE (DLE)
<D1>                    /x11    <U0011> DEVICE CONTROL ONE (DC1)
<D2>                    /x12    <U0012> DEVICE CONTROL TWO (DC2)
<D3>                    /x13    <U0013> DEVICE CONTROL THREE (DC3)
<D4>                    /x14    <U0014> DEVICE CONTROL FOUR (DC4)
<NK>                    /x15    <U0015> NEGATIVE ACKNOWLEDGE (NAK)
<SY>                    /x16    <U0016> SYNCHRONOUS IDLE (SYN)
<EB>                    /x17    <U0017> END OF TRANSMISSION BLOCK(ETB)
<CN>                    /x18    <U0018> CANCEL (CAN)
<EM>                    /x19    <U0019> END OF MEDIUM (EM)
<SB>                    /x1A    <U001A> SUBSTITUTE (SUB)
<EC>                    /x1B    <U001B> ESCAPE (ESC)
<FS>                    /x1C    <U001C> FILE SEPARATOR (IS4)
<GS>                    /x1D    <U001D> GROUP SEPARATOR (IS3)
<RS>                    /x1E    <U001E> RECORD SEPARATOR (IS2)
<US>                    /x1F    <U001F> UNIT SEPARATOR (IS1)
<SP>                    /x20    <U0020> SPACE
<!>                     /x21    <U0021> EXCLAMATION MARK
<">                     /x22    <U0022> QUOTATION MARK
<Nb>                    /x23    <U0023> NUMBER SIGN
<DO>                    /x24    <U0024> DOLLAR SIGN
<%>                     /x25    <U0025> PERCENT SIGN
<&>                     /x26    <U0026> AMPERSAND
<'>                     /x27    <U0027> APOSTROPHE
<(>                     /x28    <U0028> LEFT PARENTHESIS
<)>                     /x29    <U0029> RIGHT PARENTHESIS
<*>                     /x2A    <U002A> ASTERISK
```

```
<+>                  /x2B    <U002B>  PLUS SIGN
<,>                  /x2C    <U002C>  COMMA
<->                  /x2D    <U002D>  HYPHEN-MINUS
<.>                  /x2E    <U002E>  FULL STOP
<//>                 /x2F    <U002F>  SOLIDUS
<0>                  /x30    <U0030>  DIGIT ZERO
<1>                  /x31    <U0031>  DIGIT ONE
<2>                  /x32    <U0032>  DIGIT TWO
<3>                  /x33    <U0033>  DIGIT THREE
<4>                  /x34    <U0034>  DIGIT FOUR
<5>                  /x35    <U0035>  DIGIT FIVE
<6>                  /x36    <U0036>  DIGIT SIX
<7>                  /x37    <U0037>  DIGIT SEVEN
<8>                  /x38    <U0038>  DIGIT EIGHT
<9>                  /x39    <U0039>  DIGIT NINE
<:>                  /x3A    <U003A>  COLON
<;>                  /x3B    <U003B>  SEMICOLON
<<>                  /x3C    <U003C>  LESS-THAN SIGN
<=>                  /x3D    <U003D>  EQUALS SIGN
</>>                 /x3E    <U003E>  GREATER-THAN SIGN
<?>                  /x3F    <U003F>  QUESTION MARK
<At>                 /x40    <U0040>  COMMERCIAL AT
<A>                  /x41    <U0041>  LATIN CAPITAL LETTER A
<B>                  /x42    <U0042>  LATIN CAPITAL LETTER B
<C>                  /x43    <U0043>  LATIN CAPITAL LETTER C
<D>                  /x44    <U0044>  LATIN CAPITAL LETTER D
<E>                  /x45    <U0045>  LATIN CAPITAL LETTER E
<F>                  /x46    <U0046>  LATIN CAPITAL LETTER F
<G>                  /x47    <U0047>  LATIN CAPITAL LETTER G
<H>                  /x48    <U0048>  LATIN CAPITAL LETTER H
<I>                  /x49    <U0049>  LATIN CAPITAL LETTER I
<J>                  /x4A    <U004A>  LATIN CAPITAL LETTER J
<K>                  /x4B    <U004B>  LATIN CAPITAL LETTER K
<L>                  /x4C    <U004C>  LATIN CAPITAL LETTER L
<M>                  /x4D    <U004D>  LATIN CAPITAL LETTER M
<N>                  /x4E    <U004E>  LATIN CAPITAL LETTER N
<O>                  /x4F    <U004F>  LATIN CAPITAL LETTER O
<P>                  /x50    <U0050>  LATIN CAPITAL LETTER P
<Q>                  /x51    <U0051>  LATIN CAPITAL LETTER Q
<R>                  /x52    <U0052>  LATIN CAPITAL LETTER R
<S>                  /x53    <U0053>  LATIN CAPITAL LETTER S
<T>                  /x54    <U0054>  LATIN CAPITAL LETTER T
<U>                  /x55    <U0055>  LATIN CAPITAL LETTER U
<V>                  /x56    <U0056>  LATIN CAPITAL LETTER V
<W>                  /x57    <U0057>  LATIN CAPITAL LETTER W
<X>                  /x58    <U0058>  LATIN CAPITAL LETTER X
```

```
<Y>          /x59   <U0059> LATIN CAPITAL LETTER Y
<Z>          /x5A   <U005A> LATIN CAPITAL LETTER Z
<<(>         /x5B   <U005B> LEFT SQUARE BRACKET
</////>      /x5C   <U005C> REVERSE SOLIDUS
<)/>>        /x5D   <U005D> RIGHT SQUARE BRACKET
<'/>>        /x5E   <U005E> CIRCUMFLEX ACCENT
<_>          /x5F   <U005F> LOW LINE
<'!>         /x60   <U0060> GRAVE ACCENT
<a>          /x61   <U0061> LATIN SMALL LETTER A
<b>          /x62   <U0062> LATIN SMALL LETTER B
<c>          /x63   <U0063> LATIN SMALL LETTER C
<d>          /x64   <U0064> LATIN SMALL LETTER D
<e>          /x65   <U0065> LATIN SMALL LETTER E
<f>          /x66   <U0066> LATIN SMALL LETTER F
<g>          /x67   <U0067> LATIN SMALL LETTER G
<h>          /x68   <U0068> LATIN SMALL LETTER H
<i>          /x69   <U0069> LATIN SMALL LETTER I
<j>          /x6A   <U006A> LATIN SMALL LETTER J
<k>          /x6B   <U006B> LATIN SMALL LETTER K
<l>          /x6C   <U006C> LATIN SMALL LETTER L
<m>          /x6D   <U006D> LATIN SMALL LETTER M
<n>          /x6E   <U006E> LATIN SMALL LETTER N
<o>          /x6F   <U006F> LATIN SMALL LETTER O
<p>          /x70   <U0070> LATIN SMALL LETTER P
<q>          /x71   <U0071> LATIN SMALL LETTER Q
<r>          /x72   <U0072> LATIN SMALL LETTER R
<s>          /x73   <U0073> LATIN SMALL LETTER S
<t>          /x74   <U0074> LATIN SMALL LETTER T
<u>          /x75   <U0075> LATIN SMALL LETTER U
<v>          /x76   <U0076> LATIN SMALL LETTER V
<w>          /x77   <U0077> LATIN SMALL LETTER W
<x>          /x78   <U0078> LATIN SMALL LETTER X
<y>          /x79   <U0079> LATIN SMALL LETTER Y
<z>          /x7A   <U007A> LATIN SMALL LETTER Z
<(!>         /x7B   <U007B> LEFT CURLY BRACKET
<!!>         /x7C   <U007C> VERTICAL LINE
<!)>         /x7D   <U007D> RIGHT CURLY BRACKET
<'?>         /x7E   <U007E> TILDE
<DT>         /x7F   <U007F> DELETE (DEL)
<PA>         /x80   <U0080> PADDING CHARACTER (PAD)
<HO>         /x81   <U0081> HIGH OCTET PRESET (HOP)
<BH>         /x82   <U0082> BREAK PERMITTED HERE (BPH)
<NH>         /x83   <U0083> NO BREAK HERE (NBH)
<IN>         /x84   <U0084> INDEX (IND)
<NL>         /x85   <U0085> NEXT LINE (NEL)
<SA>         /x86   <U0086> START OF SELECTED AREA (SSA)
```

`<ES>`	`/x87`	`<U0087>`	END OF SELECTED AREA (ESA)
`<HS>`	`/x88`	`<U0088>`	CHARACTER TABULATION SET (HTS)
`<HJ>`	`/x89`	`<U0089>`	TABULATION JUSTIFICATION (HTJ)
`<VS>`	`/x8A`	`<U008A>`	LINE TABULATION SET (VTS)
`<PD>`	`/x8B`	`<U008B>`	PARTIAL LINE FORWARD (PLD)
`<PU>`	`/x8C`	`<U008C>`	PARTIAL LINE BACKWARD (PLU)
`<RI>`	`/x8D`	`<U008D>`	REVERSE LINE FEED (RI)
`<S2>`	`/x8E`	`<U008E>`	SINGLE-SHIFT TWO (SS2)
`<S3>`	`/x8F`	`<U008F>`	SINGLE-SHIFT THREE (SS3)
`<DC>`	`/x90`	`<U0090>`	DEVICE CONTROL STRING (DCS)
`<P1>`	`/x91`	`<U0091>`	PRIVATE USE ONE (PU1)
`<P2>`	`/x92`	`<U0092>`	PRIVATE USE TWO (PU2)
`<TS>`	`/x93`	`<U0093>`	SET TRANSMIT STATE (STS)
`<CC>`	`/x94`	`<U0094>`	CANCEL CHARACTER (CCH)
`<MW>`	`/x95`	`<U0095>`	MESSAGE WAITING (MW)
`<SG>`	`/x96`	`<U0096>`	START OF GUARDED AREA (SPA)
`<EG>`	`/x97`	`<U0097>`	END OF GUARDED AREA (EPA)
`<SS>`	`/x98`	`<U0098>`	START OF STRING (SOS)
`<GC>`	`/x99`	`<U0099>`	SINGLE GRAPH CHAR INTRO (SGCI)
`<SC>`	`/x9A`	`<U009A>`	SINGLE CHAR INTRODUCER (SCI)
`<CI>`	`/x9B`	`<U009B>`	CONTROL SEQUENCE INTRO (CSI)
`<ST>`	`/x9C`	`<U009C>`	STRING TERMINATOR (ST)
`<OC>`	`/x9D`	`<U009D>`	OPERATING SYSTEM COMMAND (OSC)
`<PM>`	`/x9E`	`<U009E>`	PRIVACY MESSAGE (PM)
`<AC>`	`/x9F`	`<U009F>`	APPLICATION PROGRAM CMD (APC)
`<NS>`	`/xA0`	`<U00A0>`	NO-BREAK SPACE
`<!I>`	`/xA1`	`<U00A1>`	INVERTED EXCLAMATION MARK
`<Ct>`	`/xA2`	`<U00A2>`	CENT SIGN
`<Pd>`	`/xA3`	`<U00A3>`	POUND SIGN
`<Cu>`	`/xA4`	`<U00A4>`	CURRENCY SIGN
`<Ye>`	`/xA5`	`<U00A5>`	YEN SIGN
`<BB>`	`/xA6`	`<U00A6>`	BROKEN BAR
`<SE>`	`/xA7`	`<U00A7>`	SECTION SIGN
`<':>`	`/xA8`	`<U00A8>`	DIAERESIS
`<Co>`	`/xA9`	`<U00A9>`	COPYRIGHT SIGN
`<-a>`	`/xAA`	`<U00AA>`	FEMININE ORDINAL INDICATOR
`<<<>`	`/xAB`	`<U00AB>`	LEFT-POINT DOUBLE ANGLE QUOTE
`<NO>`	`/xAC`	`<U00AC>`	NOT SIGN
`<-->`	`/xAD`	`<U00AD>`	SOFT HYPHEN
`<Rg>`	`/xAE`	`<U00AE>`	REGISTERED SIGN
`<'m>`	`/xAF`	`<U00AF>`	MACRON
`<DG>`	`/xB0`	`<U00B0>`	DEGREE SIGN
`<+->`	`/xB1`	`<U00B1>`	PLUS-MINUS SIGN
`<2S>`	`/xB2`	`<U00B2>`	SUPERSCRIPT TWO
`<3S>`	`/xB3`	`<U00B3>`	SUPERSCRIPT THREE
`<''>`	`/xB4`	`<U00B4>`	ACUTE ACCENT

`<My>`	`/xB5`	`<U00B5>`	MICRO SIGN
`<PI>`	`/xB6`	`<U00B6>`	PILCROW SIGN
`<.M>`	`/xB7`	`<U00B7>`	MIDDLE DOT
`<',>`	`/xB8`	`<U00B8>`	CEDILLA
`<1S>`	`/xB9`	`<U00B9>`	SUPERSCRIPT ONE
`<-o>`	`/xBA`	`<U00BA>`	MASCULINE ORDINAL INDICATOR
`</>/>>`	`/xBB`	`<U00BB>`	RIGHT-POINT DOUBLE ANGLE QUOTE
`<14>`	`/xBC`	`<U00BC>`	VULGAR FRACTION ONE QUARTER
`<12>`	`/xBD`	`<U00BD>`	VULGAR FRACTION ONE HALF
`<34>`	`/xBE`	`<U00BE>`	VULGAR FRACTION THREE QUARTERS
`<?I>`	`/xBF`	`<U00BF>`	INVERTED QUESTION MARK
`<A!>`	`/xC0`	`<U00C0>`	LATIN CAP LETTER A GRAVE
`<A'>`	`/xC1`	`<U00C1>`	LATIN CAP LETTER A ACUTE
`<A/>>`	`/xC2`	`<U00C2>`	LATIN CAP LETTER A CIRCUMFLEX
`<A?>`	`/xC3`	`<U00C3>`	LATIN CAP LETTER A TILDE
`<A:>`	`/xC4`	`<U00C4>`	LATIN CAP LETTER A DIAERESIS
`<AA>`	`/xC5`	`<U00C5>`	LATIN CAP LETTER A RING ABOVE
`<AE>`	`/xC6`	`<U00C6>`	LATIN CAP LETTER AE
`<C,>`	`/xC7`	`<U00C7>`	LATIN CAP LETTER C CEDILLA
`<E!>`	`/xC8`	`<U00C8>`	LATIN CAP LETTER E GRAVE
`<E'>`	`/xC9`	`<U00C9>`	LATIN CAP LETTER E ACUTE
`<E/>>`	`/xCA`	`<U00CA>`	LATIN CAP LETTER E CIRCUMFLEX
`<E:>`	`/xCB`	`<U00CB>`	LATIN CAP LETTER E DIAERESIS
`<I!>`	`/xCC`	`<U00CC>`	LATIN CAP LETTER I GRAVE
`<I'>`	`/xCD`	`<U00CD>`	LATIN CAP LETTER I ACUTE
`<I/>>`	`/xCE`	`<U00CE>`	LATIN CAP LETTER I CIRCUMFLEX
`<I:>`	`/xCF`	`<U00CF>`	LATIN CAP LETTER I DIAERESIS
`<D->`	`/xD0`	`<U00D0>`	LATIN CAP LETTER ETH (Iceland)
`<N?>`	`/xD1`	`<U00D1>`	LATIN CAP LETTER N TILDE
`<O!>`	`/xD2`	`<U00D2>`	LATIN CAP LETTER O GRAVE
`<O'>`	`/xD3`	`<U00D3>`	LATIN CAP LETTER O ACUTE
`<O/>>`	`/xD4`	`<U00D4>`	LATIN CAP LETTER O CIRCUMFLEX
`<O?>`	`/xD5`	`<U00D5>`	LATIN CAP LETTER O TILDE
`<O:>`	`/xD6`	`<U00D6>`	LATIN CAP LETTER O DIAERESIS
`<*X>`	`/xD7`	`<U00D7>`	MULTIPLICATION SIGN
`<O//>`	`/xD8`	`<U00D8>`	LATIN CAP LETTER O STROKE
`<U!>`	`/xD9`	`<U00D9>`	LATIN CAP LETTER U GRAVE
`<U'>`	`/xDA`	`<U00DA>`	LATIN CAP LETTER U ACUTE
`<U/>>`	`/xDB`	`<U00DB>`	LATIN CAP LETTER U UMFLEX
`<U:>`	`/xDC`	`<U00DC>`	LATIN CAP LETTER U DIAERESIS
`<Y'>`	`/xDD`	`<U00DD>`	LATIN CAP LETTER Y ACUTE
`<TH>`	`/xDE`	`<U00DE>`	LATIN CAP LETTER THORN
`<ss>`	`/xDF`	`<U00DF>`	LATIN SMALL LETTER SHARP S
`<a!>`	`/xE0`	`<U00E0>`	LATIN SMALL LETTER A GRAVE
`<a'>`	`/xE1`	`<U00E1>`	LATIN SMALL LETTER A ACUTE
`<a/>>`	`/xE2`	`<U00E2>`	LATIN SMALL LETTER A CIRCUMFLX

```
<a?>                /xE3    <U00E3> LATIN SMALL LETTER A TILDE
<a:>                /xE4    <U00E4> LATIN SMALL LETTER A DIAERESIS
<aa>                /xE5    <U00E5> LATIN SMALL LETTER A RING
<ae>                /xE6    <U00E6> LATIN SMALL LETTER AE
<c,>                /xE7    <U00E7> LATIN SMALL LETTER C CEDILLA
<e!>                /xE8    <U00E8> LATIN SMALL LETTER E GRAVE
<e'>                /xE9    <U00E9> LATIN SMALL LETTER E ACUTE
<e/>>               /xEA    <U00EA> LATIN SMALL LETTER E CIRCUMFLX
<e:>                /xEB    <U00EB> LATIN SMALL LETTER E DIAERESIS
<i!>                /xEC    <U00EC> LATIN SMALL LETTER I GRAVE
<i'>                /xED    <U00ED> LATIN SMALL LETTER I ACUTE
<i/>>               /xEE    <U00EE> LATIN SMALL LETTER I CIRCUMFLX
<i:>                /xEF    <U00EF> LATIN SMALL LETTER I DIAERESIS
<d->                /xF0    <U00F0> LATIN SMALL LETTER ETH
<n?>                /xF1    <U00F1> LATIN SMALL LETTER N TILDE
<o!>                /xF2    <U00F2> LATIN SMALL LETTER O GRAVE
<o'>                /xF3    <U00F3> LATIN SMALL LETTER O ACUTE
<o/>>               /xF4    <U00F4> LATIN SMALL LETTER O CIRCUMFLX
<o?>                /xF5    <U00F5> LATIN SMALL LETTER O TILDE
<o:>                /xF6    <U00F6> LATIN SMALL LETTER O DIAERESIS
<-:>                /xF7    <U00F7> DIVISION SIGN
<o//>               /xF8    <U00F8> LATIN SMALL LETTER O STROKE
<u!>                /xF9    <U00F9> LATIN SMALL LETTER U GRAVE
<u'>                /xFA    <U00FA> LATIN SMALL LETTER U ACUTE
<u/>>               /xFB    <U00FB> LATIN SMALL LETTER U CIRCUMFLX
<u:>                /xFC    <U00FC> LATIN SMALL LETTER U DIAERESIS
<y'>                /xFD    <U00FD> LATIN SMALL LETTER Y ACUTE
<th>                /xFE    <U00FE> LATIN SMALL LETTER THORN dic)
<y:>                /xFF    <U00FF> LATIN SMALL LETTER Y DIAERESIS
<NUL>               /x00    <U0000> NULL
<SOH>               /x01    <U0001> START OF HEADING (SOH)
<STX>               /x02    <U0002> START OF TEXT (STX)
<ETX>               /x03    <U0003> END OF TEXT (ETX)
<EOT>               /x04    <U0004> END OF TRANSMISSION (EOT)
<ENQ>               /x05    <U0005> ENQUIRY (ENQ)
<ACK>               /x06    <U0006> ACKNOWLEDGE (ACK)
<alert>             /x07    <U0007> BELL (BEL)
<BEL>               /x07    <U0007> BELL (BEL)
<backspace>         /x08    <U0008> BACKSPACE (BS)
<tab>               /x09    <U0009> CHARACTER TABULATION (HT)
<newline>           /x0A    <U000A> LINE FEED (LF)
<vertical-tab>      /x0B    <U000B> LINE TABULATION (VT)
<form-feed>         /x0C    <U000C> FORM FEED (FF)
<carriage-return>   /x0D    <U000D> CARRIAGE RETURN (CR)
<DLE>               /x10    <U0010> DATALINK ESCAPE (DLE)
<DC1>               /x11    <U0011> DEVICE CONTROL ONE (DC1)
```

`<DC2>`	`/x12`	`<U0012>`	DEVICE CONTROL TWO (DC2)
`<DC3>`	`/x13`	`<U0013>`	DEVICE CONTROL THREE (DC3)
`<DC4>`	`/x14`	`<U0014>`	DEVICE CONTROL FOUR (DC4)
`<NAK>`	`/x15`	`<U0015>`	NEGATIVE ACKNOWLEDGE (NAK)
`<SYN>`	`/x16`	`<U0016>`	SYNCHRONOUS IDLE (SYN)
`<ETB>`	`/x17`	`<U0017>`	END TRANSMISSION BLOCK (ETB)
`<CAN>`	`/x18`	`<U0018>`	CANCEL (CAN)
`<SUB>`	`/x1A`	`<U001A>`	SUBSTITUTE (SUB)
`<ESC>`	`/x1B`	`<U001B>`	ESCAPE (ESC)
`<IS4>`	`/x1C`	`<U001C>`	FILE SEPARATOR (IS4)
`<IS3>`	`/x1D`	`<U001D>`	GROUP SEPARATOR (IS3)
`<intro>`	`/x1D`	`<U001D>`	GROUP SEPARATOR (IS3)
`<IS2>`	`/x1E`	`<U001E>`	RECORD SEPARATOR (IS2)
`<IS1>`	`/x1F`	`<U001F>`	UNIT SEPARATOR (IS1)
`<DEL>`	`/x7F`	`<U007F>`	DELETE (DEL)
`<space>`	`/x20`	`<U0020>`	SPACE
`<exclamation-mark>`	`/x21`	`<U0021>`	EXCLAMATION MARK
`<question-mark>`	`/x3F`	`<U003F>`	QUESTION MARK
`<number-sign>`	`/x23`	`<U0023>`	NUMBER SIGN
`<dollar-sign>`	`/x24`	`<U0024>`	DOLLAR SIGN
`<percent-sign>`	`/x25`	`<U0025>`	PERCENT SIGN
`<ampersand>`	`/x26`	`<U0026>`	AMPERSAND
`<apostrophe>`	`/x27`	`<U0027>`	APOSTROPHE
`<left-parenthesis>`	`/x28`	`<U0028>`	LEFT PARENTHESIS
`<right-parenthesis>`	`/x29`	`<U0029>`	RIGHT PARENTHESIS
`<asterisk>`	`/x2A`	`<U002A>`	ASTERISK
`<plus-sign>`	`/x2B`	`<U002B>`	PLUS SIGN
`<comma>`	`/x2C`	`<U002C>`	COMMA
`<hyphen>`	`/x2D`	`<U002D>`	HYPHEN-MINUS
`<hyphen-minus>`	`/x2D`	`<U002D>`	HYPHEN-MINUS
`<period>`	`/x2E`	`<U002E>`	FULL STOP
`<full-stop>`	`/x2E`	`<U002E>`	FULL STOP
`<slash>`	`/x2F`	`<U002F>`	SOLIDUS
`<solidus>`	`/x2F`	`<U002F>`	SOLIDUS
`<zero>`	`/x30`	`<U0030>`	DIGIT ZERO
`<one>`	`/x31`	`<U0031>`	DIGIT ONE
`<two>`	`/x32`	`<U0032>`	DIGIT TWO
`<three>`	`/x33`	`<U0033>`	DIGIT THREE
`<four>`	`/x34`	`<U0034>`	DIGIT FOUR
`<five>`	`/x35`	`<U0035>`	DIGIT FIVE
`<six>`	`/x36`	`<U0036>`	DIGIT SIX
`<seven>`	`/x37`	`<U0037>`	DIGIT SEVEN
`<eight>`	`/x38`	`<U0038>`	DIGIT EIGHT
`<nine>`	`/x39`	`<U0039>`	DIGIT NINE
`<colon>`	`/x3A`	`<U003A>`	COLON
`<semicolon>`	`/x3B`	`<U003B>`	SEMICOLON

```
<less-than-sign>           /x3C   <U003C> LESS-THAN SIGN
<equals-sign>              /x3D   <U003D> EQUALS SIGN
<greater-than-sign>        /x3E   <U003E> GREATER-THAN SIGN
<question-mark>            /x3F   <U003F> QUESTION MARK
<commercial-at>           /x40   <U0040> COMMERCIAL AT
<left-square-bracket>     /x5B   <U005B> LEFT SQUARE BRACKET
<backslash>               /x5C   <U005C> REVERSE SOLIDUS
<reverse-solidus>         /x5C   <U005C> REVERSE SOLIDUS
<right-square-bracket>    /x5D   <U005D> RIGHT SQUARE BRACKET
<circumflex>              /x5E   <U005E> CIRCUMFLEX ACCENT
<circumflex-accent>       /x5E   <U005E> CIRCUMFLEX ACCENT
<underscore>              /x5F   <U005F> LOW LINE
<low-line>                /x5F   <U005F> LOW LINE
<grave-accent>            /x60   <U0060> GRAVE ACCENT
<left-brace>              /x7B   <U007B> LEFT CURLY BRACKET
<left-curly-bracket>      /x7B   <U007B> LEFT CURLY BRACKET
<vertical-line>           /x7C   <U007C> VERTICAL LINE
<right-brace>             /x7D   <U007D> RIGHT CURLY BRACKET
<right-curly-bracket>     /x7D   <U007D> RIGHT CURLY BRACKET
<tilde>                   /x7E   <U007E> TILDE
END CHARMAP
```

13.3.3 Locale Definition Files

Here is an example `localedef` file for the POSIX locale:

```
# POSIX Standard Locale
#
# As per ISO/IEC 9945-2:1993 specifications
# except for these additional identifying comments
#
# Source: ISO/IEC JTC1/SC22/WG15 RIN
# Address: C/O DKUUG, Fruebjergvej 3
#    DK-2900 Copenhagen O, Denmark
# Contact: Keld Simonsen
# Email: Keld.Simonsen@dkuug.dk
# Tel: +45 - 39179944
# Fax: +45 - 39179897
# Language: POSIX
# Territory:
# Revision: 1.0
# Date: 1994-04-02
# Application: general
# Users: general
# Repertoiremap: POSIX
```

```
# Charset: ISO646:1993
# Distribution and use is free,
# also for commercial purposes.

LC_CTYPE
# The following is the POSIX Locale LC_CTYPE.
# "alpha" is by default "upper" and "lower"
# "alnum" is by definiton "alpha" and "digit"
# "print" is by default "alnum", "punct" and the <space> character
# "graph" is by default "alnum" and "punct"
#
upper    <A>;<B>;<C>;<D>;<E>;<F>;<G>;<H>;<I>;<J>;<K>;<L>;<M>\
         <N>;<O>;<P>;<Q>;<R>;<S>;<T>;<U>;<V>;<W>;<X>;<Y>;<Z>
#
lower    <a>;<b>;<c>;<d>;<e>;<f>;<g>;<h>;<i>;<j>;<k>;<l>;<m>\
         <n>;<o>;<p>;<q>;<r>;<s>;<t>;<u>;<v>;<w>;<x>;<y>;<z>
#
digit    <zero>;<one>;<two>;<three>;<four>;\
         <five>;<six>;<seven>;<eight>;<nine>
#
space    <tab>;<newline>;<vertical-tab>;<form-feed>;\
         <carriage-return>;<space>
#
cntrl    <alert>;<backspace>;<tab>;<newline>;<vertical-tab>;\
         <form-feed>;<carriage-return>;\
         <NUL>;<SOH>;<STX>;<ETX>;<EOT>;<ENQ>;<ACK>;<SO>;<SI>\
         <DLE>;<DC1>;<DC2>;<DC3>;<DC4>;<NAK>;<SYN>;<ETB>;<CAN>;\
         <EM>;<SUB>;<ESC>;<IS4>;<IS3>;<IS2>;<IS1>;<DEL>
#
punct    <exclamation-mark>;<quotation-mark>;<number-sign>;\
         <dollar-sign>;<percent-sign>;<ampersand>;<apostrophe>;\
         <left-parenthesis>;<right-parenthesis>;<asterisk>;\
         <plus-sign>;<comma>;<hyphen>;<period>;<slash>;\
         <colon>;<semicolon>;<less-than-sign>;<equals-sign>;\
         <greater-than-sign>;<question-mark>;<commercial-at>;\
         <left-square-bracket>;<backslash>;<right-square-bracket>;\
         <circumflex>;<underscore>;<grave-accent>;\
         <left-curly-bracket>;<vertical-line>;\
         <right-curly-bracket>;<tilde>;
#
xdigit
<zero>;<one>;<two>;<three>;<four>;<five>;<six>;<seven>;<eight>;\
         <nine>;<A>;<B>;<C>;<D>;<E>;<F>;<a>;<b>;<c>;<d>;<e>;<f>
#
blank    <space>;<tab>
#
```

```
tolower (<A>,<a>);(<B>,<b>);(<C>,<c>);(<D>,<d>);(<E>,<e>);\
        (<F>,<f>);(<G>,<g>);(<H>,<h>);(<I>,<i>);(<J>,<j>);\
        (<K>,<k>);(<L>,<l>);(<M>,<m>);(<N>,<n>);(<O>,<o>);\
        (<P>,<p>);(<Q>,<q>);(<R>,<r>);(<S>,<s>);(<T>,<t>);\
        (<U>,<u>);(<V>,<v>);(<W>,<w>);(<X>,<x>);(<Y>,<y>);(<Z>,<z>);
#
toupper (<a>,<A>);(<b>,<B>);(<c>,<C>);(<d>,<D>);(<e>,<E>);\
        (<f>,<F>);(<g>,<G>);(<h>,<H>);(<i>,<I>);(<j>,<J>);\
        (<k>,<K>);(<l>,<L>);(<m>,<M>);(<n>,<N>);(<o>,<O>);\
        (<p>,<P>);(<q>,<Q>);(<r>,<R>);(<s>,<S>);(<t>,<T>);\
        (<u>,<U>);(<v>,<V>);(<w>,<W>);(<x>,<X>);(<y>,<Y>);(<z>,<Z>);
END LC_CTYPE

LC_COLLATE
# This is the POSIX Locale definition for the LC_COLLATE category.
# The order is the same as in the ASCII code set.
order_start forward
<NUL>
<SOH>
<STX>
<ETX>
<EOT>
<ENQ>
<ACK>
<alert>
<backspace>
<tab>
<newline>
<vertical-tab>
<form-feed>
<carriage-return>
<SI>
<SO>
<DLE>
<DC1>
<DC2>
<DC3>
<DC4>
<NAK>
<SYN>
<ETB>
<CAN>
<EM>
<SUB>
<ESC>
<IS4>
```

```
<IS3>
<IS2>
<IS1>
<space>
<exclamation-mark>
<quotation-mark>
<number-sign>
<dollar-sign>
<percent-sign>
<ampersand>
<apostrophe>
<left-parenthesis>
<right-parenthesis>
<asterisk>
<plus-sign>
<comma>
<hyphen>
<period>
<slash>
<zero>
<one>
<two>
<three>
<four>
<five>
<six>
<seven>
<eight>
<nine>
<colon>
<semicolon>
<less-than-sign>
<equals-sign>
<greater-than-sign>
<question-mark>
<commercial-at>
<A>
<B>
<C>
<D>
<E>
<F>
<G>
<H>
<I>
<J>
```

```
<K>
<L>
<M>
<N>
<O>
<P>
<Q>
<R>
<S>
<T>
<U>
<V>
<W>
<X>
<Y>
<Z>
<left-square-bracket>
<backslash>
<right-square-bracket>
<circumflex>
<underscore>
<grave-accent>
<a>
<b>
<c>
<d>
<e>
<f>
<g>
<h>
<i>
<j>
<k>
<l>
<m>
<n>
<o>
<p>
<q>
<r>
<s>
<t>
<u>
<v>
<w>
<y>
```

```
<z>
<left-curly-bracket>
<vertical-line>
<right-curly-bracket>
<tilde>
<DEL>
order_end
#
END LC_COLLATE

LC_MONETARY
# This is the POSIX Locale definition for
# the LC_MONETARY category.
#
int_curr_symbol       ""
currency_symbol       ""
mon_decimal_point     ""
mon_thousands_sep     ""
mon_grouping          -1
positive_sign         ""
negative_sign         ""
int_frac_digits       -1
frac_digits           -1
p_cs_precedes         -1
p_sep_by_space        -1
n_cs_precedes         -1
n_sep_by_space        -1
p_sign_posn           -1
n_sign_posn           -1
#
END LC_MONETARY

LC_NUMERIC
# This is the POSIX Locale definition for
# the LC_NUMERIC category.
#
decimal_point    "<period>"
thousands_sep    ""
grouping         -1
#
END LC_NUMERIC

LC_TIME
# This is the POSIX Locale definition for
# the LC_TIME category.
#
```

```
# Abbreviated weekday names (%s)
abday   "<S><u><n>";"<M><o><n>";"<T><u><e>";"<W><e><d>";\
        "<T><h><u>";"<F><r><i>";"<S><a><t>"
#
# Full weekday names (%A)
day     "<S><u><n><d><a><y>";"<M><o><n><d><a><y>";\
        "<T><u><e><s><d><a><y>";"<W><e><d><n><e><s><d><a><y>";\
        "<T><h><u><r><s><d><a><y>";"<F><r><i><d><a><y>";\
        "<S><a><t><u><r><d><a><y>"
#
# Abbreviated month names (%b)
abmon   "<J><a><n>";"<F><e><b>";"<M><a><r>";\
        "<A><p><r>";"<M><a><y>";"<J><u><n>";\
        "<J><u><l>";"<A><u><g>";"<S><e><p>";\
        "<O><c><t>";"<N><o><v>";"<D><e><c>"
#
# Full month names (%B)
mon     "<J><a><n><u><a><r><y>";"<F><e><b><r><u><a><r><y>";\
        "<M><a><r><c><h>";"<A><p><r><i><l>";\
        "<M><a><y>";"<J><u><n><e>";\
        "<J><u><l><y>";"<A><u><g><u><s><t>";\
        "<S><e><p><t><e><m><b><e><r>";"<O><c><t><o><b><e><r>";\
        "<N><o><v><e><m><b><e><r>";"<D><e><c><e><m><b><e><r>"
#
# Equivalent of AM/PM (%p)       "AM"/"PM"
am_pm   "<A><M>";"<P><M>"
#
# Appropriate date and time representation (%c)
#       "%a %b %e %H:%M:%S %Y"
d_t_fmt "<percent-sign><a><space><percent-sign><b><space><percent-sign><e>\
<space><percent-sign><H><colon><percent-sign><M>\
<colon><percent-sign><S><space><percent-sign><Y>"
#
# Appropriate date representation (%x)   "%m/%d/%y"
d_fmt   "<percent-sign><m><slash><percent-sign><d><slash><percent-sign><y>"
#
# Appropriate time representation (%X)   "%H:%M:%S"
t_fmt   "<percent-sign><H><colon><percent-sign><M><colon><percent-sign><S>"
#
# Appropriate 12 h time representation (%Xr   "%I:%M:%S %p"
t_fmt_ampm "<percent-sign><I><colon><percent-sign><M><colon>\
<percent-sign><S><space><percent-sign><p>"
#
END LC_TIME
```

```
LC_MESSAGES
# This is the POSIX Locale definition for
# the LC_NUMERIC category.
#
yesexpr "<circumflex><left-square-bracket><y><Y><right-square-bracket>"
#
noexpr  "<circumflex><left-square-bracket><n><N><right-square-bracket>"
END LC_MESSAGES
```

13.3.4 Localization Files

Here is a list of localization directories and files used in Solaris 2.5. Many other UNIX systems share a similar locale directory structure, except that they have catgets(3C) style message catalogs instead of gettext(3intl) style *.mo files installed under LC_MESSAGES.

Locale directories:
/usr/lib/locale/*locale*/LC_COLLATE
/usr/lib/locale/*locale*/LC_CTYPE
/usr/lib/locale/*locale*/LC_MESSAGES
/usr/lib/locale/*locale*/LC_MONETARY
/usr/lib/locale/*locale*/LC_NUMERIC
/usr/lib/locale/*locale*/LC_TIME

Message files:
/usr/lib/locale/*locale*/LC_MESSAGES/*.mo
/usr/lib/locale/*locale*/LC_MESSAGES/*.cat

Other files:
/usr/lib/iconv/*origcs%destcs*.so (.so for code conversion)

13.3.5 Translate Message Files

On Solaris systems, software message files are organized by domain, under the SUNW_* directories. In these directories are *.po files for various commands.

The letters "po" are an acronym for portable object; portable object files are human-readable and intended for editing. There are also various *.cm comment files, which serve as hints to the translator. These files give helpful commentary, list words not to translate, and serve as a repository for translators' comments.

The SUNW_OST_LANGINFO directory contains *.cat files, for use with the gencat(1) messaging scheme.

Translators must fill in the `msgstr` lines in the `*.po` files with appropriate language translations. After this, run `msgfmt`(1) on the `*.po` files to produce corresponding `*.mo` files. The letters "mo" are an acronym for message object; these files are machine-readable and contain binary trees of message IDs plus translated messages.

13.3.6 Install Message Files

You don't need to install the `*.po` files, but only the `*.mo` files. Put system messages in `/usr/lib/locale/`*lang*`/LC_MESSAGES`, where *lang* indicates the locale name you selected in step #1 on page 199. If you translate utility help files, also put them somewhere under `/usr/lib/locale/`*lang*`/LC_MESSAGES`.

Actually you can install `*.mo` files anywhere, as long as the related application calls `bindtextdomain`(3intl) to associate the directory with a message domain. You can also install `catgets`(3C) message catalogs anywhere, as long as the related application sets the `NLSPATH` environment variable properly.

13.3.7 Codeset Conversion

Certain locales may require implementation of codeset conversion routines, typically for sending and receiving e-mail. East Asian locales (among others) employ combinations of different codesets. Western European locales may need to handle unsupported codesets, such as ISO 8859 variants.

The `iconv`(1) manual page lists currently supported codesets.

For certain locales, you must define a set of functions to convert text from one codeset to another. The modules `/usr/lib/iconv/`*origcs*`%`*destcs*`.so` are shared objects to convert the codeset *origcs* to codeset *destcs*.

13.3.8 Installing Localized Applications

If you are creating localized software that is intended only for Solaris systems, you might want to consider placing your localization files in a directory such as:
`/opt/`*your-product-package-name*`/lib/locale/`*locale*`/`

For instance, if you have message catalogs for a product called ACMEtool, you might store translated message objects under:
`/opt/ACMEtool/lib/locale/`*locale*`/LC_MESSAGES/*.mo`

13

13.4 Summary

The beginning of this chapter outlined a market-driven approach for determining appropriate levels of localization for various geographies, and described typical localization processes and schedules. That information should be useful to most marketing and engineering managers.

Creating a Locale Definition on page 198 details how Solaris locales are defined. That information is useful only for system localization teams.

Standards Organizations 14 ☰

Standardization is a growing force in the Information Technology (IT) industry. This chapter presents some organizations that are important in setting international standards.

14.1 The Case for Standardization

Standardization should be viewed as one of the things for which users of a system will ask—when it is appropriate to their business needs. If standardization is seen as a product attribute—along with price, performance, safety, or any of the many other things that cause customers to buy—then it is correctly positioned. There are times when it may not appeal to some customers at some level, but there are times when it is nearly always mandatory, depending upon the nature and intent of the user. The end user (ultimate user) doesn't really care about the collision detection schema (ISO/IEEE 8802-3) used in his or her LAN but is very interested as to whether or not the keyboard has a QWERTY layout. Conversely, the software designer needs to know when to use a standardized interface for shell and utilities (IEEE 1003.2) or if a multi-octet character set (ISO 10646) is specified.

In any case involving voluntary standards, there is the option of not adhering to a standard. Regulatory standards are a different matter. They deal with safety, telephonic network interconnect, and environmental concerns and are usually required by law. Products that do not meet these standards are illegal. Voluntary standards, by contrast, are a price of doing business; if a user demands them and you don't have them, you don't make a sale. In some cases, you can convince a buyer that the nonstandard solution you offer is significantly better, but it must be better by a margin large enough to justify the extra expense of ignoring a standard. Ultimately, standardization comes down to a matter of economics.

Internationalization is an emerging focus of standardization, a focus that has been implicit for many years but is now coming into its own as a special field. In the past, internationalization was achieved by consensus around a single standard, usually derived from current practice in the United States, where a majority of IT standards were originally created. However, as computers have become more ubiquitous and powerful, they have been modified to reflect national characteristics: this is the intent of internationalization. Basically, computers have become advanced and powerful enough to begin to respond to the needs of the users, rather than requiring users to respond to the needs of the system.

This response has created a need for an entirely new set of standardization rules and metrics called Internationalization (i18n). In the standardization arena, it is most often demonstrated by the multi-octet character set (MOC), ISO 10646. Other arenas—from power cords through display graphics to keyboards—have national and international activities. Additionally, standards that have nothing to do with i18n are becoming accepted as requirements for internationalized products: standards such as the ISO 9000-9004 quality standards, ISO TC 159 ergonomics standards, and others that will be covered briefly.

Governments specify standardization so that they can compare two or more dissimilar products and make a business decision; many governments are required by law to specify standards in their procurements for exactly this reason. Users specify standards because they believe standards promote interworking and interconnection. Providers use standardization as a base from which to expand capabilities or provide expandability of a system into areas in which they have little expertise. SCSI disk drives are one example, and the use of OSI or TCP/IP for communications is another.

The key thing to remember as you read this chapter is that standards are a business tool and should be used for business reasons. This chapter describes some of the more important standardization organizations and their products. However, keep in mind that standards are an enabler; if you do not have the standards that a user wants, then you will not even have a chance to sell a product, no matter how good or advanced it is. On the other hand, if you have standards in your product and the product is inferior, you probably will also not win too many sales. Standards do not sell products—they merely make it possible for you to enter the market to try to sell your efforts.

14.2 Sources and Types of Standards

Two distinct types of standards exist: de jure standards and de facto standards. De jure standards are created by Standards Developing Organizations (SDOs), organizations that operate under specific rules to create standards. No consortia produce de jure standards, because consortia limit participation in their specification-producing processes.

De facto standards are volume standards; that is, a true de facto standard is a product that leads in market share, in the industry, and from this gains standing as the "industry standard." Consortia try to develop de facto standards from their specification by having large numbers of users and providers adopt their specifications. Ultimately, most consortia wish to have their specifications made into standards by submitting them to an SDO and gaining a national and international seal of approval.

In this chapter, "standards" refers to technical descriptions formally accepted and endorsed by an SDO, "specification" refers to a consortium document, and the term "de facto standard" indicates a product that is a dominant market leader.

14.3 Standards Developing Organizations

Two important Standards Developing Organizations (SDOs) are discussed below: ISO and ANSI. The latter is a national standards organization.

14.3.1 International Organisation for Standardisation (ISO)

ISO is the premier standardization organization in the world. Based in Geneva, ISO standardizes everything from screw threads to mica to ornamental garden rocks. It has, in conjunction with the International Electrotechnical Commission (IEC), one joint technical committee, called ISO/IEC Joint Technical Committee 1 (JTC 1), which is charged with information technology standardization. JTC 1 is also the largest and most prolific standards committee in existence. It currently has 22 primary (or voting) members and 19 observer (nonvoting but contributing) members, with 2,500 standards documents and 3,500 volunteers in 41 nations.

JTC 1 is composed of subcommittees (SCs) to deal with specific areas of IT. JTC 1 currently has 18 SCs, with the areas of interest and national Secretariats listed in Table 14-1. (Note that subcommittee numbers, once used, are not reused when the committee goes out of existence to ensure that duplicate document numbers are never created.)

Table 14-1   ISO Subcommittees by Activity

SC #	Interest Areas	Secretariat
SC 1	Vocabulary	France
SC 2	Character Sets and Information Coding	France
SC 6	Data Communications	USA
SC 7	Design and Documentation	Canada
SC 11	Flexible Magnetic Media	USA

Table 14-1   ISO Subcommittees by Activity

SC #	Interest Areas	Secretariat
SC 14	Representation of Data Elements	Sweden
SC 15	Labeling and File Structure	Japan
SC 17	Identification and Credit Cards	Switzerland
SC 18	Text and Office Systems	USA
SC 21	Open Systems Support Services	USA
SC 22	Languages	Canada
SC 23	Optical Digital Data Disks	Japan
SC 24	Graphics	Germany
SC 25	Interconnection and Information Technology	Germany
SC 26	Microprocessor Systems	Japan
SC 27	Security Techniques	Germany
SC 28	Office Machinery and Standalone Printers	Japan
SC 29	Coded Representation for Hypermedia	France

These subcommittees and their subordinate working groups (WGs) are the standards-creating organizations of JTC 1. This is where the need for a standard is reviewed and accepted, where a draft is written and circulated, and where the technical accuracy of the standard is ensured, as far as possible.

Upon the completion of the working draft, the Working Group votes to determine if the working draft should be made into a committee draft. If the committee draft is approved, the subcommittee forwards it for further voting, for acceptance as a Draft International Standard (DIS). Again a vote is taken, and, if successful, the document becomes an International Standard after review, discussion, and approval by the JTC 1.

These steps can take up to six years to complete, with the variance in time resulting from technical complexity, political and national infighting, and any of a host of other reasons, including technical obsolescence.

The standards produced by ISO/IEC JTC 1 are the dominant information technology standards in the world and are usually the standards to which procurements point.

14.3.2 American National Standards Institute (ANSI)

Most nations have a single SDO that oversees creation of national standards. In Germany, the organization is the Deutsches Institut für Normung e.V. (DIN); in Canada, the Canadian Standards Association; in Japan, the Japanese Institute of Standards (JIS) and so on. In the United States, an umbrella organization, ANSI, keeps the rules by which standards are written, accredits organizations that write standards by the ANSI rules, but does not itself write standards.

The rules are aimed at two things: allowing free and open participation to any concerned party and obtaining consensus in the creation of a standard. Consensus can best be defined as a state achieved when all parties reach a substantial agreement. The definition indicates more than majority approval but does not imply unanimity. Rather, it indicates that all arguments have been heard, addressed, and dealt with in a constructive fashion.

Any organization that agrees to follow ANSI rules in writing standards usually receives ANSI accreditation. This policy has led to accreditation of more than 230 separate SDOs in the United States, usually with poorly defined charters and overlapping responsibilities.

ANSI's position in the U.S. standards hierarchy is derived from its authority in two areas: the sole right to publish American National Standards (ANS) and all that this implies, and its position as the sole U.S. representative to ISO. National input to ISO (and hence to JTC 1) is through ANSI, which votes the U.S. national position. However, because ANSI does not have the technical competence to create an opinion, it uses an organization called a Technical Advisory Group (TAG). The TAG that advises ANSI on JTC 1 matters is called the JTC 1 TAG, and is composed of all impacted U.S. SDOs, including ASC X3, AO IEEE, ASC T1, and AO EIA (see below).

The most important standards organization in the IT arena is Accredited Standards Committee (ASC) X3. ASC X3 produces approximately 90% of the IT standards in the U.S. and contributes to approximately 90% of the worldwide IT standards. The IEEE produces the bulk of the remainder of the IT standards in the U.S. but has little impact on the course of international standardization except in the areas of POSIX and LANs.

ASC X3 consists of a general committee of the whole that meets approximately three times a year, three management committees, and seven general Technical Committees. Additionally, X3 members are part of the JTC 1 by virtue of being part of X3. Voting is by organization; that is, no company can flood a committee and gain a disproportionate advantage in standards creation. X3 sets broad policy and general direction and votes on each proposed standard that comes to it for action from the Technical Committees.

The Technical Committees (TCs) of X3 are divided into of eight major areas, with Technical Management Committees overseeing the TCs. These areas are listed in Table 14-2.

Table 14-2   ANSI Technical Committees by Activity

Technical Committee	Area of Concern
X3A – Recognition	
X3A1	OCR and MICR
X3B – Media	
X3B6	Instrumentation Tape
X3B7	Magnetic Disks
X3B8	Flexible Disk Cartridges
X3B9	Paper Forms/Layouts
X3B10	Credit/ID Cards
X3B11	Optical Digital Data Disks
X3H,J – Languages	
X3H2	Database
X3H3	Computer Graphics
X3H4	Information Resource and Dictionary (IRDS)
X3H5	Parallel Processing Constructs for High-Level Programming Languages
X3H6	Case Tools
X3H7	Object-Oriented Languages
X3J1	PL/1
X3J2	BASIC
X3J3	FORTRAN
X3J4	COBOL
X3J7	APT
X3J9	Pascal
X3J10	APL
X3J11	C
X3J12	DIBOL
X3J13	Common LISP
X3J14	FORTH

Table 14-2   ANSI Technical Committees by Activity (Continued)

Technical Committee	Area of Concern
X3J15	Databus
X3J16	C++
X3J17	Prologue
X3J18	REXX
X3K – Documentation	
X3X1	Computer Documentation
X3K5	Vocabulary for Information Processing Standards
X3L – Data Representation	
X3L2	Codes and Character Sets
X3L3	Audio/Picture Coding
X3L8	Data Representation
X3S – Communication	
X3S3	Data Communication
X3T,V – Systems Technology	
X3T1	Data Encryption
X3T2	Data Interchange
X3T3	Open Distributed Processing
X3T4	Security Techniques
X3T5	Open Systems Interconnection (OSI)
X3T6	Noncontact Information Systems Interfaces
X3T7	Internationalization
X3T9	I/O Interface
X3V1	Text and Office Publishing Systems
X3W1 – Office Machines	

While many of these committees are simple to explain (for example, the COBOL committee is concerned with COBOL), it is important to understand that each of these committees retains liaison with most of the of the other committees that will impact its activities. Thus, the COBOL committee must be aware of changes in the way that languages are used, and it must be able to respond to these changes as they impact COBOL. If object-orientation or network management is seen as necessary in environments in which COBOL is specified, then the COBOL committee must understand these activities and merge them into the next iteration of the COBOL standard. This form of activity accounts for much of the work of the older committees. As the technology changes, the standards must change to be able to take advantage of the newer technology.

This requirement to ensure that a standard is updated and compatible with other standards is usually one of the major benefits of an SDO standard.

14.4 International Standards Activity

This section briefly discusses the histories and purposes of some organizations responsible for creating the specifications and standards discussed in this guide. Most computer companies recognize the importance of complying with existing and evolving standards and claim they are firmly committed to support and participate in ongoing efforts toward standardization. Moreover, most companies eventually conform to and adapt important new standards as they evolve.

Organizations are listed below in alphabetic order, not in order of importance.

14.4.1 European Computer Manufacturer's Association (ECMA)

ECMA, as the name indicates, is a European vendors' consortium mostly concerned with standardizing hardware interfaces. They have set standards for CD-ROM format, floppy disk and cartridge tape interchange, and thickness and trim size of printer paper. In addition, they have established numerous coded character set standards, some of which have been subsumed into ISO coded character set standards.

14.4.2 IEEE and POSIX.1

/usr/group, a group of UNIX users, established a committee with the objective of proposing a set of standards for application-level interfaces. After publishing the 1984 /usr/group Standard, the group decided to seek IEEE status for the standard. (IEEE stands for the Institute of Electrical and Electronics Engineers.) In early 1984, the /usr/group Standards Committee closed its activities in its own name; its members were encouraged to become involved in the IEEE POSIX committee so that the work could become the basis for an official international standard.

The first externally visible result of this initiative was the publication of the IEEE Trial-Use Standard in March 1986, with the formal approval in August 1988 of IEEE Standard 1003.1-1988, a "Portable Operating System Interface for Computer Environments" (POSIX). POSIX was the first step toward a truly portable operating system.

Although originally planned to refer to the IEEE Standard 1003.1-1988, the name POSIX has come to refer to a family of related standards and parts of the International Standard ISO/IEC 9945 (see below). A preferred term, POSIX.1, emerged, which did not confuse the 1003.1 standard with the POSIX family of standards. The 1003.1-1988 POSIX standard has also been accepted as an ISO standard, ISO/IEC 9945-1:1989. Note that use of, or compliance with, an IEEE standard is wholly voluntary.

14.4.3 IETF

The Internet Engineering Task Force (IETF) electronically proposes and ratifies networking standards and has gained importance with the growth of the Web.

14.4.4 ISO and the IEC

The International Standards Organization (ISO) and International Electrotechnical Commission (IEC) together form a system for worldwide standardization. National bodies that are members of ISO or IEC participate in the development of international standards through technical committees established to deal with particular fields of technical activity. Technical committees collaborate in fields of mutual interest. Other organizations, governmental and nongovernmental, also take part in the work.

ISO divides topics of standardization into a number of areas, each assigned to a technical committee. One of these committees, the Open Systems Interconnection (OSI), was organized to deal with the complexity of communicating systems and the required protocol standards.

14.4.5 Unicode Consortium

The Unicode Consortium is a U.S. vendors' organization established to promote the 16-bit worldwide coded character set called Unicode. In 1992 the Unicode consortium managed to get this codeset accepted as a subset of ISO 10646, a 32-bit codeset. Unicode is considered the Basic Multilingual Plane (BMP) of ISO 10646. Members of the Unicode consortium are Adobe, Borland, Digital, GO, H/P, IBM, Lotus, Metaphor, Microsoft, NeXT, Novell, Sun, Taligent, and WordPerfect. Coding of archaic scripts and rare Han characters is still in progress.

14.4.6 UniForum (/usr/group)

The UniForum Technical Committee, formerly /usr/group, is an association of individuals, corporations, and institutions with an interest in the UNIX system. This organization provides input to POSIX and other standards committees and consortia to aid the development of independent, industry-driven standards.

UniForum members represent a cross-section of the UNIX system community: more than 450 members represent hardware manufacturers, vendors of operating systems and software development tools, software designers, consultants, academics, authors, applications programmers, and others.

14.4.7 Open Group (X Consortium and OSF)

The X Consortium was organized to develop and extend the X Window System, originally written at MIT. The Open Software Foundation (OSF) devised Motif, a popular graphical user interface based on X Windows. In 1996 the X Consortium and OSF were merged to form the Open Group. Computer vendors and academic institutions contribute new software to X Windows and meet to decide how to extend the system in the next release. Although X11 hasn't been at the forefront of internationalization technology, the widespread acceptance of X Windows means that Open Group has great influence on window system programming practices.

14.4.8 X/Open and XPG

Founded in 1984, X/Open is a worldwide consortium of vendors attempting to adopt existing standards and adapt them into a consistent environment called the Common Applications Environment (CAE). X/Open is a trademark of the X/Open Company Limited in the UK and in other countries.

Through establishment of the Common Applications Environment and awarding of the X/Open brand trademark to products that comply with the X/Open definitions, X/Open aims to ensure portability and connectivity of applications. If no official standard is agreed upon, X/Open policy is to work closely with standards bodies to encourage the emergence of needed standards.

Many of the world's major hardware suppliers are now X/Open or Open Group members. Most of X/Open's technical work is accomplished by people from its member companies. Each member company has a contractual agreement with the consortium to provide compliant versions of the products specified.

X/Open publishes its specifications in the X/Open Portability Guide (XPG). The X/Open Portability Guide defines the interfaces identified as components of the Common Applications Environment. It contains an evolving portfolio of applications programming interfaces that enhance portability of application programs at source code level. The interfaces are supported by an extensive set of conformance tests and the distinct trademark, the X/Open brand. The third version of the Portability Guide, XPG3, encompasses the IEEE POSIX.1 operating system interface.

Internationalization Checklist

15≣

This chapter presents an internationalization software requirements matrix and provides a "do" and "don't" list for internationalization.

15.1 Internationalized Software Requirements

The software requirements outlined in this section are intended to replace the software internationalization guidelines introduced in 1993, (more commonly known as Levels 1–4), and described in the first edition of this book.

The impetus for changing the software internationalization guidelines was driven by evolving market requirements for language support and by the recognition of some basic inadequacies in the Level 1–4 definitions. Level 1–4 definitions were open to interpretation, unclear on required versus optional content, and often resulted in implementations that were not global in nature.

Table 15-1 identifies required features for internationalized software support. Where standard application programming interfaces (APIs) are available, it has been noted. If no standard APIs exists, you will need to create your own.

Internationalized software requirements have been grouped into the following classes:

- *Foundation class*—basic framework upon which other internationalization work is dependent
- *I/O class*—internationalization features that enable input, display, and printing of native language text
- *Data representation class*—internationalization features that enable access to application data in culturally acceptable formats

Dependencies between internationalization features are identified in a separate column to assist you in determining the appropriate order of implementation.

In using this matrix, you may find that some required features do not apply to your product. Exceptions can and should be made, based on the characteristics of the product itself but not on the basis of supporting unique needs of specific markets for which you intend to localize.

Table 15-1   Internationalization Software Planning Matrix

	Internationalization Feature	Subcategory	Standard API	Dependent Upon
	Foundation Class			
1	Locale Aware	Locale Announcement	XPG	-
2	Codeset Support	Code Set Independent$_a$	XPG	-
	I/O Class			
3-1	Font Handling	Composite Font Support in Window System	X11	1, 2
3-2		Composite Font Support in Console $_b$		1, 2
3-3		Composite Font Support for Printing	X11	1, 2
3-4		Rasterizer		1, 2
4-1	Printing	Format Filter		1, 2, 3-3, 3-4
4-2		Page size		1, 2, 3-3, 3-4
5-1	Text Rendering $_c$	with Preprocessing	X11, X/Open	1, 2, 3
6-1	User Interface Layout	GUI		1, 2, 3, 5, 9-6
6-2		CUI		1, 2, 3, 5, 9-6
7-1	Language Input$_d$	with Postprocessing	X11, X/Open	1, 2, 3
8-1	Data Interchange	ICCCM compliant	X11	1, 2
8-2		MIME compliant	MIME	1, 2

Table 15-1   *Internationalization Software Planning Matrix*

Internationalization Feature		Subcategory	Standard API	Dependent Upon
Data Representation Class				
9-1	Cultural Data	Time	XPG	1, 2
9-2		Date	XPG	1, 2
9-3		Monetary	XPG	1, 2
9-4		Numeric	XPG	1, 2
9-5		Collation	XPG	1, 2
9-6		Character Classification	XPG	1, 2
9-7		Messages	XPG, Sun	1, 2, 3, 5
9-8		Calendar		**
9-9		Names		1, 2, 3, 4, 5
9-10		Addresses		1, 2, 3, 4, 5
9-11		Telephone		1, 2, 3, 4, 5
9-12		Measurements		1, 2, 3, 4, 5
9-13		Icons		1, 2
9-14		Images		1, 2
9-15		Colors		1, 2
10-1	Linguistic	Word Separation		1, 2, 9-5, 9-6
10-2		Parsing		1, 2, 9-5, 9-6
10-3		Hyphenation		1, 2, 4, 5, 9-5, 9-6
10-4		Justification		1, 2, 4, 5, 9-5, 9-6
10-5		Punctuation		1, 2, 9-5, 9-6
10-6		Spellchecking		1, 2, 9-5, 9-6
10-7		Word Expansion		1, 2, 9-5, 9-6

a. Code Set Independence development is currently limited to support only UNIX file system safe codesets.

b. Console display of Eastern European, East Asian, Southeast Asian, and Middle Eastern languages is currently not available due to limitations in the console driver.

c. Text rendering for various Southeast Asian and Middle Eastern languages (such as Thai and Arabic) requires the Complex Text Language (CTL) framework, which is based on the interfaces defined in the X/Open Portable Layout Services: Context-dependent and Directional Text snapshot document.

d. Language input for Southeast Asian languages (such as Thai) requires the Complex Text Language (CTL) framework, which is based on the interfaces defined in the X/Open Portable Layout Services: Context-dependent and Directional Text snapshot document.

15

15.2 Do and Don't List

Here is a "do" and "don't" list, organized according to the internationalization matrix presented above.

15.2.1 Locale Awareness

When testing, always be aware of the values of the `LANG` and `LC_*` environment variables. You can check the current settings using the `locale`(1) command.

In X toolkit (Xt) window programs, remember that `XtSetLanguageProc()` does not itself change the locale; the locale doesn't actually change until the program later calls `XtAppInitialize()`.

15.2.2 Codeset Support

Ensure that your programs are 8-bit clean.

Be careful about sign extension when using the `char` and `signed char` data types.

Do not make assumptions beyond those guaranteed by Standard C about the way characters are encoded.

Use appropriate string functions. For example, calls to `strchr()` are usually wrong; use `wcschr()` instead.

15.2.3 Composite Font Support in Window System

Be sure your resource files specify fonts appropriate to the locale.

When testing, be aware of the value of the `XFILESEARCHPATH` environment variable.

15.2.4 GUI Layout

Use Xlib metric functions to determine string display dimensions.

Let the window system's geometry manager determine the dimensions and positions of objects.

When testing, be aware of the value of the `XFILESEARCHPATH` environment variable.

15.2.5 Accelerator Keys

Allow localization teams to change accelerator key mnemonics.

15.2.6 CUI Layout

Don't assume that all characters are the same width, even when using a fixed-width font.

15.2.7 Time and Date

Use `strftime()` to format dates and times.

15.2.8 Monetary

Use `strfmon()` to format monetary amounts.

15.2.9 Numeric

Remember that the `%f` format for `scanf()` and `printf()` uses a decimal separator appropriate to the locale.

15.2.10 Collation

When testing strings for exact equality, use `strcmp()`, not `strcoll()`.

15.2.11 Character Classification

Don't assume a one-to-one mapping between lowercase and uppercase letters. Some letters in one case may have no single-letter equivalent in the other case.

15.2.12 Messages

Create message catalogs for strings that must be translated.

Use `catgets()` or `gettext()` (but not both).

When testing, be aware of the value of the `NLSPATH` environment variable.

Write messages that will be clear to a non-native speaker of your language. Avoid jargon, abbreviations, and acronyms.

Do not split messages into multiple strings.

15.2.13 Names

Don't assume that all names fit a First/Middle/Last format.

Don't assume that names are sorted by family name.

15.2.14 Telephone Numbers

Don't assume telephone numbers are of fixed length or in any particular format.

15.2.15 Addresses

Recognize that address styles vary greatly around the world, so allow flexibility for input, storage, and output.

15.2.16 Images

In bitmap images, don't include text that must be translated.

15.2.17 Color

Allow localization teams to change color schemes. With X Windows this is seldom a problem.

Languages, Territories, and Locale Names

This appendix lists Solaris locale names, along with the ISO language and territory names recommended for distributed computing.

A.1 Language and Territory

An internationalized program makes no assumptions about the language and format of text it is designed to handle. It must work equally well in any locale for all of these things: data generated internally, text read from or written to files, and messages presented to the user.

To determine locale-specific conventions at runtime, programs query system databases, installed in `/usr/lib/locale`, for cultural data. Applications should identify the proper locale, using the Solaris standard names shown in Table A-1. This identification is especially important in distributed computing environments where servers need to recognize client locales, and vice versa.

Because locale information includes things like monetary formats, a language might be the same for two locales, but other locale categories might differ. For example, computer messages in French might please users in both France and Belgium, but Belgium would need a locale of its own because it uses a currency different from the French Franc.

A.2 Solaris Locale Names

Solaris follows the locale naming convention specified by XPG4. A locale name can consist of a language name, a territory name, and a codeset name.

Language codes (all lowercase) are specified by the ISO 639 standard. Territory codes (all uppercase) are specified by the ISO 3166 standard. These standards are always subject to updates, particularly ISO 3166 in this post-Cold War era when political boundaries change rapidly.

A

In the Solaris locale names listed in Table A-1, language is separated from territory by an underscore, and territory is optional.

Table A-1   Solaris Locale Names

Locale Name	Language	Territory	Encoding
C	English	default	ASCII (7-bit)
ca	Catalan	Spain	ISO 8859-1
cz	Czech	Czech Republic	ISO 8859-2
da	Danish	Denmark	ISO 8859-1
de	German	Germany	ISO 8859-1
de_AT	German	Austria	ISO 8859-1
de_CH	German	Switzerland	ISO 8859-1
el	Greek	Greece	ISO 8859-7
en_AU	English	Australia	ISO 8859-1
en_CA	English	Canada	ISO 8859-1
en_IE	English	Ireland	ISO 8859-1
en_NZ	English	New Zealand	ISO 8859-1
en_UK	English	Great Britain	ISO 8859-1
en_US	English	United States	ISO 8859-1
en_US.UTF-8	English	United States	UTF-8
es	Spanish	Spain	ISO 8859-1
es_AR	Spanish	Argentina	ISO 8859-1
es_BO	Spanish	Bolivia	ISO 8859-1
es_CL	Spanish	Chile	ISO 8859-1
es_CO	Spanish	Columbia	ISO 8859-1
es_CR	Spanish	Costa Rica	ISO 8859-1
es_EC	Spanish	Ecuador	ISO 8859-1
es_GT	Spanish	Guatemala	ISO 8859-1
es_MX	Spanish	Mexico	ISO 8859-1
es_NI	Spanish	Nicaragua	ISO 8859-1
es_PA	Spanish	Panama	ISO 8859-1
es_PE	Spanish	Peru	ISO 8859-1
es_PY	Spanish	Paraguay	ISO 8859-1
es_SV	Spanish	El Salvador	ISO 8859-1

A ≡

Table A-1   Solaris Locale Names

Locale Name	Language	Territory	Encoding
es_UY	Spanish	Uruguay	ISO 8859-1
es_VE	Spanish	Venezuela	ISO 8859-1
et	Estonian	Estonia	ISO 8859-10
fr	French	France	ISO 8859-1
fr_BE	French	Belgium	ISO 8859-1
fr_CA	French	Canada	ISO 8859-1
fr_CH	French	Switzerland	ISO 8859-1
hu	Hungarian	Hungary	ISO 8859-2
is	Icelandic	Iceland	ISO 8859-1
it	Italian	Italy	ISO 8859-1
ja	Japanese	Japan	Japanese EUC
ja_JP.PCK	Japanese	Japan	PC-Kanji
ko	Korean	Korea	Korean
ko.UTF-8	Korean	Korea	UTF-8
lt	Lithuanian	Lithuania	ISO 8859-10
lv	Latvian	Latvia	ISO 8859-10
nl	Dutch	Netherlands	ISO 8859-1
nl_BE	Dutch	Belgium	ISO 8859-1
no	Norwegian	Norway	ISO 8859-1
pl	Polish	Poland	ISO 8859-2
POSIX	English	default	ASCII (7-bit)
pt	Portuguese	Portugal	ISO 8859-1
pt_BR	Portuguese	Brazil	ISO 8859-1
ru	Russian	Russian Federation	ISO 8859-5
su	Finnish	Finland	ISO 8859-1
sv	Swedish	Sweden	ISO 8859-1
tr	Turkish	Turkey	ISO 8859-9
zh	Simplified Chinese	China (PRC)	Simplified Chinese EUC
zh_TW	Traditional Chinese	Taiwan (ROC)	Traditional Chinese EUC
zh_TW.BIG5	Traditional Chinese	Taiwan (ROC)	Big 5

A

A.3 Languages

The following tables list ISO language codes, from which Solaris locale names are formed. Table A-2 lists ISO 639 alphabetically by code.

Table A-2   ISO 639 Language Codes Listed Alphabetically by Code

Code	Language	Code	Language	Code	Language
aa	Afar	eo	Esperanto	is	Icelandic
ab	Abkhazian	es	Spanish	it	Italian
af	Afrikaans	et	Estonian	iu	Eskimo, Inuktitut
am	Amharic	eu	Basque		
ar	Arabic			ja	Japanese
as	Assamese	fa	Persian	jw	Javanese
ay	Aymara	fi	Finnish		
az	Azerbaijani	fj	Fiji	ka	Georgian
		fo	Faeroese	kk	Kazakh
ba	Bashkir	fr	French	kl	Greenlandic
be	Byelorussian	fy	Frisian	km	Cambodian
bg	Bulgarian			kn	Kannada
bh	Bihari	ga	Irish	ko	Korean
bi	Bislama	gd	Scots Gaelic	ks	Kashmiri
bn	Bengali; Bangla	gl	Galician	ku	Kurdish
bo	Tibetan	gn	Guarani	ky	Kirghiz
br	Breton	gu	Gujarati		
				la	Latin
ca	Catalan	ha	Hausa	ln	Lingala
co	Corsican	he	Hebrew	lo	Laotian
cs	Czech	hi	Hindi	lt	Lithuanian
cy	Welsh	hr	Croatian	lv	Latvian, Lettish
		hu	Hungarian		
da	Danish	hy	Armenian	mg	Malagasy
de	German			mi	Maori
dz	Bhutani	ia	Interlingua	mk	Macedonian
		id	Indonesian	ml	Malayalam
el	Greek	ie	Interlingue	mn	Mongolian
en	English	ik	Inupiak	mo	Moldavian

Table A-2   *ISO 639 Language Codes Listed Alphabetically by Code*

Code	Language	Code	Language	Code	Language
mr	Marathi	sa	Sanskrit	tr	Turkish
ms	Malay	sd	Sindhi	ts	Tsonga
mt	Maltese	sg	Sangro	tt	Tatar
my	Burmese	sh	Serbo-Croatian	tw	Twi
		si	Singhalese		
na	Nauru	sk	Slovak	ug	Uigur
ne	Nepali	sl	Slovenian	uk	Ukrainian
nl	Dutch	sm	Samoan	ur	Urdu
no	Norwegian	sn	Shona	uz	Uzbek
		so	Somali		
oc	Occitan	sq	Albanian	vi	Vietnamese
om	(Afan) Oromo	sr	Serbian	vo	Volapuk
or	Oriya	ss	Siswati		
		st	Sesotho	wo	Wolof
pa	Punjabi	su	Sudanese		
pl	Polish	sv	Swedish	xh	Xhosa
ps	Pashto, Pushto	sw	Swahili		
pt	Portuguese			yi	Yiddish
		ta	Tamil	yo	Yoruba
qu	Quechua	te	Tegulu		
		tg	Tajik	za	Zhuang
rm	Rhaeto-Romance	th	Thai	zh	Chinese
rn	Kirundi	ti	Tigrinya	zu	Zulu
ro	Romanian	tk	Turkmen		
ru	Russian	tl	Tagalog		
rw	Kinyarwanda	tn	Setswana		
		to	Tonga		

A

Table A-2 lists ISO 639 alphabetically by language.

Table A-3   *ISO 639 Language Codes Listed Alphabetically by Language*

Language	Code	Language	Code	Language	Code
Abkhazian	ab	English	en	Japanese	ja
Afar	aa	Eskimo, Inuktitut	iu	Javanese	jw
Afrikaans	af	Esperanto	eo		
Albanian	sq	Estonian	et	Kannada	kn
Amharic	am			Kashmiri	ks
Arabic	ar	Faeroese	fo	Kazakh	kk
Armenian	hy	Fiji	fj	Kinyarwanda	rw
Assamese	as	Finnish	fi	Kirghiz	ky
Aymara	ay	French	fr	Kirundi	rn
Azerbaijani	az	Frisian	fy	Korean	ko
				Kurdish	ku
Bashkir	ba	Galician	gl		
Basque	eu	Georgian	ka	Laotian	lo
Bengali; Bangla	bn	German	de	Latin	la
Bhutani	dz	Greek	el	Latvian, Lettish	lv
Bihari	bh	Greenlandic	kl	Lingala	ln
Bislama	bi	Guarani	gn	Lithuanian	lt
Breton	br	Gujarati	gu		
Bulgarian	bg			Macedonian	mk
Burmese	my	Hausa	ha	Malagasy	mg
Byelorussian	be	Hebrew	he	Malay	ms
		Hindi	hi	Malayalam	ml
Cambodian	km	Hungarian	hu	Maltese	mt
Catalan	ca			Maori	mi
Chinese	zh	Icelandic	is	Marathi	mr
Corsican	co	Indonesian	id	Moldavian	mo
Croatian	hr	Interlingua	ia	Mongolian	mn
Czech	cs	Interlingue	ie		
		Inupiak	ik	Nauru	na
Danish	da	Irish	ga	Nepali	ne
Dutch	nl	Italian	it	Norwegian	no

Table A-3   ISO 639 Language Codes Listed Alphabetically by Language

Language	Code	Language	Code	Language	Code
Occitan	oc	Setswana	tn	Turkish	tr
Oriya	or	Shona	sn	Turkmen	tk
(Afan) Oromo	om	Sindhi	sd	Twi	tw
		Singhalese	si		
Pashto, Pushto	ps	Siswati	ss	Uigur	ug
Persian	fa	Slovak	sk	Ukrainian	uk
Polish	pl	Slovenian	sl	Urdu	ur
Portuguese	pt	Somali	so	Uzbek	uz
Punjabi	pa	Spanish	es		
		Sudanese	su	Vietnamese	vi
Quechua	qu	Swahili	sw	Volapuk	vo
		Swedish	sv		
Rhaeto-Romance	rm			Welsh	cy
Romanian	ro	Tagalog	tl	Wolof	wo
Russian	ru	Tajik	tg		
		Tamil	ta	Xhosa	xh
Samoan	sm	Tatar	tt		
Sangro	sg	Tegulu	te	Yiddish	yi
Sanskrit	sa	Thai	th	Yoruba	yo
Scots Gaelic	gd	Tibetan	bo		
Serbian	sr	Tigrinya	ti	Zhuang	za
Serbo-Croatian	sh	Tonga	to	Zulu	zu
Sesotho	st	Tsonga	ts		

A

A.4 Territories

The following tables list ISO territory codes, from which Solaris locale names are formed. Table A-4 lists ISO 3166 alphabetically by code.

Table A-4   ISO 3166 Territory Codes Listed Alphabetically by Code

Code	Territory	Code	Territory
AD	Andorra	BR	Brazil
AE	United Arab Emirates	BS	Bahamas
AF	Afghanistan	BT	Bhutan
AG	Antigua and Barbuda	BV	Bouvet Island
AI	Anguilla	BW	Botswana
AL	Albania	BY	Belarus
AM	Armenia	BZ	Belize
AN	Netherlands Antilles		
AO	Angola	CA	Canada
AQ	Antarctica	CC	Cocos (Keeling) Islands
AR	Argentina	CF	Central African Republic
AS	American Samoa	CG	Congo
AT	Austria	CH	Switzerland
AU	Australia	CI	Cote D'Ivoire
AW	Aruba	CK	Cook Islands
AZ	Azerbaijan	CL	Chile
		CM	Cameroon
BA	Bosnia and Herzegowina	CN	China
BB	Barbados	CO	Colombia
BD	Bangladesh	CR	Costa Rica
BE	Belgium	CU	Cuba
BF	Burkina Faso	CV	Cape Verde
BG	Bulgaria	CX	Christmas Island
BH	Bahrain	CY	Cyprus
BI	Burundi	CZ	Czech Republic
BJ	Benin		
BM	Bermuda	DE	Germany
BN	Brunei Darussalam	DJ	Djibouti
BO	Bolivia	DK	Denmark

Table A-4   ISO 3166 Territory Codes Listed Alphabetically by Code

Code	Territory	Code	Territory
DM	Dominica	GS	South Georgia and the South Sandwich Islands
DO	Dominican Republic	GT	Guatemala
DZ	Algeria	GU	Guam
		GW	Guinea-bissau
EC	Ecuador	GY	Guyana
EE	Estonia		
EG	Egypt	HK	Hong Kong
EH	Western Sahara	HM	Heard and McDonald Islands
ER	Eritrea	HN	Honduras
ES	Spain	HR	Croatia
ET	Ethiopia	HT	Haiti
		HU	Hungary
FI	Finland		
FJ	Fiji	ID	Indonesia
FK	Falkland Islands (Malvinas)	IE	Ireland
FM	Micronesia, Federated States of	IL	Israel
FO	Faeroe Islands	IN	India
FR	France	IO	British Indian Ocean Territory
FX	France, Metropolitan	IQ	Iraq
		IR	Iran (Islamic Republic of)
GA	Gabon	IS	Iceland
GB	United Kingdom	IT	Italy
GD	Grenada		
GE	Georgia	JM	Jamaica
GF	French Guiana	JO	Jordan
GH	Ghana	JP	Japan
GI	Gibraltar		
GL	Greenland	KE	Kenya
GM	Gambia	KG	Kyrgyzstan
GN	Guinea	KH	Cambodia
GP	Guadeloupe	KI	Kiribati
GQ	Equatorial Guinea	KM	Comoros
GR	Greece	KN	Saint Kitts and Nevis

A

Table A-4   ISO 3166 Territory Codes Listed Alphabetically by Code

Code	Territory	Code	Territory
KP	Korea, Democratic People's Republic of	MU	Mauritius
KR	Korea, Republic of	MV	Maldives
KW	Kuwait	MW	Malawi
KY	Cayman Islands	MX	Mexico
KZ	Kazakhstan	MY	Malaysia
		MZ	Mozambique
LA	Lao People's Democratic Republic		
LC	Saint Lucia	NA	Namibia
LI	Liechtenstein	NC	New Caledonia
LK	Sri Lanka	NE	Niger
LR	Liberia	NF	Norfolk Island
LS	Lesotho	NG	Nigeria
LT	Lithuania	NI	Nicaragua
LU	Luxembourg	NL	Netherlands
LV	Latvia	NO	Norway
LY	Libyan Arab Jamahiriya	NP	Nepal
		NR	Nauru
MA	Morocco	NU	Niue
MC	Monaco	NZ	New Zealand
MD	Moldova, Republic of		
MG	Madagascar	OM	Oman
MH	Marshall Islands		
MK	Macedonia, former Yugoslav Republic of	PA	Panama
ML	Mali	PE	Peru
MM	Myanmar	PF	French Polynesia
MN	Mongolia	PG	Papua New Guinea
MO	Macau	PH	Philippines
MP	Northern Mariana Islands	PK	Pakistan
MQ	Martinique	PL	Poland
MR	Mauritania	PM	St. Pierre and Miquelon
MS	Montserrat	PN	Pitcairn
MT	Malta	PR	Puerto Rico

Table A-4   ISO 3166 Territory Codes Listed Alphabetically by Code

Code	Territory	Code	Territory
PT	Portugal	TF	French Southern Territories
PW	Palau	TG	Togo
PY	Paraguay	TH	Thailand
		TJ	Tajikistan
QA	Qatar	TK	Tokelau
		TM	Turkmenistan
RE	Reunion	TN	Tunisia
RO	Romania	TO	Tonga
RU	Russian Federation	TP	East Timor
RW	Rwanda	TR	Turkey
		TT	Trinidad and Tobago
SA	Saudi Arabia	TV	Tuvalu
SB	Solomon Islands	TW	Taiwan, Province of China
SC	Seychelles	TZ	Tanzania, United Republic of
SD	Sudan		
SE	Sweden	UA	Ukraine
SG	Singapore	UG	Uganda
SH	St. Helena	UM	United States minor outlying islands
SI	Slovenia	US	United States
SJ	Svalbard and Jan Mayen Islands	UY	Uruguay
SK	Slovakia (Slovak Republic)	UZ	Uzbekistan
SL	Sierra Leone		
SM	San Marino	VA	Vatican City State (Holy See)
SN	Senegal	VC	Saint Vincent and the Grenadines
SO	Somalia	VE	Venezuela
SR	Suriname	VG	Virgin Islands (British)
ST	Sao Tome and Principe	VI	Virgin Islands (U.S.)
SV	El Salvador	VN	Viet Nam
SY	Syrian Arab Republic	VU	Vanuatu
SZ	Swaziland		
		WF	Wallis and Futuna Islands
TC	Turks and Caicos Islands	WS	Samoa
TD	Chad		

Table A-4   ISO 3166 Territory Codes Listed Alphabetically by Code

Code	Territory	Code	Territory
YE	Yemen	ZM	Zambia
YT	Mayotte	ZR	Zaire
YU	Yugoslavia	ZW	Zimbabwe
ZA	South Africa		

Table A-5 lists ISO 3166 alphabetically by territory.

Table A-5   ISO 3166 Territory Codes Listed Alphabetically by Territory

Territory	Code	Territory	Code
Afghanistan	AF	Brunei Darussalam	BN
Albania	AL	Bulgaria	BG
Algeria	DZ	Burkina Faso	BF
American Samoa	AS	Burundi	BI
Andorra	AD		
Angola	AO	Cambodia	KH
Anguilla	AI	Cameroon	CM
Antarctica	AQ	Canada	CA
Antigua and Barbuda	AG	Cape Verde	CV
Argentina	AR	Cayman Islands	KY
Armenia	AM	Central African Republic	CF
Aruba	AW	Chad	TD
Australia	AU	Chile	CL
Austria	AT	China	CN
Azerbaijan	AZ	Christmas Island	CX
		Cocos (Keeling) Islands	CC
Bahamas	BS	Colombia	CO
Bahrain	BH	Comoros	KM
Bangladesh	BD	Congo	CG
Barbados	BB	Cook Islands	CK
Belarus	BY	Costa Rica	CR
Belgium	BE	Cote D'Ivoire	CI
Belize	BZ	Croatia	HR
Benin	BJ	Cuba	CU
Bermuda	BM	Cyprus	CY
Bhutan	BT	Czech Republic	CZ
Bolivia	BO		
Bosnia and Herzegowina	BA	Denmark	DK
Botswana	BW	Djibouti	DJ
Bouvet Island	BV	Dominica	DM
Brazil	BR	Dominican Republic	DO
British Indian Ocean Territory	IO		

Table A-5   ISO 3166 Territory Codes Listed Alphabetically by Territory

Territory	Code	Territory	Code
East Timor	TP	Guinea-bissau	GW
Ecuador	EC	Guyana	GY
Egypt	EG		
El Salvador	SV	Haiti	HT
Equatorial Guinea	GQ	Heard and McDonald Islands	HM
Eritrea	ER	Honduras	HN
Estonia	EE	Hong Kong	HK
Ethiopia	ET	Hungary	HU
		Iceland	IS
Falkland Islands (Malvinas)	FK	India	IN
Faeroe Islands	FO	Indonesia	ID
Fiji	FJ	Iran (Islamic Republic of)	IR
Finland	FI	Iraq	IQ
France	FR	Ireland	IE
France, Metropolitan	FX	Israel	IL
French Guiana	GF	Italy	IT
French Polynesia	PF		
French Southern Territories	TF	Jamaica	JM
		Japan	JP
Gabon	GA	Jordan	JO
Gambia	GM		
Georgia	GE	Kazakhstan	KZ
Germany	DE	Kenya	KE
Ghana	GH	Kiribati	KI
Gibraltar	GI	Korea, Democratic People's Republic of	KP
Greece	GR	Korea, Republic of	KR
Greenland	GL	Kuwait	KW
Grenada	GD	Kyrgyzstan	KG
Guadeloupe	GP		
Guam	GU	Lao People's Democratic Republic	LA
Guatemala	GT	Latvia	LV
Guinea	GN	Lebanon	LB

Table A-5   ISO 3166 Territory Codes Listed Alphabetically by Territory

Territory	Code	Territory	Code
Lesotho	LS	Nepal	NP
Liberia	LR	Netherlands	NL
Libyan Arab Jamahiriya	LY	Netherlands Antilles	AN
Liechtenstein	LI	New Caledonia	NC
Lithuania	LT	New Zealand	NZ
Luxembourg	LU	Nicaragua	NI
		Niger	NE
Macau	MO	Nigeria	NG
Macedonia, former Yugoslav Republic of	MK	Niue	NU
Madagascar	MG	Norfolk Island	NF
Malawi	MW	Northern Mariana Islands	MP
Malaysia	MY	Norway	NO
Maldives	MV		
Mali	ML	Oman	OM
Malta	MT		
Marshall Islands	MH	Pakistan	PK
Martinique	MQ	Palau	PW
Mauritania	MR	Panama	PA
Mauritius	MU	Papua New Guinea	PG
Mayotte	YT	Paraguay	PY
Mexico	MX	Peru	PE
Micronesia, Federated States of	FM	Philippines	PH
Moldova, Republic of	MD	Pitcairn	PN
Monaco	MC	Poland	PL
Mongolia	MN	Portugal	PT
Montserrat	MS	Puerto Rico	PR
Morocco	MA		
Mozambique	MZ	Qatar	QA
Myanmar	MM		
		Reunion	RE
Namibia	NA	Romania	RO
Nauru	NR	Russian Federation	RU
		Rwanda	RW

Table A-5   ISO 3166 Territory Codes Listed Alphabetically by Territory

Territory	Code	Territory	Code
Saint Kitts and Nevis	KN	Tajikistan	TJ
Saint Lucia	LC	Tanzania, United Republic of	TZ
Saint Vincent and the Grenadines	VC	Thailand	TH
Samoa	WS	Togo	TG
San Marino	SM	Tokelau	TK
Sao Tome and Principe	ST	Tonga	TO
Saudi Arabia	SA	Trinidad and Tobago	TT
Senegal	SN	Tunisia	TN
Seychelles	SC	Turkey	TR
Sierra Leone	SL	Turkmenistan	TM
Singapore	SG	Turks and Caicos Islands	TC
Slovakia (Slovak Republic)	SK	Tuvalu	TV
Slovenia	SI		
Solomon Islands	SB	Uganda	UG
Somalia	SO	Ukraine	UA
South Africa	ZA	United Arab Emirates	AE
South Georgia and the South Sandwich Islands	GS	United Kingdom	GB
Spain	ES	United States	US
Sri Lanka	LK	United States minor outlying islands	UM
St. Helena	SH	Uruguay	UY
St. Pierre and Miquelon	PM	Uzbekistan	UZ
Sudan	SD		
Suriname	SR	Vanuatu	VU
Svalbard and Jan Mayen Islands	SJ	Vatican City State (Holy See)	VA
Swaziland	SZ	Venezuela	VE
Sweden	SE	Viet Nam	VN
Switzerland	CH	Virgin Islands (British)	VG
Syrian Arab Republic	SY	Virgin Islands (U.S.)	VI
Taiwan, Province of China	TW	Wallis and Futuna Islands	WF

Table A-5   *ISO 3166 Territory Codes Listed Alphabetically by Territory*

Territory	Code	Territory	Code
Western Sahara	EH	Zaire	ZR
		Zambia	ZM
Yemen	YE	Zimbabwe	ZW
Yugoslavia	YU		

Locale Summaries and Keyboard Layouts

This appendix depicts various keyboard layouts used in western Europe and east Asia. All keyboards shown here are SPARC type-5. SPARC type-4 keyboards were also delivered in similar international designs, but their layouts were different (not PC-compatible). The PC keyboards used on x86 machines are similar to the type-5 layout, with a few exceptions: both the left-hand keypad of window system functions, and the top row help key and volume controls, are missing. Also, more PC keyboards are available than shown here, and more SPARC keyboards will be available in the future.

B.1 European and Asian Locales

Keys with an accent mark above a square are called "dead keys" because they do not advance the cursor. Note that the French/Belgian keyboard is an AZERTY, not a QWERTY keyboard, and that the German keyboard is a QWERTZ keyboard. Interestingly, the Swiss French keyboard uses the German rather than the French layout. On keyboards where a supported character does not exist, it can always be produced with the Compose key.

Asian keyboard layouts are based on the U.S.-English layout, but have local language markings on the right-hand side of many keycaps. On the Japanese keyboard only, the space bar was split to form extra keys. The Japanese keyboard has Hiragana characters marked, the Korean keyboard has Hangul elements, and the traditional Chinese keyboard has Bopomofo symbols and ideographic character components (radicals).

Keyboards are depicted on the following pages in order of DIP switch settings, from 33 to 49. Type-4 keyboards are numbered from 1 to 17. At boot time, or when a new keyboard is plugged in, SPARC keyboards identify themselves by returning the number of their internal DIP switch setting. This number can be retrieved with a KIOCLAYOUT call to ioctl(). The kernel keeps track of keyboards using files in /usr/share/lib/keytables. OpenWindows uses different files, located in $OPENWINHOME/etc/keytables. For an easy-to-read list of supported keyboard types, see the keytables.map file in that directory.

B

B.2 US English Locale

Name of Locale

en_US

Collation Order

Aa Bb Cc Dd Ee Ff Gg Hh Ii Jj Kk Ll Mm Nn Oo Pp Qq Rr Ss Tt Uu Vv Ww Xx Yy Zz

Monetary Format

US dollar (USD) $1,234.50

Numeric Format

9,876,543.21

Date and Time

Sunday August 20, 1995   8/20/95

9:30 AM – 5:30 PM

Days and Months

Sunday Monday Tuesday Wednesday Thursday Friday Saturday

January February March April May June July August September October November December

B.3 US UNIX Keyboard

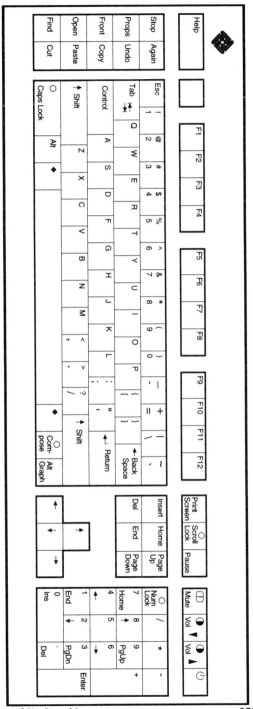

B.4 French Locale

Name of Locale

fr

Collation Order

Aaàâ Bb CcÇç Dd Eeéèêë Ff Gg Hh Iiîï Jj Kk Ll Mm Nn Ooô Pp Qq Rr Ss Tt Uuùûü Vv Ww Xx Yyÿ Zz

Monetary Format

French Franc (FRF)   1 234,50 F

Numeric Format

9 876 543,21

Date and Time

dimanche, 20 août 1995   20.8.95

9 h 30 – 17 h 30

Days and Months

dimanche lundi mardi mercredi jeudi vendredi samedi

janvier février mars avril mai juin juillet août septembre octobre novembre décembre

B.5 French Keyboard

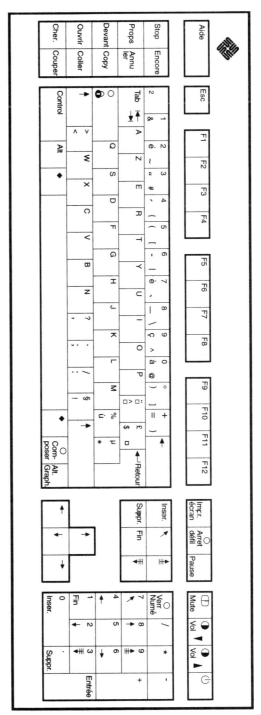

B.6 Danish Locale

Name of Locale

da

Collation Order

Aaà Bb Cc Dd EeÉé Ff Gg Hh Ii Jj Kk Ll Mm Nn Oo Pp Qq Rr Ss Tt Uu Vv Ww Xx YyÜü Zz Ææ Øø Åå

Monetary Format

Danish Krone (DKK)   Kr 1.234,50

Numeric Format

9.876.543,21

Date and Time

søndag 20. august 1995   20/8-95

9:30 – 17:30

Days and Months

søndag mandag tirsdag onsdag torsdag fredag lørdag

januar februar marts april maj juni juli august september oktober november december

B.7 Danish Keyboard

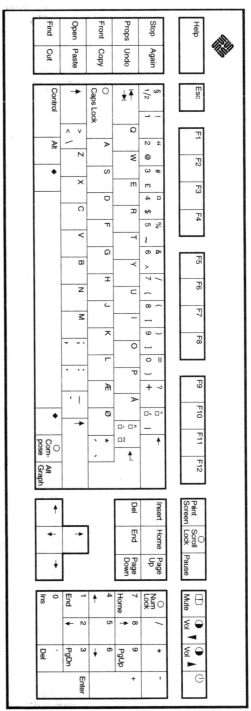

B

B.8 German Locale

Name of Locale

de

Collation Order

AaÄä Bb Cc Dd Ee Ff Gg Hh Ii Jj Kk Ll Mm Nn OoÖö Pp Qq Rr Ssß Tt UuÜü Vv Ww Xx Yy Zz

Monetary Format

Deutsche Mark (DEM)   DM 1.234,50

Numeric Format

9.876.543,21

Date and Time

Sonntag 20. august 1995   20.8.95

9:30 Uhr – 17:30 Uhr

Days and Months

Sonntag Montag Dienstag Mittwoch Donnerstag Freitag Samstag

Januar Februar März April Mai Juni Juli August September Oktober November Dezember

B.9 German Keyboard

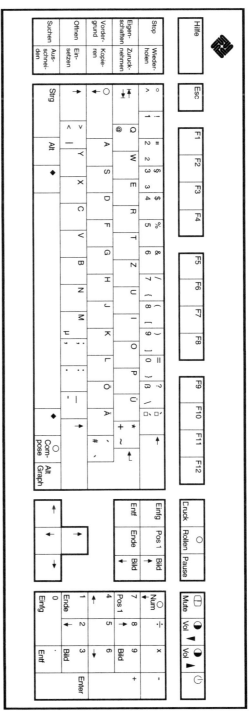

B.10 Italian Locale

Name of Locale

it

Collation Order

AaÀà Bb CcÇç Dd EeÈèÉé Ff Gg Hh IiÌì Jj Kk Ll Mm Nn OoÒò Pp Qq Rr Ss Tt UuÙù Vv Ww Xx Yy Zz

Monetary Format

Italian Lire (ITL)   L 1 234,50

Numeric Format

9 876 543,21

Date and Time

domenica, 20 agosto 1995   20.8.95

9:30 – 17:30

Days and Months

domenica lunedì martedì mercoledì giovedì venerdì sabato

gennaio febbraio marzo aprile maggio giugno luglio agosto settembre ottobre novembre dicembre

B.11 Italian Keyboard

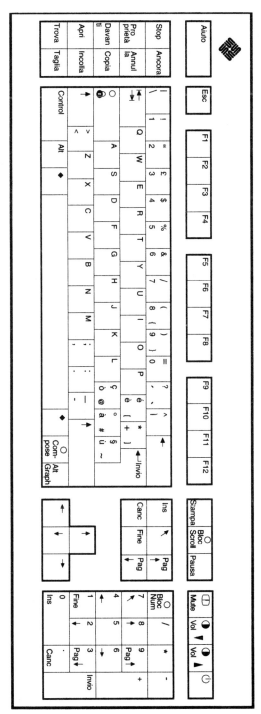

B

B.12 Dutch Locale

Name of Locale

nl

Collation Order

Aa Bb Cc Dd Ee Ff Gg Hh Ii Jj Kk Ll Mm Nn Oo Pp Qq Rr Ss Tt Uu Vv Ww Xx Yy Zz

Monetary Format

Dutch Guilder (NLG)   FL 1.234,50

Numeric Format

9.876.543,21

Date and Time

zondag 20 augustus 1995   20.8.95

9:30 uur – 17:30 uur

Days and Months

zondag maandag dinsdag woensdag donderdag vrijdag zaterdag

januari februari maart april mei juni juli augustus september oktober november december

B.13 Dutch Keyboard

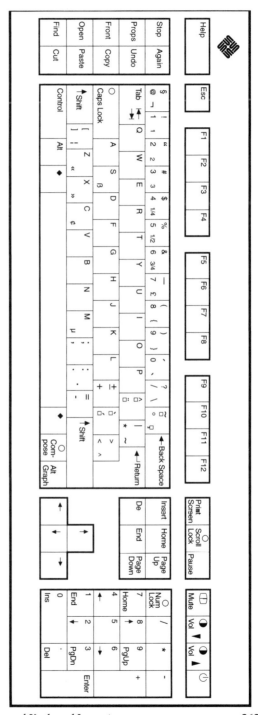

B

B.14 Norwegian Locale

Name of Locale

no

Collation Order

Aa Bb Cc Dd Ee Ff Gg Hh Ii Jj Kk Ll Mm Nn Oo Pp Qq Rr Ss Tt Uu Vv Ww Xx Yy Zz Ææ Øø Åå

Monetary Format

Norwegian Krone (NOK)   Kr. 1 234,50

Numeric Format

9 876 543,21

Date and Time

søndag 20. august 1995   20.8.95

kl 9.30 – kl 17.30

Days and Months

søndag mandag tirsdag onsdag torsdag fredag lørdag

januar februar marts april mai juni juli august september oktober november desember

B.15 Norwegian Keyboard

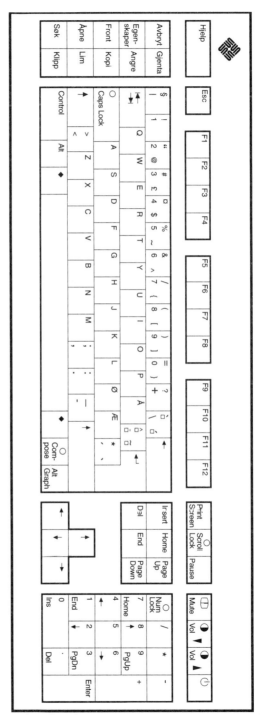

B

B.16 Portuguese Locale

Names of Locales

pt

Collation Order

AaÀàÁáÂâÃã Bb CcÇç Dd EeÉéÊê Ff Gg Hh IiÍí Jj Ll Mm Nn OoÓóÔôÕõ Pp Qq Rr Ss Tt UuÚú Vv Xx Zz

Monetary Format

Porguguese Escudo (PTE)   1.234$50

Numeric Format

9.876.543,21

Date and Time

domingo 20 agosto 1995   20.8.95

9:30 – 17:30

Days and Months

domingo segunda-feira terça-feira quarta-feira quinta-feira sexta-feira sábado

janiero fevereiro março abril maio junho julho agosto setembro outubro novembro dezembro

B.17 Portuguese Keyboard

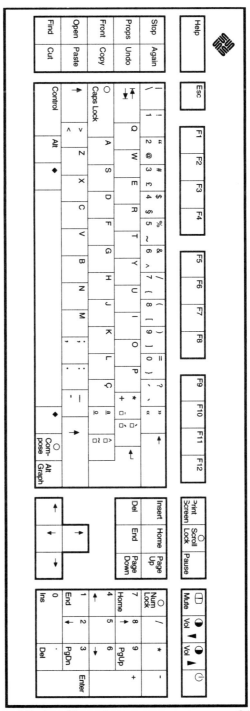

B.18 Spanish Locales

Names of Locales

es

es_AR, es_BO, es_CL, es_CO, es_EC, es_GT, es_CR, es_MX, es_PE, es_UY, es_VE

Collation Order

Aaá Bb Cc {Ch,ch} Dd Eeé Ff Gg Hh Iií Jj Kk Ll {Ll,ll} Mm Nn Ññ Ooó Pp Qq Rr Ss Tt Uuú Vv Ww Xx Yy Zz

Monetary Format

Spanish Peseta (ESP)   1.234,50 Pts

Numeric Format

9.876.543,21

Date and Time

Domingo 20 Agosto 1995   20-8-95

9:30 – 17:30

Days and Months

Domingo Lunes Martes Miércoles Jueves Viernes Sabado

Enero Febrero Marzo Abril Mayo Junio Julio Agosto Septiembre Octubre Noviembre Diciembre

B.19 Spanish Keyboard

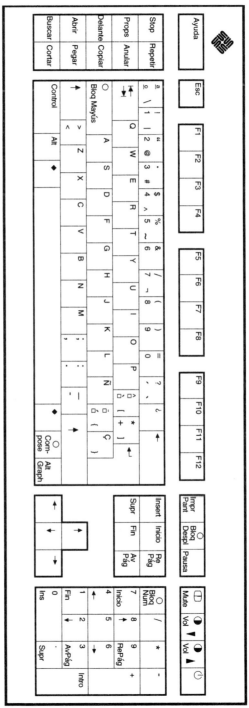

B

B.20 Swedish Locale

Name of Locale

sv

Collation Order

Aa Bb Cc Dd Eeé Ff Gg Hh Ii Jj Kk Ll Mm Nn Oo Pp Qq Rr Ss Tt Uu Vv Ww Xx Yy Zz Åå Ää Öö

Monetary Format

Swedish Krone (SEK)   Kr 1.234,50

Numeric Format

9.876.543,21

Date and Time

söndag 20 august 1995   20-8-95

kl 9.30 – kl 17.30

Days and Months

söndag måndag tisdag onsdag torsdag fredag lördag

januari februari mars april maj juni juli augusti september oktober november december

B.21 Swedish Keyboard

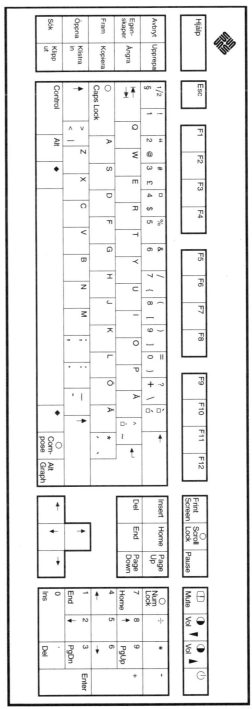

B

B.22 Swiss French Locale

Name of Locale

fr_CH

Collation Order

Aaàâ Bb CcÇç Dd Eeéèêë Ff Gg Hh Iiîï Jj Kk Ll Mm Nn Ooô Pp Qq Rr Ss Tt Uuùûü Vv Ww Xx Yyÿ Zz

Monetary Format

Swiss Franc (CHF)   fr 1'234.50

Numeric Format

9'876'543,21

Date and Time

dimanche, 20 août 1995   20.8.95

9.30 h – 17.30 h

Days and Months

dimanche lundi mardi mercredi jeudi vendredi samedi

janvier février mars avril mai juin juillet août septembre octobre novembre décembre

B.23 Swiss French Keyboard

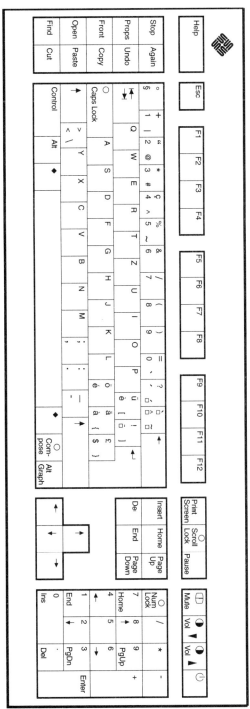

B.24 Swiss German Locale

Name of Locale

de_CH

Collation Order

AaÄä Bb Cc Dd Ee Ff Gg Hh Ii Jj Kk Ll Mm Nn OoÖö Pp Qq Rr Ssß Tt UuÜü Vv Ww Xx Yy Zz

Monetary Format

Swiss Franc (CHF)   Fr 1'234.50

Numeric Format

9'876'543,21

Date and Time

Sonntag 20. august 1995   20.8.95

9.30 Uhr – 17.30 Uhr

Days and Months

Sonntag Montag Dienstag Mittwoch Donnerstag Freitag Samstag

Januar Februar März April Mai Juni Juli August September Oktober November Dezember

B.25 Swiss German Keyboard

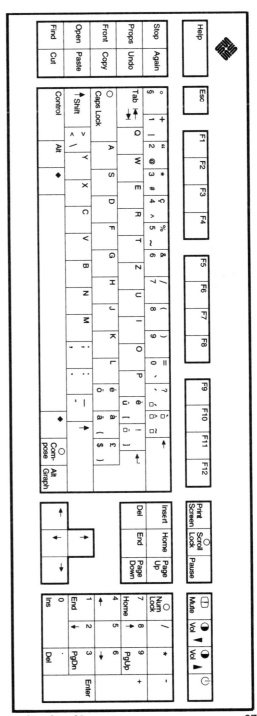

B.26 UK English Locale

Name of Locale

en_UK

Collation Order

Aa Bb Cc Dd Ee Ff Gg Hh Ii Jj Kk Ll Mm Nn Oo Pp Qq Rr Ss Tt Uu Vv Ww Xx Yy Zz

Monetary Format

British Pound (GBP) £1,234.50

Numeric Format

9,876,543.21

Date and Time

Sunday 20th August 1995 20/8/95

9:30 AM – 5:30 PM

Days and Months

Sunday Monday Tuesday Wednesday Thursday Friday Saturday

January February March April May June July August September October November December

B.27 UK-English Keyboard

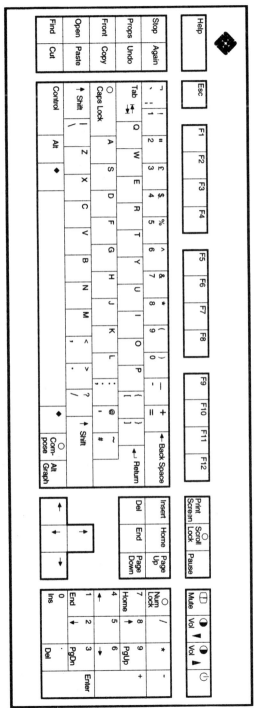

B.28 Korean Locale

Name of Locale

ko

Collation Order

usually follows KSC ordering

Monetary Format

South Korean won (W) = 100 chun

Numeric Format

9,876,543.21

B.29 Korean Keyboard

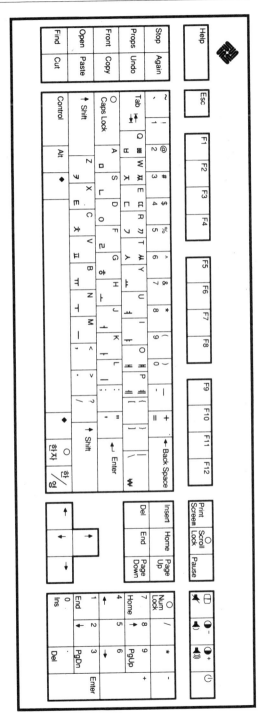

B

B.30 Chinese Locales

Names of Locales

zh *and* zh_TW

Collation Order

usually follows stroke ordering

Monetary Format

1 yuan (¥) = 10 jiao (People's Republic of China)

1 new Taiwan dollar (NT$) = 100 cents

Numeric Format

often 9,876,543.21

B.31 Chinese Keyboard

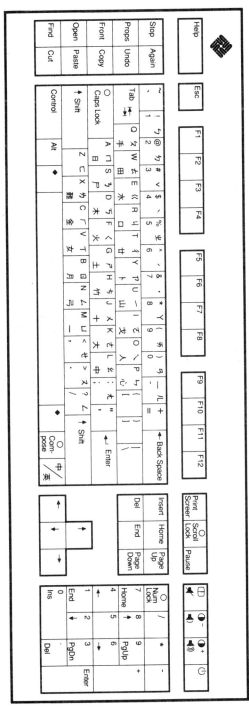

B.32 Japanese Locale

Name of Locale

ja

Collation Order

usually follows JIS ordering

Monetary Format

Japanese Yen · ¥1,234

Numeric Format

9,876,543.21

Date and Time

1995年08月20日

23時59分

B.33 Japanese Keyboard

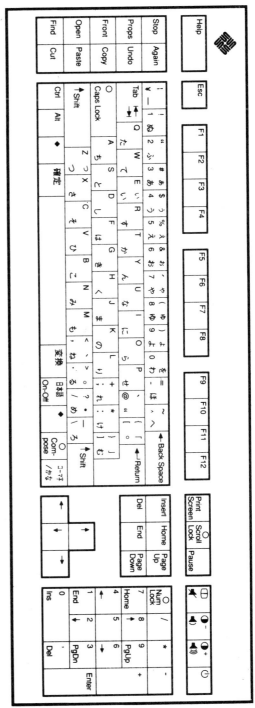

OpenWindows and DevGuide

This chapter describes how to write internationalized OpenWindows code, using either the XView or OLIT toolkits, or, more easily, using DevGuide.

Asian OpenWindows was integrated into mainstream OpenWindows 3.2 in the Solaris 2.2 release. As a result, international software no longer requires separate releases for Asia; it can be released as a single binary. The XView and OLIT toolkits now support level-3 and level-4 internationalization, enabling both message translation and multibyte characters. Previously, software released on OpenWindows 3.1 could be internationalized to level 3, to provide translated messages for Western Europe. However, software had to be prepared for East Asia by using Asian OpenWindows, which necessitated a separate binary release.

Note – 8-bit characters in the upper half of the Latin-1 codeset do not appear by default. `LC_CTYPE` must be set to `iso_8859_1` first.

C.1 Choice of Toolkits

XView 3.x has a complete interface for localization and is itself fully international. Thus, an XView application and its window objects (such as frame, menus, text subwindow, and panel) can appear properly localized. See the *XView Developer's Notes* for details.

Applications built with OLIT 3.x could be internationalized for Western Europe, using the messaging scheme of your choice. OLIT has also been internationalized to support East Asian locales. See the *OLIT Reference Manual* for details.

You may want to develop applications with OpenWindows Developer's Guide 3.0.1, a window-based tool designed specifically for building user interfaces. Usually DevGuide is available about one month after the associated release of OpenWindows. DevGuide 3.0.1 offers many aids for localizing as well as internationalizing applications. Specific approaches are discussed in the Internationalization appendix of the *DevGuide 3.0.1 User's Guide*. Briefly, GXV or GOLIT—DevGuide's XView and OLIT code generators—helps you to internationalize your application by placing `dgettext()` function calls around strings associated with the user interface. Furthermore, GXV has an option for adding the object size and position attributes discussed in the section on XView.

C.2 Window System Features

OpenWindows 3.2, released in the spring of 1993, was based on Sun's X/NeWS® server. OpenWindows 3.3, released in the fall of 1993, featured an X server based on Display PostScript instead of NeWS. The XView and OLIT toolkits remained upward compatible despite this change.

SunSoft now supports COSE, the Common Open Software Environment. As part of this agreement, OpenWindows was merged into the Motif specification, resulting in CDE, the Common Desktop Environment. This was submitted to X/Open for testing and branding. OLIT applications should be relatively easy to port to Motif, since both are Xt-based.

C.3 International Windowing Issues

Window systems have to take care of three things that operating systems don't have to worry about: object layout, input method, and font handling. The following section describes how XView applications might deal with these issues. If you are programming with OLIT, you might want to skip the rest of this chapter.

C.3.1 Window Object Layout

Window objects include push-pins, pop-up menus, control buttons, and scrollbars. Layout of objects containing strings (such as menus and buttons) can change because the dimensions of those strings often change when switching languages. For example, a control button in English is probably shorter than the equivalent in German. Also, a control button in Japanese is probably taller than the equivalent in English. Even in the same language, control buttons can grow and overlap when the font size increases. In XView, here's how you would determine the length and height of a text string:

```
extern Xv_Font font;
Font_string_dims dims;
(void) xv_get(font, FONT_STRING_DIMS, "string", &dims);
```

The `dims` structure now contains the string width as its first element and the string height as its second element.

XView application layout may be *implicit* or *explicit*. Implicit layout relies on the toolkit to position objects. Explicit layout relies on the programmer to specify pixel values (or row and column values) both for position (*x*, *y*) and dimension (width, height, and gaps).

If you create a series of controls without specifying location information, the toolkit will position items based on its built-in spacing rules. Implicit layout will very likely make localization easier, since control objects will often be repositioned for you as required. So, if you have time, try using implicit layout whenever possible. DeskSet™ tools use a custom library for implicit layout.

The XView toolkit provides a limited implicit layout facility. Basically, control area objects, such as buttons, are positioned according to default spacing rules. However, if button width increases so that the right-most button is outside the control area, the toolkit wraps that button to the next line, rather than expanding the control area. DeskSet tools such as Mail Tool and Calendar Manager re-lay out gracefully because developers have added code to properly center and size objects, based on current window size and font size.

C.3.2 Object Size and Positioning

XView contains attributes to allow runtime configuration of the size and position of objects making up an application's interface. Size and positioning information is retrieved from an X11 windows-style resource database. Attributes associated with sizing and positioning are described below:

XV_INSTANCE_NAME
Provides a mechanism to give each XView object a unique name, so that it can be queried from the database.

XV_USE_DB
Allows specification of a null-terminated list of attributes value pairs. Each attribute's value will be looked up in the database; if not found, the specified value is used as the default.

XV_LOCALE_DIR

An xv_init() attribute, this tells XView where the app-defaults directory is located. The resource database file resides in a directory called app-defaults. Like the scheme used by the message object files, the parent of the app-defaults directory is the name of the locale. The name of the resource database file is the name of the application with a .db suffix appended to it.

To understand the use of these attributes, see how the following portion of code from the file my_app.c is modified:

```
xv_init(XV_INIT_ARGC_PTR_ARGV, &argc, argv, 0);
frame = xv_create(XV_NULL, FRAME, XV_NULL);
control = xv_create(frame, PANEL, XV_NULL);
button = xv_create(control, PANEL_BUTTON,
        PANEL_LABEL_STRING, "Quit", XV_X, 10, XV_NULL);
```

Assuming the resource database (.db) file for the Spanish locale resides in /home/locale/es/app-defaults, here's how to modify the code:

```
bindtextdomain("my_app_strings", "/home/locale");
xv_init(XV_INIT_ARGC_PTR_ARGV, &argc, argv,
        XV_LOCALE_DIR, "/home/locale",
        XV_USE_LOCALE, TRUE,
0);
frame = xv_create(XV_NULL, FRAME,
        XV_INSTANCE_NAME, "base_frame",
XV_NULL);
control = xv_create(frame, PANEL,
        XV_INSTANCE_NAME, "control1",
XV_NULL);
button = xv_create(control, PANEL_BUTTON,
        XV_INSTANCE_NAME, "button1",
        PANEL_LABEL_STRING, dgettext("my_app_strings", "Quit")
        XV_USE_DB,
        XV_X, 10, XV_Y, 10, XV_NULL,
XV_NULL);
```

When the application runs, it builds a path, using the directory pointed to by XV_LOCALE_DIR, the name of the current locale, and app-defaults. This path is used to search for the resource database (.db) file. Any attribute specified in the `XV_USE_DB` attribute list, whose parent is given a name with `XV_INSTANCE_NAME`, will have its value looked up in the file. If the attribute is found, the value in the database is used; if the attribute isn't found, the value specified in the source code is used.

For the example above, the entries in the resource database file `my_app.db` would look like this:

```
my_app.base_frame.control1.button1.xv_x:  10
my_app.base_frame.control1.button1.xv_y:  10
```

If the layout has changed for a specific locale, an interface object may need to be repositioned. For example, let's say that for the Spanish locale, the interface looks more presentable if the above button is positioned at position 20,11 rather than position 10,10. All the developer needs to do is to change the x and y values in the .db file and rerun the application (without recompiling!).

In this case, the above database lines would be changed to:

```
my_app.base_frame.control1.button1.xv_x:  20
my_app.base_frame.control1.button1.xv_y:  11
```

The button would then appear at position 20,11.

C.3.3 Input Method

Phonetic-based languages such as English are easy to type on a keyboard. However, typing is much more complicated for East Asian languages based on ideographs. When entering Japanese, for example, the typist must select among Kanji, Hiragana, Katakana, and Romaji (Roman letters used phonetically to produce Japanese words). There must also be a way to convert phonetic characters into Kanji. Input is further complicated because a given syllable can frequently be represented by several different Kanji characters—the user must select the Kanji character that is appropriate for the specific context. Here's how to type Japanese with a Japanese keyboard under OpenWindows:

1. Select the Japanese locale from the Workspace Properties Localization menu, or set the LANG environment to ja.

2. The initial input mode simulates a type-4 US keyboard. To switch input modes, press the Nihongo (Japanese) key.

3. Type words using phonetic values in Romaji, or press the Romaji/Kana toggle key and type words in Hiragana. Japanese engineers often prefer typing in Romaji, but most clerks prefer Hiragana, because it requires fewer keystrokes. With either method, the system echoes Hiragana letters in reverse video.

4. If that Hiragana word is the one you want, press the Commit key.

5. To convert the word to Kanji, press the Conversion key. The system shows a Kanji spelling in the pre-edit region. If that's the desired spelling, press the Commit key. If not, press the Conversion key again to see the next choice.

C.3.4 Font Handling

In OpenWindows 3.x, all 57 OpenFonts™ in all sizes include ISO Latin-1 characters. Most other OpenWindows fonts do not.

Solaris 2.x fully supports EUC encoding, as did releases of Asian OpenWindows. Refer to Chapter 3 for more information on EUC. Note the many different instantiations of EUC; SunSoft supports four of them—for China, Japan, Korea, and Taiwan. These different EUC implementations are not interoperable.

To support languages with multiple character fonts, XView applications can open a *font set*. Here's an example of a call to open the Minchou font with International XView:

```
Xv_Font_Set font_set;
font_set = (Xv_Font_Set) xv_find(frame, FONT_SET,
        FONT_FAMILY, FONT_FAMILY_MINCHOU,
        FONT_STYLE, FONT_STYLE_NORMAL,
        FONT_LOCALE, xv_get(server, XV_LC_DISPLAY_LANG),
NULL);
```

Additionally, Xlib text functions can handle multibyte and wide characters. For example, XwcDrawString is the wide character equivalent of XDrawString, and XwcTextWidth is the wide character equivalent of XTextWidth. See the *Programmer's Supplement for Release 5* manual for more details.

C.4 Internationalization with DevGuide

OpenWindows Developer's Guide 3.0.1 (DevGuide) is a user interface builder for developing OPEN LOOK applications. DevGuide enables developers to visually design and test the user interface for an application. The DevGuide main window is shown in Figure C-1. No programming is required to generate a user interface, so that those without programming experience, such as interface or graphic designers, can use the product.

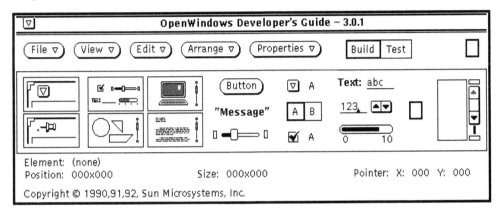

Figure C-1   DevGuide Window

The user-interface description is saved in a Guide Interface Language (GIL) file. It can be read into DevGuide and modified as many times as necessary. The GIL file is independent of the particular toolkit used for the interface to the application. One of several conversion programs is used to convert the GIL language into toolkit code for the chosen toolkit.

After the user interface has been designed, a code generator is run to generate the appropriate toolkit code. The code generators available with DevGuide are GXV, GXV++, and GOLIT. GXV generates C code that is used with the XView toolkit; C++ code is generated when GXV++ is used. GOLIT generates files for the OLIT toolkit.

When internationalizing an application, you must address two main issues. Initially, the text of the application needs to be translated into other languages. Additionally, depending on the language family (Indo-European or Asian, for example) and the font, the characters being displayed may require varying amounts of space on the screen. The default size of user interface objects is partially determined by the font of the characters displayed within them.

C

DevGuide aids the developer's internationalization efforts in two ways. First, the code generators provide a method of collecting interface text strings for translation. Second, a grouping package provides automatic resizing and repositioning of user interface elements after their text has been translated. This package ensures that an application's layout remains correct after the new font has been introduced.

C.4.1 Translation

DevGuide code generators enable the collection of user interface text. This text is stored in a file for translation into the appropriate language. This process differs slightly among the code generators and is discussed below.

C.4.1.1 XView Code Generator (GXV)

GXV optionally generates wrappers around all the user interface labels. These wrappers are `gettext()` function calls, inserted directly into the application source code. During runtime, these calls are used to look up text strings in other languages. Once these "hooks" are in the source code, the system utility `xgettext` is run against the source to produce a specially formatted text file, called a portable object file. This file contains the original text strings and placeholders for their translations. Here is a sample portable object file before translation:

```
domain "guide notices"
msgid "Cannot open %s: %s\n"
msgstr
msgid "Continue"
msgstr
msgid "Connect"
msgstr
```

Someone (usually someone other than the developer) translates the strings into the local language. After translation, the same file for the Spanish locale would look like this:

```
domain "guide notices"
msgid "Cannot open %s: %s\n"
msgstr "No es posible abrir %s: %s\n"
msgid "Continue"
msgstr "Sigue"
msgid "Connect"
msgstr "Conectar"
```

After translation, the `msgfmt` utility creates a binary version of the portable object file, called a message object file. For each language, different object files are generated. During runtime, the appropriate language file is accessed to display the correct language.

C.4.1.2 OLIT Code Generator (GOLIT)

Like the GXV code generator, GOLIT provides an option to generate a resource file that lists all user interface strings requiring translation. A translator replaces the English text with foreign text directly in the resource file. A separate resource file is required for each language. During runtime, the correct resource file displays the correct messages for a language.

C.4.2 Size and Position of Elements

You can position objects in two ways: by grouping or from a resource database.

The most general method is to use relative layout or "grouping," in which object positions are based on other objects. Grouping facilitates the use of multiple fonts and sizes, ensuring that the user interface layout continues to be displayed correctly when a different font is used. One of the most common problems in multilanguage layout is dealing with the varying lengths and heights of the foreign language words and fonts. Grouping resolves these problems. Figure C-2 shows the DevGuide panel that controls grouping.

There are multiple schemes to set a group's layout: As Is, Row, Column, and Matrix. For each layout, the appropriate alignment scheme is determined. The primary advantage of grouping is that it allows for automatic layout adjustment to support different fonts.

Another method for positioning objects requires explicit object size and position. This method uses an X windows-style resource database. The application retrieves the size and position information of the objects from the resource database.

If relative layout is used, the size and position database is not needed. If x,y coordinates for interface objects are explicitly requested, the size and position database is required.

The code generator produces function calls and attributes for the interface that allow an application to access the locale-specific databases. The code generator can also generate the X resource database for the developer, if desired.

If you do not use grouping, you can activate a utility after the text strings have been translated, allowing DevGuide to display the user interface using the new language. This allows you to change the layout to support the translated interface.

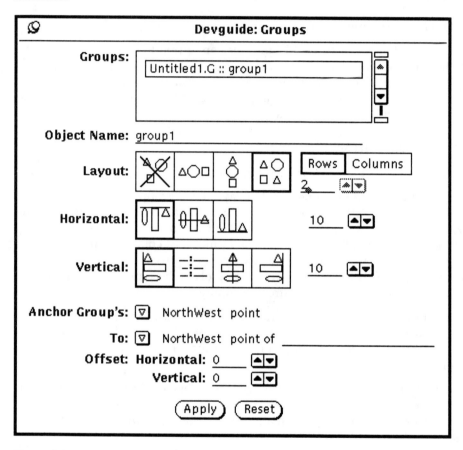

Figure C-2   Groups Window

For more information, refer to the *OpenWindows Developer's Guide 3.0.1 User's Guide* and either the *Programmer's Guide to the XView Toolkit Code Generator* or the *Programmer's Guide to the OLIT Toolkit Code Generator.*

XView Programming

XView 3.2 is a user interface toolkit based on the X Window System and the OPEN LOOK graphical user interface. It is included in the Solaris 2.x release. By supporting East Asian and Western European languages and locales, XView allows you to internationalize your OpenWindows applications. You do not have to redesign or recompile internationalized applications. The goal is to have a single application binary operate in all of the supported locales.

Western European (ISO Latin-1) languages and East Asian languages are supported with locale settings, localized text handling, and customized object layout. For East Asian languages, additional support is provided for multibyte codesets, wide characters, input method, and font set selection.

In an internationalized XView application, language-specific application data (message strings, labels, and so on) is separate from the rest of the application. To localize the application—that is, to adapt the application to support a specific language—you need to modify only the language-specific data. Thus, the task of porting an internationalized application consists of, among other things, translating application-specific strings and modifying object layout.

The information in this chapter builds on the contents of several manuals and books published. In particular, you may want to obtain the *Solaris 2.x XView Developer's Notes* from SunSoft and the *XView Programming Manual Version 3* from O'Reilly and Associates.

D.1 Internationalization Features

The internationalization of XView applications is broadly outlined in the *XView Programming Manual, Version 3*. Specifically, XView supports the following internationalization features described in that programming manual:

- *Locale setting*
  Before running an internationalized application, users must select the language to run in. The locale setting allows the user to choose the language or cultural environment.

D

- *Localized text handling*
  Application strings—error messages, menu labels, button labels—written in the developer's native language must be retrievable in the language specified by the locale. This process is called localized text handling.

- *Object layout*
  When an application runs in a non-native language, the layout of various objects may change. For example, the dimensions of objects containing strings, such as buttons and panels, may be different. Object layout is the mechanism by which the screen location of objects is modified (depending on the display language) to accommodate these kinds of changes.

This chapter summarizes additional internationalization features that are *not* documented in the *XView Programming Manual* but that are fully documented in part 2 of the *XView 3.2 Developer's Notes* from SunSoft:

- Wide character and multibyte characters

- Input method

- Font sets

D.1.1 Wide Characters and Multibyte Characters

English language applications use ASCII encoding to represent characters. Each character is encoded in a single byte (actually only 7 out of the 8 bits). Other languages have multiple character sets that sometimes contain large numbers of characters. These languages require more than one byte to represent each character and must be encoded differently. XView 3.2 uses the Extended UNIX Code (EUC) encoding method.

Certain XView 3.2 attributes and functions have been modified to handle EUC multibyte characters. There are also wide character attributes and functions. Wide character attributes are suffixed with _WC (wide character) or _WCS (wide character string). Similarly, wide character functions are suffixed with _wc or _wcs. See Chapter 3, *Encoding Character Sets* for more information on wide character functions.

D.1.2 Input Method

Input method refers to how users enter text in an application. For example, to enter data in a typical European language application, users simply type the information. Many Asian languages, however, consist of multiple character sets; for example, Japanese has two phonetic alphabets and one ideographic character set. These multiple character sets can consist of many thousands of characters and contain numerous homonyms for any particular word. Entering data in these languages requires special input handling. See Chapter 7, *Handling Language Input* for background information.

D.1.3 Font Sets

Most Western European languages consist of a single character set, and only one font is necessary to support the language. Languages with multiple character sets require multiple fonts, which are grouped into font sets. The font handling API has been extended in XView 3.2 to handle font sets. See Chapter 6, *Displaying Localized Text* for background information.

D.2 Character Encoding

In order to support a wide range of languages, XView 3.2 uses EUC as its primary encoding method. EUC encoding is suited for internationalized applications because it is compatible with ASCII and, at the same time, supports multiple character sets.

XView 3.2's new multibyte API is upward compatible with earlier versions of XView, such as XView 3.1, which used ASCII or ISO Latin-1 characters. The new multibyte API is derived from and is compatible with earlier versions of Asian XView.

The character sets you use depend on the locale(s) associated with your application. Non-Asian locales can use a single character set. For example, ASCII or ISO Latin-1 is suited for English or Western European languages. East Asian locales use multiple character sets.

EUC characters and text strings use either *multibyte* or *wide character* representation. In multibyte representation, characters are represented by a varying number of bytes. In wide character representation, characters are represented by a fixed number of bytes (four).

In XView 3.2, attributes and functions have been modified to handle multibyte strings, and additional attributes and functions accommodate wide characters.

XView 3.2 also uses Compound Text encoding for transferring data between X clients.

For detailed discussions on encoding, refer to these documents:

- For EUC, multibyte, and wide characters: Chapter 3 of this book.
- Compound Text: *Compound Text Encoding, Version 1.1, MIT X Consortium Standard, X Version 11, Release 5* by Robert W. Scheifler.

D.3 Encodings Used in Asian Locales

As you write your program, you will need to choose a suitable character encoding and API. Figure D-1 shows how you can use different encodings (EUC wide character and multibyte, and Compound Text) within the same application.

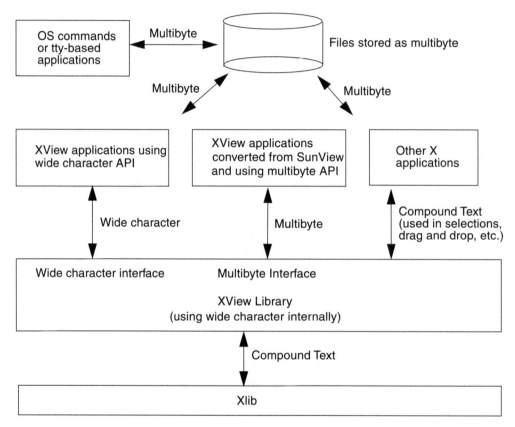

Figure D-1   Encodings Used for Asian Locales

D.3.1 Using Multibyte and Wide Character

The wide character API (type `wchar_t`) consists of wide character string handling attributes and functions. The so-called multibyte API (type `char`) is the same as in earlier, single byte versions of XView.

You can mix wide character and multibyte characters within the same application. Be sure to consider the following guidelines.

- Use multibyte for:
  - File names
  - System names
  - Operating system commands
  - Data storage to files
- Use wide character for:
  - Performance optimization
  - Strings internal to the application
  - Data storage for private use

D.3.2 Using Compound Text

The character encodings or coded character sets used in multibyte and wide character implementations may differ among vendors. For an application to communicate with other applications, a common encoding scheme is needed. XView relies on Compound Text, which is specified by the X Consortium.

Use Compound Text encoding in these situations:

- When an application needs to send a string composed of characters other than ISO Latin-1 across the X server to another application. XView uses Compound Text for data transfers to and from other X clients; for example, selection services (including drag and drop operations) and sending properties to the window manager.
- When an application implements its own interclient communication; for example, a canvas-based application that uses selection service.

Note that an application is free to use a private encoding scheme for its own use, as long as the Inter-Client Communication Conventions Manual (ICCCM) is followed.

D.4 EUC Programming Issues

The following sections discuss special programming issues related to screen column definitions and to passing multibyte strings among functions.

D.4.1 Defining Screen Columns

A screen column is defined as the pixel space required by a single ASCII character. In previous releases (such as domestic XView 3.1), a screen column was the space occupied by one character, which was represented by one byte. Thus, the following was true:

screen columns == character count == byte count

Asian characters may use a wider screen space than ASCII characters and are generally represented by more than one byte. Thus, in Asian locales:

screen columns != character count != byte count

Asian characters may also be interspersed with ASCII characters. In Asian locales, a fixed unit in pixels is needed to specify the space required by a screen column. Then, wide Asian characters can occupy two or more columns, as shown in Figure D-2.

Figure D-2   ASCII and Japanese Characters

A number of functions and attributes use screen columns as arguments or returned values.

For example, PANEL_VALUE_STORED_LENGTH limits the number of characters that can be entered into a panel item. In Asian locales, PANEL_VALUE_STORED_LENGTH is measured in bytes. However, this attribute is screen-column based. If PANEL_VALUE_STORED_LENGTH and PANEL_VALUE_DISPLAY_LENGTH are specified as 80, the programmer has allocated 80 screen columns, but not necessarily 80 characters, for display of a message string. In traditional Chinese, a Han character can be composed of 4 bytes and can occupy 2 columns. Therefore, the PANEL_VALUE_STORED_LENGTH limit can be reached at 20 characters, yet only 40 screen columns are occupied.

This screen column concept is only applicable in the case of fixed-width fonts. By default, the C locale uses fixed-width fonts for textsw and ttysw, and variable-width fonts for frame and panel. Currently, Asian locales use only fixed-width fonts.

D.4.2 Passing Multibyte Strings

The XView library implementation uses the EUC wide character representation. Thus, every time the multibyte API is used, multibyte data is converted to wide character before it is used internally.

If your application uses the same multibyte string repeatedly, convert the multibyte string to a wide character string, then pass the wide character string. This procedure avoids the conversion that the XView library makes each time the multibyte string is passed.

D.5 Wide Character Attributes and Functions

All XView 3.2 multibyte attributes and functions that take a string or character as an argument have wide character analogs. These wide character attributes and functions have similar names composed of the original names suffixed with _WCS, _WC, _ws, or _wcs:

- _WC for wide character attributes
- _wc for wide character functions
- _WCS for wide character string attributes
- _wcs for wide character string functions

D.6 Input Method

An input method is a method by which an application directs the user to type, select, and send text to an application. Input methods differ for each language, depending on the language's structure and conventions. Input methods for Japanese, Chinese, and Korean are provided with Solaris.

The XView 3.2 programming environment follows the X Window System Version 11 Release 5 specifications for input methods. Refer to *Xlib—C Language X Interface MIT X Consortium Standard X Version 11, Release 5* for additional information. XView supports the X input method in panels, tty subwindows, text subwindows, and canvases.

D.7 Purpose of Input Methods

English text is entered into an application directly by typing letters from the keyboard. In the Asian locales, an input method for text entry is required because users cannot enter all characters into an application directly from the keyboard. It

D

is often impractical to map all Asian alphabets and characters onto a keyboard; many Asian languages have extremely large character sets and several alphabets. For example:

- Japanese text uses three different writing systems: Hiragana, Katakana, and Kanji. Hiragana and Katakana are phonetic alphabets. Users enter them directly from the keyboard by using Romaji, a way to spell out Hiragana and Katakana sounds with a western alphabet. Hiragana and Katakana combinations can be converted to ideographic Kanji characters.

- Korean uses two different writing systems: Hangul and Hanja. Hangul is a phonetic alphabet users can enter from the keyboard and then convert to Hanja (ideographic) characters.

- Chinese employs numerous input methods, including phonetic spelling, stroke combinations, and phrase compositions.

For further information on specific input method operations, refer to the *JFP Programmer's Guide*, or the Korean or Chinese Solaris 2.x application developer's reference manuals.

D.7.1 Using an Input Method

In typical Asian language input method(s), the following occurs:

1. The user selects a phonetic alphabet in which to enter characters.

2. The user types the word, which appears in inverse video in an area of the screen called the *pre-edit region*.

3. To convert the word in the pre-edit region to another alphabet or an ideographic character, the user presses the Select Start key.

4. Phonetically equivalent choices are displayed in the *lookup choice region*, and the user selects the most appropriate choice to replace the word in the pre-edit region.

D.7.2 Using Input Method Screen Regions

Each Asian language has its own input method, but the screen regions are similar from language to language. Japanese, for example, has three screen regions:

- *Pre-edit region*
  The pre-edit region is activated when input method conversion is enabled. Entered text is displayed in inverse video. When pre-edit text is committed, the text is sent to the client and displayed in normal video.

- *Lookup choice region*
  In many Asian languages one phonetic representation of a word can have several ideographic representations. The lookup choice region displays the multiple ideographic choices that correspond to one phonetic representation. For example, in Japanese, the user can type in a word phonetically, then display the lookup choice region, and finally, select the appropriate Kanji, Hiragana, or Katakana representation.

- *Status region*
  The status region provides feedback on the state of the input method. Some languages are very complex and have several input methods. For example, in Chinese, users can choose from TsangChieh, Chuyin, ChienI, Neima, ChuanHsing, or Telecode input methods. In the Japanese input method, the status region displays the alphabet (Hiragana or Katakana) that is being used. The status region is part of the frame window and is displayed above the frame footer.

The screen regions for the Japanese input method for XView 3.2 are shown in Figure D-3.

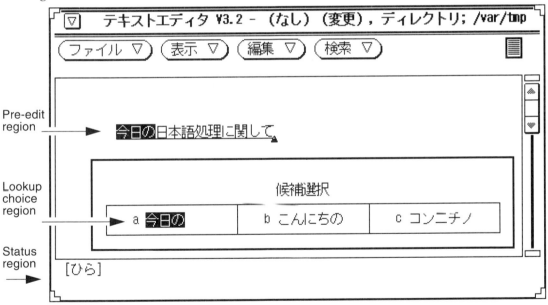

Figure D-3   Japanese Input Method Screen Regions

D

D.8 Input Method Styles

Xlib supports a variety of input method styles, which allow for different user interaction and display models for pre-edit and status regions. XView supports many of these styles. In particular, XView 3.2 supports the following `XIMStyle` values:

- Xlib pre-edit styles:
  - `XIMPreeditCallbacks`
  - `XIMPreeditPosition`
  - `XIMPreeditNothing`
  - `XIMPreeditNone`
- Xlib status styles:
  - `XIMStatusCallbacks`
  - `XIMStatusArea`
  - `XIMStatusNothing`
  - `XIMStatusNone`

D.8.1 Specifying Styles

Input method styles can be specified in the following ways (listed in order of precedence):

- XView attribute
- User-specified command-line options
- User-specified, locale-specific X resources (`~/.Xdefaults`)
- User-specified X resources (`~/.Xdefaults`)

XView attributes override user-specified styles, and command-line entries override X resource settings. Table D-1 and Table D-2 show the pre-edit and status style values. By default, XView requests the use of an on-the-spot pre-edit style and a client-displays status style.

Table D-1   Pre-Edit Style Values

XView Attribute	Command-line Option	X Resources
WIN_X_IM_STYLE_MASK	-preedit_style	OpenWindows.ImPreeditStyle
XIMPreeditCallbacks	onTheSpot	onTheSpot
XIMPreeditPosition	overTheSpot	overTheSpot
XIMPreeditNothing	rootWindow	rootWindow
XIMPreeditNone	none	none

Table D-2   Status Style Values

XView Attribute	Command-Line Option	X Resources
WIN_X_IM_STYLE_MASK	-status_style	OpenWindows.ImStatusStyle
XIMStatusCallbacks	clientDisplays	clientDisplays
XIMStatusArea	imDisplaysInClient	imDisplaysInClient
XIMStatusNothing	imDisplaysInRoot	imDisplaysInRoot
XIMStatusNone	none	none

D.8.2 Determining the Default Style

XView clients can request a particular input method (IM) style; however, the requested style is only considered to be a hint. The actual IM styles used by the application depend on what styles are supported by both the toolkit and the input method server.

XView attempts to accommodate the requested IM style. If, however, the style requested is not supported, then the default IM style is set to a root-window pre-edit style and an im-displays-in-root status style.

The attribute XV_IM_STYLES can be used to determine what styles are supported. It returns an XIMStyles structure.

D

D.9 Input Method Enabling and Disabling

If you expect a window to use Asian text input, request the use of an input method during xv_create(). The WIN_USE_IM attribute is considered to be a hint for enabling or disabling the input method for a given window. If an input method is available (that is, if the locale-specific resource xview.needIM is TRUE), then setting WIN_USE_IM to TRUE will enable the input method. Setting WIN_USE_IM to FALSE will disable use of the input method.

WIN_USE_IM can be set on any frame, panel, tty subwindow, text subwindow, or canvas. By default, WIN_USE_IM is TRUE if the input language specified by XV_LC_INPUT_LANG supports an input method. WIN_USE_IM is an inheritable attribute; therefore, subwindows inherit the value of WIN_USE_IM from the parent frame if the value is not set explicitly.

If a subwindow does not require Asian text input—say, a panel containing buttons or a read-only text subwindow—create it with WIN_USE_IM set to FALSE. This choice avoids requiring the toolkit to create and maintain unnecessary input context (IC) resources and avoids the overhead of connecting with the input method server.

Once an input method is enabled, the user can compose Asian text by interacting with the various input method screen regions.

D.10 Input Method Architecture

Internationalized applications receive user text input by communicating with an input method. XView makes a single input method connection with Xlib upon calling xv_init() and operates in the specified input language locale.

Different Xlib implementations provide input method support in various ways. Shown in is one possible example of an application connecting with an Asian input method, which is based on the input method server. In this example, the client is connected with the input method server by means of a back-end method. One input method server can provide input method service to multiple X clients.

Various Xlib implementations exist today to support input methods. For instance, European input methods may not require pre-edit feedback or dictionary lookup and may be implemented directly within Xlib. Conversely, many Asian input methods are implemented with Xlib establishing a connection with another process called the input method server. Input method servers may also connect with a language engine process that aids in dictionary lookup.

Creating Worldwide Software

Additionally, an input method can be further characterized as a *front-end* or *back-end method*, depending on whether the event is intercepted before it reaches the application.

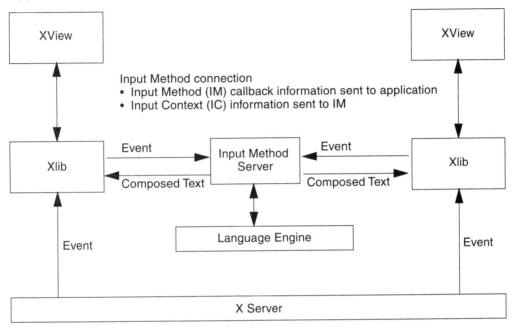

Figure D-4   High-Level Overview of Input Method

By default, XView provides an on-the-spot and client-displays input method style, in which the input method makes requests to the application to display pre-edit and status information through a series of callback functions. In Xlib terminology, both the XIMStyle of XIMPreeditCallbacks and XIMStatusCallbacks are supported.

XView automatically handles communication between the application and the input method by creating an X input context (IC) and registering default pre-edit callbacks and status callbacks for each panel, canvas, text subwindow, or tty subwindow that has input method enabled. Xlib supports the concept of the input context (IC), which is essentially an abstraction of a data structure that contains information about the state of an input method area.

Only one IC is registered per subwindow, even if there are multiple input areas within a subwindow. For instance, a panel with multiple text items will have each text item share the same IC.

D

D.11 Implicit Commit of Pre-Edit Text

Certain mouse and keyboard actions automatically commit a pre-edit string without requiring the user to enter a commit key sequence. Implicit commit actions are listed in Table D-3. In some cases, key actions are consumed by the language conversion engine. The language conversion engine can also implicitly commit text. For example, in the Japanese input method, when a pre-edit string has been converted by means of the Control-N key, subsequent pre-edit input implicitly commits the pre-edit string. Refer to the specific Asian Language Environment documentation for implicit commit behavior of a particular language's conversion engine.

Implicit commit can also be triggered programmatically by certain attributes and functions in panels and text subwindows. Refer to the *Solaris 2.x XView Developer's Notes* for details.

Table D-3   Implicit Commit Actions

Function Keys/Actions	Panel	Textsw	Ttysw
Left arrow key (R10)	Y	Y	Y
Down arrow key (R14)	Y	Y	Y
Right arrow key (R12)	Y	Y	Y
Up arrow key (R8)	Y	Y	Y
Home key (R7)	N	Y	N
End key (R13)	N	Y	N
PgUp key (R9)	N	Y	N
PgDn key (R15)	N	Y	N
Paste (L8)	Y	Y	Y
Find (L9)	Y	Y	N
Again (L2)	N	Y	N
Undo (L4)	Y	Y	N
Carriage Return	Y*	Y*	Y*
Tab	Y*	Y*	Y*
Select (mouse left button)	Y	Y	Y
Adjust (mouse middle button)	Y	Y	N

*. Denotes key actions known to be consumed by some language conversion engine.

D.12 Input Method Callback Customization

A default user interface is provided for the pre-edit and status regions when on-the-spot and client-displays styles are used. To customize the user interface, you can specify your own callback functions for pre-edit and status regions by using the WIN_IC_PREEDIT_* and WIN_IC_STATUS_* attributes. The lookup choice region is not customizable, because it is displayed by the input method and not by the toolkit. Refer to the *Solaris 2.x XView Developer's Notes* for details on enabling input methods and attributes available for customizing the input method interface.

D.13 XView 3.2 Program Compilation

Use the following command line to compile your XView 3.2 application:

```
cc -DOW_I18N -I$OPENWINHOME/include file.c
    -L$OPENWINHOME/lib -lxview -lolgx -lX11 {-lintl -lw}
```

where

-DOW_I18N enables internationalization support

-lxview is an XView library

-lolgx is an OPEN LOOK graphics library

-lX11 is an X11 Release 5 library

and the optional flags link in libraries that may be needed by the application.

-lintl is a message cataloguing library, needed if application uses gettext family of functions

-lw is a wide character support library, needed if the application uses wide character functions, such as getwchar()

Note that -lintl and -lw were merged into the C library in Solaris 2.5.

OLIT Programming

This chapter focuses on the general issues of internationalizing applications and describes how new features of OLIT 3.2 address these issues. It also provides a simple example application, which demonstrates how OLIT makes it easy to create and use internationalized applications.

The OLIT toolkit, a user interface toolkit based on the X Window System and the OPEN LOOK graphical user interface, allows developers to create international applications simply and easily, without having to modify the source code for each supported language. An application developed and compiled with OLIT will be able to operate in any of the supported languages and process data according to the rules of that language.

OLIT 3.2 features that support internationalized applications are referred to as *international OLIT* in this chapter. The first version of international OLIT supports Japanese, Korean, Chinese (Taiwan version), and Chinese (PRC version). European language handling is also supported if it is supported by the operating system.

Adding new languages to an international OLIT application consists primarily of changing messages, labels, and other strings in resource files, setting the default text format, and providing localized *input methods* (IM). The input method is the method by which text is entered into the system. Input methods are specific to each language and are provided by SunSoft. They can, however, be redefined and changed by OEMs or independent software vendors.

E.1 System Requirements

The first release of international OLIT enables developers to localize to several Asian languages. To run this release of international OLIT, you need SunOS 5.x and the *Feature Package* for the locale in which you intend to run it. For example, you need the Japanese Feature Package (JFP) for Japan and the Korean localization package for Korea. These packages consist of extensions to SunOS and incorporate numerous facilities for handling local linguistic and cultural conventions.

E

E.2 Issues Involved in Internationalizing Applications

To internationalize your application, you must address the following issues.

- *Locale setting* is the method by which the language or cultural environment is set. See *Locale Setting* on page 313.

- *Character encoding* is the method by which a language's character set is represented. Conventional applications use 7-bit ASCII encoding to represent each character. However, some languages have larger character sets that require more than the 128 character range permitted by 7-bit encoding. See *Character Encoding and Text Formats* on page 314.

- *Font set handling* is simple for the languages that conventional OLIT supports because they use only one character set. However, some languages use multiple character sets and therefore require multiple fonts or a *font set*. See *Handling Font Sets* on page 316.

- *Localized text handling.* The developer needs to be able to use application strings (that is, error messages, menu text, button text, and so forth) in the native language and have those strings retrieved in the language specified by the locale. See *Localized Text Handling* on page 317.

- *Input method* is the method by which users enter the text of a language. To enter data into a conventional application, the user simply types in the information to be processed. Some languages, however, consist of multiple alphabets that require several keystrokes to create one character. This special handling is called the input method. See *Input Method* on page 319.

- *Standards.* Software internationalization is supported by a number of standards organizations. These include IEEE (POSIX), ANSI, ISO, X/Open, and the MIT X Consortium. In order to make applications portable across a wide variety of hardware platforms, it is important to use a toolkit that follows these standards as much possible, such as international OLIT. See Section 9.8, *Standards,* on page 147.

This chapter describes each of these issues in detail and discusses how these issues are addressed by international OLIT. In addition, the chapter provides a section on compiling and linking, beginning on page 328.

E.3 Locale Setting

The X Toolkit Intrinsics layer, on which OLIT is layered, provides an application resource called XnlLanguage (class XnlLanguage) that announces the user's locale to the toolkit and to the operating system The resource is characterized in Table E-1.

Table E-1   XnlLanguage *Application Resource*

Resource	Type	Default	Access
XnlLanguage	XtNstring	NULL	I

The currently supported values for this resource are: ko, ja, zh, and zh_TW. The three ways to establish the locale are listed below:

1. Specify -xnllanguage on the command line of an OLIT application. For example, to set the locale to Korean for an application called *myapplication*, type:

```
% myapplication -xnllanguage ko
```

2. Specify *xnlLanguage: *language* in a X11 Resource Manager database file. For example, to set the locale to traditional Chinese, add the following line to your .Xdefaults file:

```
*xnlLanguage:  zh_TW
```

3. Set the LANG environment variable in the shell from which you are starting the application. For example, to set the locale to Japanese, type:

```
% setenv LANG ja
```

To set the locale to Chinese, type:

```
% setenv LANG zh
```

Establishing the OS locale is the responsibility of OLIT and Xt. You should not use the OS function setlocale(3) in your OLIT applications, since OLIT already calls this function internally.

E

E.4 Character Encoding and Text Formats

International OLIT supports three character encoding types, or *text formats:*

- Single byte, which represents each character with one byte
- Multibyte, which represents each character with a variable number of bytes
- Wide character, which represents each character with a fixed number of bytes

Applications can create single byte, multibyte, or wide character OLIT objects, or a combination of these. If you are writing an application intended for single byte locales only, you may want to use single byte text format to avoid the performance overhead incurred by processing multibyte text. However, note that if you use single byte format, it will be harder to internationalize your application at a later date.

International OLIT supports the single byte text format primarily for backward compatibility.

The multibyte text format is fully compatible with ASCII. Because each different character can potentially be a different size, programming with multibyte text can be difficult. However, the multibyte format uses memory efficiently.

Wide character text format, on the other hand, is easier to program because all characters are represented with the same number of bytes. However, the wide character format consumes more storage because it represents all characters with a fixed number of bytes. If all characters are ASCII, many of the bytes will be superfluous.

When deciding which text format is appropriate for a user interface, consider the following:

- Conversion between formats reduces performance.
- OLIT honors the requested text format inside the object implementation.
- Processing multibyte data is inherently more time consuming than processing single byte or wide character data. Objects that perform intensive data manipulation (for example, text-editing object such as OLIT's TextEdit or TextField widgets) will perform better if created as wide character objects. (If an object is certain to handle only 8-bit data, the optimal solution is to create single byte objects.)

You should design your application so that conversion between formats is minimized. For example, you may want to decide on an object-by-object basis whether textual data will be processed intensively and if it is, then use wide character format.

Note – The widget makes assumptions based on the text format. For example, specifying the single byte format and supplying a wide character label causes an error.

OLIT widget resources for presentation text are of type `OlStr`. For more information on this type, see *Setting the Default Text Format for an Entire Application* on page 315. To provide support for multiple text formats, international OLIT introduces the `XtNtextFormat` resource. This resource allows you to inform widgets what text format to expect for resources associated with presentation text. This is an interface for programmers only; there is no equivalent interface for users to specify widget text formats. The text format of an object is persistent for the lifetime of the object; it is established at object creation time and cannot be changed.

You can set the text format in several ways:

- Do nothing; if you do nothing, the text format defaults to single byte.

- Set the default text format for the entire application with the `OlSetDefaultTextFormat()` function.

- Set the default text format for an individual widget by changing the widget's `XtNtextFormat` resource.

E.4.1 Setting the Default Text Format for an Entire Application

As a convenience, OLIT maintains a default text format that widgets inherit when they are created without their text format explicitly specified in the argument list passed to one of the `XtCreateWidget()` family of functions.

For compatibility with previous OLIT releases, the default text format is single-byte unless you change it. To change it, use the function `OlSetDefaultTextFormat()`, which is defined as follows:

```
void OlSetDefaultTextFormat(OlStrRep format);
```

where *format* specifies the character representation of the text. The *format* argument can have the values listed in Table E-2:

Table E-2   Default Text Format Values

format Value	Meaning
OL_SB_STR_REP	Single byte character representation
OL_WC_STR_REP	Wide character representation
OL_MB_STR_REP	Multibyte character representation

Your application should call OlSetDefaultTextFormat() immediately after OlToolkitInitialize() and before creating the widget hierarchy. Objects subsequently created will have the text format specified in the most recent call to OlSetDefaultTextFormat(), unless overridden by explicit arguments. Note that if the application is single byte only, it does not need to call OlSetDefaultTextFormat().

You can create a widget hierarchy consisting of a combination of multibyte, wide character, and single byte objects. You can do this either by changing the default text format between widget creation calls or by specifying an object's text format explicitly when creating it.

E.4.2 Setting the Text Format for an Individual Widget

OLIT provides a resource, XtNtextFormat, which allows you to set the text format for individual widgets. See the *OLIT Reference Manual* for details.

E.4.3 Handling Font Sets

To represent data that consists of multiple character sets, Release 5 of the X Window System provides the notion of a *Font Set*. An XFontSet is an X11R5 data structure that supports this notion. From the user's perspective, an XFontSet represents a list of X11 Logical Font Description (XLFD) fonts that allows the application to fully represent the characters used in a particular locale. For full details on font sets, refer to the X11R5 documentation.

To specify a font set in a resource file, use a comma-separated list of fonts. For example, you can enter the following in your .Xdefaults file:

```
*font: -misc-fixed-medium-r-normal--20-200-75-75-c-100-iso8859-1, \
  -sun-gothic-medium-r-normal--14-120-75-75-c-120-jisx0208.1983-0, \
  -sun-gothic-medium-r-normal--14-120-75-75-c-60-jisx0201.1976-0
```

When you internationalize your application, you should specify fonts in a resource file. If you specify them within your application, it will be impossible for others to localize the application.

E.4.4 Using the OlFont Type

OLIT supports both the font and font set notions by introducing the OlFont type for objects that display text. OlFont is an opaque pointer type whose interpretation depends on the setting of its associated XtNtextFormat resource. If you create an object as multibyte or wide character, the value of the OlFont field will be a valid XFontSet identifier. If you create an object as single byte, OlFont field will be a valid pointer to an XFontStruct.

If the text format is OL_SB_STR_REP and a font set has been specified (using a comma-separated list), the first font in the list will be used to construct an Xfont structure.

E.4.5 Specifying the Default Font or Font Set

The OLIT 3.2 widget set provides an XtNolDefaultFont resource that specifies the default font or font set for an application. This resource is discussed in the *OLIT Reference Manual*.

If no font is specified for a widget's XtNfont resource, then XtNolDefaultFont determines the widget's font. In international OLIT, the default value of XtNolDefaultFont is determined as follows:

- In the C locale, the default value of XtNolDefaultFont is Lucida sans serif with Resolution_X and Resolution_Y set to 75.
- In other locales, the default value of XtNolDefaultFont is the font set required to display all the characters in the codeset of the locale.

The OlGetDefaultFont() convenience routine enables you to select the font or font set that will be used if you do not set the XtNfont resource for a widget. The syntax of OlGetDefaultFont() is:

```
OlFont OlGetDefaultFont(widget w);
```

where *w* is a widget in the application for which you want to get the default font.

If XtNolDefaultFont specifies a font that is not available, they OlGetDefaultFont() returns a null pointer.

E.5 Localized Text Handling

OLIT provides resources that enable you to set various text strings (messages, menu items, button labels, and so on) in an application. For information on the text string resources for a particular widget, see the reference section for the widget. When you create an internationalized application, remove all these resources from your application and keep them in locale-specific resource files.

E.5.1 Internationalized Help

You can register multibyte help text for a widget with OLIT's
OlRegisterHelp() function. To register single byte help, use multibyte help.
The OLIT Help API currently supports multibyte only. A wide character API will
be added in the future. The syntax for OlRegisterHelp() is as follows:

```
void OlRegisterHelp(
    OlDefine    id_type,
    XtPointer   id,
    String      tag,
    OlDefine    source_type,
    XtPointer   source);
```

To use OlRegisterHelp() with international OLIT, specify one of the following
values listed in Table E-3 for the *id_type* argument.

Table E-3   Types of Help in OLIT

id_type **Value**	**Meaning**
OL_WIDGET_HELP	Specifies multibyte format help text for an individual widget (for backward compatibility)
OL_FLAT_HELP	Specifies multibyte format help text for a flat widget (for backward compatibility

If you specify OL_DISK_SOURCE for the *source_type* argument, you must specify
a single byte or multibyte file name for the *source* argument.

Help searches the directories specified by XFILESEARCHPATH for the specified
file name. If you set the filename from within your program as an absolute path,
help ignores XFILESEARCHPATH. If the XFILESEARCHPATH expansion does not
find a file for help, the current directory is searched. Within the value of
XFILESEARCHPATH, any instance of the string "%T" is expanded to "help" and
"%N" is expanded to the file name the programmer specifies as the source
parameter to OlRegisterHelp().

For a description of other arguments of OlRegisterHelp(), see the *OLIT
Reference Manual*.

E.5.2 Localized Messages

OLIT issues textual error message in the program's locale at startup. To do this,
OLIT registers a private language procedure with the OLIT Intrinsics during
OlToolkitInitialize().

Do not register an application-specific language procedure. If you do, it will interfere with OLIT's locale-announcement mechanism and you will be responsible for it in your application. If your application requires processing before OLIT's language procedure is called, you can provide your own procedure and call OLIT's procedure from it. For the language procedure registered by OLIT, call:

```
olit_proc = XtSetLanguageProc(NULL, NULL, NULL);
```

E.5.3 Multibyte and Wide Character Text Buffer Functions

International OLIT provides multibyte and wide character equivalents to the single byte text buffer functions in previous releases. A list of these functions and their syntax is provided in the *OLIT Reference Manual*.

E.6 Input Method

The input method (IM) is the algorithm by which users enter the text of a language. The input method for each language may be different, depending on the linguistic structure and conventions of that language.

International OLIT follows the *X Window System Version 11, Input Method Specification, Draft 3.0*. This specification was derived as a result of discussions among X Consortium members on standardizing the input handling of characters in various languages by X clients.

For many languages, there isn't a one-to-one key to character mapping, regardless of how the keyboard is configured. In order to support such languages, an input method is required.

In English, users enter the desired text by typing in a sequence of letters to create a word. However, for languages based on ideographic characters, input is more complicated. For example, there are two phonetic alphabets in Japanese— Hiragana and Katakana—and the traditional ideographic alphabet, Kanji. In any piece of writing, all three alphabets may be used. Moreover, Japanese words can also be spelled out phonetically in English, called Romaji.

To handle languages for which there isn't a one-to-one key to character mapping, input methods provide features such as the following:

- A control key sequence, which selects the *input mode*
- A pre-edit region, which displays characters as the user enters them but before the user *commits* them

- A lookup choice region, which displays ideographic characters and allows the user to choose one

- A status region, which provides information such as whether conversion is activated and the state or mode of the input method

Text input widgets, in conjunction with some input methods, also can provide advanced, language-specific, pre-editing features. For instance, the OLIT TextEdit widget can detect certain conditions under which it will commit any uncommitted pre-edit text without the user having to take further action. This technique is known as *implicit commit*.

Example: In a mail application the user enters a message in Japanese and presses a "send" button to dispatch the composed message. If pre-edit text has not been committed to the text buffer, and the user's intention is that it be part of the message, then it is useful for the toolkit to intervene and cause a commit to occur before the application processes the buffer and sends the message.

Details of which operations trigger implicit commit semantics in OLIT widgets can be found in the localization documentation for the appropriate languages.

The use of these features varies with the input method. For more information, see the documentation for the input method you are using. Figure E-1 shows the input method screen regions.

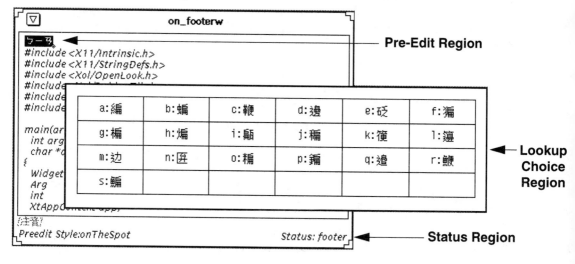

Figure E-1   Input Method Screen Regions for zh_TW *Locale*

E.6.1 Control of Input Method Pre-Edit and Status Styles

An OLIT application can control two aspects of the input method:

- The *pre-edit style*, which specifies where and how pre-edit data is presented. The pre-edit style can vary from widget to widget within a shell.

- The *status style*, which specifies where status feedback is presented. The status style, unlike the pre-edit, is an attribute of the shell and is expected to remain the same across all widgets inside the shell.

OLIT provides two new resources that specify the pre-edit and status styles: XtNimPreeditStyle and XtNimStatusStyle, described in the following sections.

E.6.2 **XtNimPreeditStyle** Resource

The XtNimPreeditStyle resource selects the pre-edit style. This resource is supported by all the OLIT widgets that allow text input. See, for example, TextEdit XtNimPreeditStyle in the *OLIT Reference Manual*. Table E-4 characterizes the resource.

Table E-4   XtNimPreeditStyle *Resource*

Resource	Type	Default	Access
XtNimPreeditStyle	OlImPreeditStyle	OL_NO_PREEDIT	GI

If the specified style is not supported by the input method, the ability to pre-edit is lost. The currently supported pre-edit styles are listed in Table E-5.

Table E-5   *Supported Pre-Edit Styles*

XtNimPreeditStyle Value	Meaning
OL_ON_THE_SPOT/ "onTheSpot"	IM directs the application to display the pre-edit data
OL_OVER_THE_SPOT/ "overTheSpot"	IM displays pre-edit data in its own window
OL_ROOT_WINDOW/ "rootWindow"	IM displays pre-edit data outside the application in a window that is a child of the base window
OL_NO_PREEDIT/"none"	IM does not display pre-edit data

See the X11R5 documentation for a full description of each of the pre-edit styles.

Figure E-2 shows an example of the on-the-spot pre-edit style. The pre-edit data is shown in reverse video. When the user commits the data, it is sent to the client and displayed in normal video.

```
┌─────────────────────────────────────────────────┐
│  ▽              on_root▼                         │
│ ┌───────────────────────────────────────────────┤
│ │これはですとです#include <X11/Intrinsic.h>        │
│ │#include <X11/StringDefs.h>                      │
│ │#include <Xol/OpenLook.h>                        │
│ │#include <Xol/RubberTile.h>                      │
│ │#include <Xol/TextEdit.h>                        │
│ │#include <Xol/ScrolledWi.h>                      │
│ │                                                 │
│ │main(argc, argv)                                 │
│ │  int argc;                                      │
│ │  char *argv[];                                  │
│ │{                                                │
│ │  Widget      toplevel, te, rb, sw;              │
│ │  Arg         wargs[5];                          │
│ │  int         n;                                 │
│ │  XtAppContext app;                              │
│ │  void        DoHelp();                          │
│ │Preedit Style:onTheSpot                          │
│ └───────────────────────────────────────────────┤
│                                                  │
│  [ひら]                                          │
│                                                  │
└─────────────────────────────────────────────────┘
```

Figure E-2   On-the-Spot Pre-Edit Style for ja *Locale*

Figure E-3 shows an example of the over-the-spot pre-edit style.

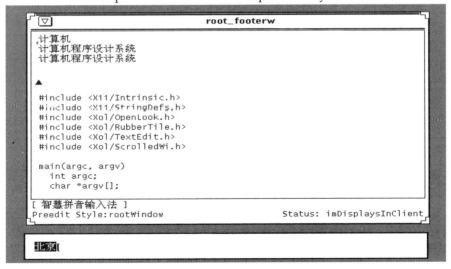

Figure E-3   *Over-the-Spot Pre-Edit Style for zh Locale*

Figure E-4 shows an example of the root window pre-edit style.

Figure E-4   *Root Window Pre-Edit Style for zh Locale.*

E.6.3 `XtNimStatusStyle` Resource

The `XtNimStatusStyle` resource, defined in the `VendorShell` class, determines the style of IM status feedback. Table E-6 characterizes the resource.

Table E-6   `XtNimStatusStyle` *Resource*

Resource	Type	Default	Access
XtNimStatusStyle	OlImStatusStyle	OL_NO_STATUS	GI

The supported styles are listed in Table E-7.

Table E-7   `XtNimStatusStyle` *Styles*

`XtNimStatusStyle` Value	Meaning
OL_IM_DISPLAYS_IN_CLIENT/ "imDisplaysInClient"	The IM generates status feedback in the footer of the shell window
OL_IM_DISPLAYS_IN_ROOT/ "imDisplaysInRoot"	The IM generates status feedback in a separate window
OL_NO_STATUS/"none"	The IM doesn't generate any status feedback

Figure E-5 shows an example of the `imDisplaysInClient` status style.

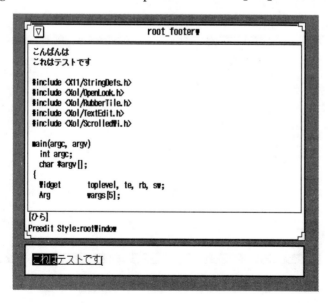

Figure E-5   `imDisplaysInClient` *Status Style for* `ja` *locale*

Figure E-6 shows an example of the `imDisplaysInRoot` status style.

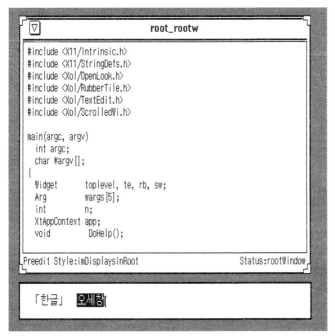

Figure E-6   `imDisplaysInRoot` Status Style for ko locale

When `XtNimStatusStyle` is set to `OL_IM_DISPLAYS_IN_CLIENT`, a number of other resources are available to set characteristics of the application footer. See *Application Resources for the IM Footer* on page 325.

E.6.4 Application Resources for the IM Footer

Table E-8 characterizes the resources for the IM footer.

Table E-8   IM Footer Resources

Resource	Type	Default	Access
XtNimFontSet	OlFont	XtDefaultFont	SGI
XtNdefaultImName	String	NULL	SGI

E.6.5 **XtNimFontSet** Resource

The `XtNimFontSet` resource specifies the internationalization IM status footer's font set.

E.6.6 **XtNdefaultImName** Resource

The XtNdefaultImName resource specifies the string to identify the IM Server.

E.6.7 **XtNshellTitle** Resource

XtNshellTitle is an OlStr resource that allows the title of shell widgets to be set. The shell being set must be a subclass of VendorShell. The use of this resource is analogous to the XtNtitle resource defined by the Intrinsic classes. XtNshellTitle and XtNtitle are synchronized by OLIT; calling XtSetValues() on either will cause both to be updated.

E.6.8 Example of Internationalizing an OLIT application

To internationalize a simple OLIT application:

1. Remove any resources that contain display text from the application code and put them in a resource file.

2. Specify the text format for widgets that display text (by specifying a default text format for the application or for individual widgets).

3. Specify a font set for resources that contain OlFont values (such as XtNfont) in the resource file.

Suppose you want to write an internationalized application that displays a StaticText widget with some wide character text in it. To do this, you would write code similar to that shown in Figure E-7.

Note that this application does not specify the string that appears in the StaticText widget. You specify this text in the resource file as follows:

```
*StaticText.string: <text>
```

Also note that this application is different from a conventional OLIT application in that it calls OlSetDefaultTextFormat() to set the default text format. OlSetDefaultTextFormat() sets the default text format for any widgets in the application that display text.

To set only the text format for an individual widget, set its XtNtextFormat resource. For example, in the application above, you would create the StaticText widget as follows:

```
msg_widget = XtVaCreateManagedWidget("msg",
    staticTextWidgetClass, toplevel,
    XtNtextFormat, OL_WC_STR_REP,
    NULL);
```

```
#include <X11/Intrinsic.h>
#include <X11/StringDefs.h>
#include <Xol/OpenLook.h>
#include <Xol/StaticText.h>

main(argc, argv)
    int      argc;
    char     *argv[];
{
    Widget toplevel, msg_widget;
    XtAppContext app;

    /* Initialize the OLIT toolkit */
    OlToolkitInitialize((XtPointer)NULL);

    /* Set the default text format to wide character */
    OlSetDefaultTextFormat(OL_WC_STR_REP);

    toplevel = XtAppInitialize(&app, "Memo",
            (XrmOptionDescList)NULL,
            0, &argc, argv, NULL,
            (ArgList) NULL, 0);

    /* Create a staticText widget. */
    msg_widget = XtVaCreateManagedWidget("msg",
            staticTextWidgetClass,
            toplevel,
            NULL);

    /* Realize the widgets and enter the event loop. */
    XtRealizeWidget(toplevel);
    XtAppMainLoop(app);
}
```

Figure E-7   OLIT Hello World Program

For some locales, you may also need to specify a font set for the application. To do this, add the following line to the resources file:

```
*StaticText.font: font set
```

Figure E-8 and Figure E-9 show the application with Korean and Japanese text.

Figure E-8   "Hello World" in Korean

Figure E-9   "Hello World" in Japanese

E.7 Compiling and Linking with Archive Libraries

To use the archive libraries when compiling and linking an Asian OLIT application, link the libraries explicitly as follows:

```
cc foo.c -o foo -Bstatic -lXol -lXt -lX11 \
    -Bdynamic -lintl -lnsl -lsocket -lw -ldl
```

The archive libraries are: -lXol, -lXt, and -lX11. The archive libraries support only the C locale. Shared libraries may contain dependencies on other shared libraries; linking resolves the dependencies for you. If you choose to link against archive libraries, you must explicitly specify any dependent libraries. However, use of archive libraries is discouraged because international support relies on dynamic linking.

E.8 Compiling and Linking with Asian OLIT

Compile and link Asian OLIT applications as follows:

```
cc foo.c -o foo -I$OPENWINHOME/include \
    -L$OPENWINHOME/lib -lXol -lXt -lX11
```

Shared libraries may contain dependencies on other shared libraries; dynamic linking resolves the dependencies for you. Static linking is discouraged because it increases executable size and doesn't allow for system fixes by upgrading. Note that -lintl and -lw were merged into the C library in Solaris 2.5.

Example Program

F.1 International Billing Program

This program performs customer billing functions, and works in many locales.

Code Example 15-1

```
 1   #include <Xm/Xm.h>
 2   #include <Xm/MainW.h>
 3   #include <Xm/RowColumn.h>
 4   #include <Xm/PushB.h>
 5   #include <Xm/Form.h>
 6   #include <Xm/Label.h>
 7   #include <Xm/Text.h>
 8   #include <Xm/TextF.h>
 9   #include <stdlib.h>
10   #include <stdio.h>
11   #include <time.h>
12   #include <monetary.h>
13   #include <nl_types.h>
14
15   struct Guest {
16      char          *name;      /* name of guest */
17      unsigned long distance;   /* distance from home */
18      double        bill;       /* amt of hotel bill */
19      time_t        recordEntryTime;
20      struct Guest  *next;      /* ptr to next guest in */
21                                /* sorted list */
22   };
23
24      /* singly-linked list of guests, sorted by name */
25   struct Guest *sortedGuestList = NULL;
26
27   static String fallback_resources[] = {
28      "*fontList: serif.r.14",
29      "*background: burlywood",
```

```
30      "*XmLabel.alignment: alignment_end",
31      "*textName.columns: 20",
32      "*textMiles.columns: 10",
33      "*textBill.columns: 10",
34      "*listGuest.columns: 57",
35      NULL
36   };
37
38   Widget    textName, textMiles, textBill, enter, listGuest;
39
40   nl_catd  catd;    /* descriptor for message catalog */
41
42   /*
43    * callback routine to enter new guest
44    */
45   void enterCB(widget, client_data, call_data)
46   Widget widget;
47   XtPointer client_data;
48   XtPointer call_data;
49   {
50      struct Guest   *newgp;       /* ptr to new guest to add */
51         /* current guest in list, for list traversal */
52      struct Guest   *gp;
53         /* previous guest in list, for list traversal */
54      struct Guest   *prevgp;
55      char  *cp;
56      char  buffer[BUFSIZ];
57
58      cp = XmTextGetString(textName);
59      if (cp[0] == '\0') { /* we want at least a name */
60         XBell(XtDisplay(widget), 0);
61         XmProcessTraversal(textName, XmTRAVERSE_CURRENT);
62         return;
63      }
64      /*
65       * create new guest
66       * NOTE:  Little validation done on input fields!
67       */
68      newgp = (struct Guest *) malloc(sizeof(struct Guest));
69      if (newgp == NULL) {
70         fprintf(stderr,"malloc failed in enterCB\n");
71         exit(1);
72      }
73      newgp->name = cp;
74
75      cp = XmTextGetString(textMiles);
```

```
76      if (sscanf(cp, "%lu", &newgp->distance) != 1) {
77          XBell(XtDisplay(widget), 0);
78          XmProcessTraversal(textMiles, XmTRAVERSE_CURRENT);
79          return;
80      }
81      XtFree(cp);
82
83      cp = XmTextGetString(textBill);
84      if (sscanf(cp, "%lf", &newgp->bill) != 1) {
85          XBell(XtDisplay(widget), 0);
86          XmProcessTraversal(textBill, XmTRAVERSE_CURRENT);
87          return;
88      }
89      XtFree(cp);
90      newgp->recordEntryTime = time((time_t) NULL);
91
92      /*
93       * insert new guest into sorted linked list of guests
94       */
95      if (sortedGuestList == NULL  ||
96           strcoll(newgp->name, sortedGuestList->name) < 0) {
97          newgp->next = sortedGuestList;
98          sortedGuestList = newgp;
99      } else {
100         for (prevgp = sortedGuestList;
101              (gp = prevgp->next) != NULL  &&
102               strcoll(newgp->name, gp->name) >= 0;
103             prevgp = gp)
104            ;
105         newgp->next = gp;
106         prevgp->next = newgp;
107     }
108     /*
109      * display sorted guest list
110      */
111     XmTextSetString(listGuest,"");
112     for (gp = sortedGuestList; gp != NULL; gp = gp->next) {
113         struct tm *timep = localtime(&gp->recordEntryTime);
114         sprintf(buffer,catgets(catd,1,1,"%-20s"), gp->name);
115         XmTextInsert(listGuest,
116                   XmTextGetLastPosition(listGuest), buffer);
117         sprintf(buffer,catgets(catd,1,2," %5d miles"),
118                                             gp->distance);
119         XmTextInsert(listGuest,
120                   XmTextGetLastPosition(listGuest), buffer);
121         strfmon(buffer, sizeof(buffer), "  %n", gp->bill);
```

```
122              XmTextInsert(listGuest,
123                      XmTextGetLastPosition(listGuest), buffer);
124           strftime(buffer, sizeof(buffer), " %c\n", timep);
125           XmTextInsert(listGuest,
126                      XmTextGetLastPosition(listGuest), buffer);
127       }
128       /*
129        * clear text input fields
130        */
131       XmTextSetString(textName,"");
132       XmTextSetString(textMiles,"");
133       XmTextSetString(textBill,"");
134       XmProcessTraversal(textName, XmTRAVERSE_CURRENT);
135   }
136
137   /*
138    * callback routine to find info about a guest
139    */
140   void findCB(widget, client_data, call_data)
141   Widget widget;
142   XtPointer client_data;
143   XtPointer call_data;
144   {
145       struct Guest   *gp;      /* current guest in list,  */
146       char   *cp;
147       char   buffer[BUFSIZ];
148
149       cp = XmTextGetString(textName);
150       if (cp[0] == '\0') { /* we need a name */
151           XBell(XtDisplay(widget), 0);
152           XmProcessTraversal(textName, XmTRAVERSE_CURRENT);
153           return;
154       }
155       /*
156        * search for guest
157        */
158       for (gp = sortedGuestList; gp != NULL; gp = gp->next) {
159           if (strcmp(gp->name, cp) == 0) {
160               sprintf(buffer, "%lu", gp->distance);
161               XmTextSetString(textMiles, buffer);
162
163               strfmon(buffer, sizeof(buffer), "%n", gp->bill);
164               XmTextSetString(textBill, buffer);
165               XmProcessTraversal(textName, XmTRAVERSE_CURRENT);
166
167               return;
```

```
168          }
169        }
170     XmTextSetString(textMiles,"");
171     XmTextSetString(textBill,"");
172     XBell(XtDisplay(widget), 0);
173     XmProcessTraversal(textName, XmTRAVERSE_CURRENT);
174 }
175
176 /*
177  * callback routine for hitting RETURN in text box
178  */
179 void textCB(widget, client_data, call_data)
180 Widget widget;
181 XtPointer client_data;
182 XtPointer call_data;
183 {
184    Widget   nextw;
185
186    if      (widget == textName) nextw = textMiles;
187    else if (widget == textMiles) nextw = textBill;
188    else if (widget == textBill) nextw = enter;
189    else return;
190    XmProcessTraversal(nextw, XmTRAVERSE_CURRENT);
191 }
192
193 /*
194  * callback routine to quit program
195  */
196 void quitCB(widget, client_data, call_data)
197 Widget widget;
198 XtPointer client_data;
199 XtPointer call_data;
200 {
201    exit(0);
202 }
203
204    /* MAIN ROUTINE */
205 int main(argc, argv)
206 int argc;
207 char **argv;
208 {
209    XtAppContext   app_context;
210    Widget      parent, mainwin, form;
211    Widget       find, quit;
212    Widget        label0, label1, label2, label3;
213    Arg       args[20];
```

```
214        Cardinal n = 0;
215        XmString str;
216
217        /*
218         * Xt set locale
219         */
220        XtSetLanguageProc(NULL, NULL, NULL);
221
222        /*
223         * initialize the X toolkit
224         */
225        parent = XtAppInitialize(&app_context,
226            "xguest", (XrmOptionDescList) NULL, 0,
227            (Cardinal*) &argc, argv, fallback_resources, args, 0);
228        /*
229         * open message catalog
230         */
231        catd = catopen("xguest", NL_CAT_LOCALE);
232        if (catd == (nl_catd) -1) {
233            fprintf(stderr, "The message catalog for the current "
234                "locale cannot be found.\nThis program will "
235                "continue in English.\n");
236        }
237        /*
238         * create main window and form
239         */
240        mainwin = XmCreateMainWindow(parent,
241            "mainwin", args, n);
242        form = XtVaCreateWidget("form",
243            xmFormWidgetClass, mainwin, NULL);
244        /*
245         * fill in guest name
246         */
247        textName = XtVaCreateManagedWidget("textName",
248            xmTextFieldWidgetClass, form,
249            XmNnavigationType,   XmTAB_GROUP,
250            XmNtopAttachment, XmATTACH_FORM,
251            XmNtopOffset,            6,
252            XmNrightAttachment,   XmATTACH_FORM,
253            XmNrightOffset,       120,
254            XmNleftAttachment,    XmATTACH_POSITION,
255            XmNleftPosition,  30,
256            NULL);
257        XtAddCallback(textName, XmNactivateCallback, textCB,
258                                                        NULL);
259
```

```
260      str = XmStringCreateSimple(catgets(catd, 2, 1,
261                                      "Guest name:"));
262      label0 = XtVaCreateManagedWidget("labelName",
263          xmLabelWidgetClass,  form,
264          XmNlabelString,      str,
265          XmNtopAttachment, XmATTACH_FORM,
266          XmNtopOffset,          10,
267          XmNleftAttachment,   XmATTACH_FORM,
268          XmNleftOffset,         5,
269          XmNrightAttachment,  XmATTACH_POSITION,
270          XmNrightPosition, 30,
271          XmNrightOffset,        3,
272          NULL);
273      XmStringFree(str);
274
275      /*
276       * fill in distance from guest's home to hotel
277       */
278      textMiles = XtVaCreateManagedWidget("textMiles",
279          xmTextFieldWidgetClass, form,
280          XmNnavigationType,    XmTAB_GROUP,
281          XmNtopAttachment, XmATTACH_WIDGET,
282          XmNtopWidget,        textName,
283          XmNleftAttachment,   XmATTACH_OPPOSITE_WIDGET,
284          XmNleftWidget,       textName,
285          NULL);
286      XtAddCallback(textMiles, XmNactivateCallback, textCB,
287                                               NULL);
288
289      str = XmStringCreateSimple(catgets(catd, 2, 2,
290                                      "Miles from home:"));
291      label1 = XtVaCreateManagedWidget("labelMiles",
292          xmLabelWidgetClass,  form,
293          XmNlabelString,      str,
294          XmNtopAttachment, XmATTACH_WIDGET,
295          XmNtopWidget,        textName,
296          XmNtopOffset,        4,
297          XmNleftAttachment,   XmATTACH_FORM,
298          XmNleftOffset,         5,
299          XmNrightAttachment,  XmATTACH_POSITION,
300          XmNrightPosition, 30,
301          XmNrightOffset,        4,
302          NULL);
303      XmStringFree(str);
304
305      /*
```

```
306        * fill in amount of hotel bill
307        */
308       textBill = XtVaCreateManagedWidget("textBill",
309          xmTextFieldWidgetClass, form,
310          XmNnavigationType,    XmTAB_GROUP,
311          XmNtopAttachment, XmATTACH_WIDGET,
312          XmNtopWidget,       textMiles,
313          XmNleftAttachment,    XmATTACH_OPPOSITE_WIDGET,
314          XmNleftWidget,      textName,
315          NULL);
316       XtAddCallback(textBill, XmNactivateCallback, textCB,
317                                                   NULL);
318
319       str = XmStringCreateSimple(catgets(catd, 2, 3, "Bill:"));
320       label2 = XtVaCreateManagedWidget("labelBill",
321          xmLabelWidgetClass,  form,
322          XmNlabelString,       str,
323          XmNtopAttachment, XmATTACH_WIDGET,
324          XmNtopWidget,       textMiles,
325          XmNtopOffset,       3,
326          XmNleftAttachment,    XmATTACH_FORM,
327          XmNleftOffset,        5,
328          XmNrightAttachment,   XmATTACH_POSITION,
329          XmNrightPosition, 30,
330          XmNrightOffset,       4,
331          NULL);
332       XmStringFree(str);
333
334       /*
335        * create enter button
336        */
337
338       str = XmStringCreateSimple(catgets(catd, 2, 4, "Enter"));
339       enter = XtVaCreateManagedWidget("btnEnter",
340          xmPushButtonWidgetClass, form,
341          XmNlabelString,        str,
342          XmNnavigationType,    XmTAB_GROUP,
343          XmNtopAttachment, XmATTACH_WIDGET,
344          XmNtopWidget,       textBill,
345          XmNleftAttachment,    XmATTACH_OPPOSITE_WIDGET,
346          XmNleftWidget,      textName,
347          NULL);
348       XmStringFree(str);
349       XtAddCallback(enter, XmNactivateCallback, enterCB, NULL);
350
351       /*
```

```
352        * create find button
353        */
354
355       str = XmStringCreateSimple(catgets(catd, 2, 5, "Find"));
356       find = XtVaCreateManagedWidget("btnFind",
357          xmPushButtonWidgetClass, form,
358          XmNlabelString,       str,
359          XmNnavigationType,    XmTAB_GROUP,
360          XmNtopAttachment, XmATTACH_WIDGET,
361          XmNtopWidget,         textBill,
362          XmNleftAttachment,    XmATTACH_WIDGET,
363          XmNleftWidget,        enter,
364          XmNleftOffset,        10,
365          NULL);
366       XmStringFree(str);
367       XtAddCallback(find, XmNactivateCallback, findCB, NULL);
368
369       /*
370        * create quit button
371        */
372
373       str = XmStringCreateSimple(catgets(catd, 2, 6, "Quit"));
374       quit = XtVaCreateManagedWidget("btnQuit",
375          xmPushButtonWidgetClass, form,
376          XmNlabelString,       str,
377          XmNtraversalOn,       False,
378          XmNtopAttachment, XmATTACH_WIDGET,
379          XmNtopWidget,         textBill,
380          XmNleftAttachment,    XmATTACH_WIDGET,
381          XmNleftWidget,        find,
382          XmNleftOffset,        10,
383          NULL);
384       XmStringFree(str);
385       XtAddCallback(quit, XmNactivateCallback, quitCB, NULL);
386
387
388       /*
389        * label sorted guest list
390        */
391
392       str = XmStringCreateSimple(catgets(catd, 2, 7,
393                                          "Guest list"));
394       label3 = XtVaCreateManagedWidget("labelGuestlist",
395          xmLabelWidgetClass,   form,
396          XmNlabelString,       str,
397          XmNtopAttachment, XmATTACH_WIDGET,
```

```
398        XmNtopWidget,        enter,
399        XmNleftAttachment,    XmATTACH_FORM,
400        NULL);
401    XmStringFree(str);
402
403    /*
404     * create guestlist area
405     */
406
407    n = 0;
408    XtSetArg(args[n], XmNtopAttachment, XmATTACH_WIDGET);
409                                                    n++;
410    XtSetArg(args[n], XmNtopWidget,      label3); n++;
411    XtSetArg(args[n], XmNleftAttachment,   XmATTACH_FORM);
412                                                    n++;
413    XtSetArg(args[n], XmNrightAttachment,  XmATTACH_FORM);
414                                                    n++;
415    XtSetArg(args[n], XmNbottomAttachment, XmATTACH_FORM);
416                                                    n++;
417    XtSetArg(args[n], XmNrows,            5); n++;
418    XtSetArg(args[n], XmNeditable,       False); n++;
419    XtSetArg(args[n], XmNeditMode,       XmMULTI_LINE_EDIT);
420                                                    n++;
421    XtSetArg(args[n], XmNcursorPositionVisible, False); n++;
422    XtSetArg(args[n], XmNtraversalOn,    False); n++;
423    listGuest =
424            XmCreateScrolledText(form, "listGuest", args, n);
425    XtManageChild(listGuest);
426    /*
427     * form's inital focus is textName
428     */
429    XtVaSetValues(form, XmNinitialFocus, textName, NULL);
430    /*
431     * manage window elements and realize parent widget
432     */
433    XtManageChild(form);
434    XtManageChild(mainwin);
435    XtRealizeWidget(parent);
436    /*
437     * loop forever waiting for user commands
438     */
439    XtAppMainLoop(app_context);
440    return 0;
441 }
```

Annotated Bibliography

G.1 Trade Press Books

Compound Text Encoding, Version 1.1, MIT X Consortium Standard, X Version 11 Release 5, by Robert W. Scheifler, 1989, available in the X11 release 5 source under `mit/doc/CTEXT`, or as an appendix of the *X Window System* book by Scheifler and Getty (see below).

> This six-page document describes X11's compound text format for representing data in multiple character sets. Compound text encoding was first described in X11 release 4 as a text interchange method for interclient communication.

Digital Guide to Developing International Software, by the Corporate User Publications Group, Digital Press and Prentice-Hall, 1991.

> Concentrates mostly on how to develop software for the VAX/VMS environment. Has valuable, though sometimes inaccurate, appendices on locale data formats.

Digital Guide to Developing International User Information, by Scott Jones, Cynthia Kennelly, Claudia Mueller, Marcia Sweezy, Bill Thomas, and Lydia Velez, Digital Press and Prentice-Hall, 1992.

> User information is Digital-speak for documentation, and this is a good introduction to that topic. Contains the same appendices on locale data formats as the book above.

Global Software: Developing Applications for the International Market, by Dave Taylor with a foreword by John Sculley, Springer Verlag, 1992.

> This was the only general introduction to software internationalization on the market as of spring 1993. All other books concentrated on a single vendor's environment. The chapter on "Pitfalls" is excellent; the book is worth obtaining for this alone.

Guide to Macintosh Software Localization, Apple Computer, Addison-Wesley, 1993.

> The official publication from Apple Computer on how to localize software for the Macintosh. As such it also covers internationalization topics. Contains many great charts printed in a variety of scripts.

Internationally Yours, Writing and Communicating Successfully In Today's Global Marketplace, by Mary A. DeVries, Houghton Mifflin, 1994.

> Provides guidelines for international correspondence and communications.

OSF/Motif Programmer's Guide, Open Software Foundation, Prentice-Hall, 1992.

> Presents Motif, a popular X windows toolkit. Chapter 11 covers internationalization, including text input for Asian languages. A Motif reference guide is also available in the series, as is a style guide.

PostScript Language Reference Manual, Second Edition, Adobe Systems, Inc. and Addison-Wesley, 1990.

> The updated red book, including material on level-2 PostScript and composite fonts.

Programmer's Supplement for Release 5, by David Flanagan, continuation of a series, O'Reilly & Associates, 1992.

> A complete update, in a single volume, for the X11 release 4 volumes 1, 2, 4 and 5 of the O'Reilly series. Look at Chapters 4 and 5 for eighty pages discussing internationalization and international text input issues.

Programming for the World, A Guide to Internationalization, by Sandra Martin O'Donnell, Prentice Hall, 1994.

> Excellent overview of computer software internationalization. Covers a wide range of topics including writing methods of the world, international software design, and specific I18N programming issues.

Solaris Porting Guide, from SunSoft ISV Engineering, by Michele Ann Goodman, Manoj Goyal, and Robert A. Massoudi, Prentice-Hall, 1993.

> Presents lots of information about porting applications to Solaris, now and in the future. Chapter 7 discusses internationalization, though not in any greater depth than Chapters 2 and 3 of this book.

The Unicode Standard: Worldwide Character Encoding, Version 2.0, Volume 1, by the Unicode Consortium, Addison-Wesley, 1996.

> Contains charts of symbols and scripts for all the world's major living languages (except Han characters for Chinese/Japanese/Korean) plus cross-reference tables to various existing codeset standards. Also contains implementation hints for character properties and a bidirectional algorithm.

The Unicode Standard: Worldwide Character Encoding, Version 2.0, Volume 2, by the Unicode Consortium, Addison-Wesley, 1996.

> Contains charts of unified Han characters for Chinese/Japanese/Korean, which weren't in the first volume. Also has information on Unicode version 1.1, plus implementation hints including character shaping algorithms for Arabic, Devanagari, and Tamil. A good coffee-table book.

Writing Applications for the Solaris Environment, A Guide for Windows Programmers, from SunSoft, Inc. and Addison-Wesley, 1992.

> A succinct introduction to application development on Solaris, not as up-to-date as the *Solaris Porting Guide,* but still useful.

XView Programming Manual, An OPEN LOOK Toolkit for X11, for Version 3, by Dan Heller, volume 7 of a series, O'Reilly & Associates, 1992.

> The standard introduction to programming OpenWindows with the XView toolkit. Includes a chapter on internationalization for locales in Western Europe, but doesn't cover issues for locales in East Asia.

XView Reference Manual, for XView Version 3, edited by Thomas Van Raalte, a companion to volume 7, O'Reilly & Associates, 1992.

> A complete reference manual to be used in conjunction with the *XView Programming Manual* listed above.

X Window System C Library and Protocol Reference, Release 5 Version, by Robert W. Scheifler and James Getty, Digital Press, 1992.

> The original source for X11 release 5 information; content is similar to that of the Flanagan book, *Programmer's Supplement for Release 5.*

The X Window System Programming & Applications with Xt, OPEN LOOK Edition, by Douglas A. Young and John A. Pew, Prentice-Hall, 1992.

> The standard introduction to programming OpenWindows with OLIT (OPEN LOOK Intrinsics Toolkit). Contains little information on internationalization.

G.2 Solaris Documentation

JFP User's Guide, Nihon Sun and SunSoft, Inc., part number 802-4507-10.

> Describes specific features of the Japanese Feature Package.

Japanese Solaris Introduction, Nihon Sun and SunSoft, part number 802-4508-10.

> Provides an overview of Japanese Solaris.

ATOK7 User's Guide, Nihon Sun and SunSoft, Inc., part number 802-4509-10.

> Documents the ATOK7 input method.

cs00 User's Guide, Nihon Sun and SunSoft, Inc., part number 802-4510-10.

> Documents the `cs00` input method used by `htt`.

JFP Reference Manual, Nihon Sun and SunSoft, Inc., part number 802-4511-10.

> JFP manual pages and many Solaris manual pages translated into Japanese.

JFP Developer's Guide, Nihon Sun and SunSoft, Inc., part number 802-4513-10.

> Describes how to program the Japanese Feature Package.

G

Korean Solaris Release Overview, SunSoft, Inc., part number 802-3090-10.
Release notes for Korean Solaris 2.5; later releases will have different part numbers.

Korean Solaris User's Guide, SunSoft, Inc., part number 802-3088-10.
Describes for users the unique features of Korean Solaris.

Korean Solaris System Administration Guide, SunSoft, Inc., part number 802-3089-10.
Describes the unique features of Korean Solaris system administration.

Traditional Chinese Solaris Release Overview, SunSoft, Inc., part number 802-3084-10.
Release notes for Traditional Chinese Solaris 2.5; later releases will have different part numbers.

Traditional Chinese Solaris User's Guide, SunSoft, Inc., part number 802-3082-10.
Describes for users the unique features of Traditional Chinese Solaris.

Traditional Chinese Solaris System Administration Guide, SunSoft, Inc., part number 802-3083-10.
Describes the features of Traditional Chinese Solaris system administration.

Simplified Chinese Solaris Release Overview, SunSoft, Inc., part number 802-3079-10.
Release notes for Simplified Chinese Solaris 2.5; later releases will have different part numbers.

Simplified Chinese Solaris User's Guide, SunSoft, Inc., part number 802-3080-10.
Describes for users the unique features of Simplified Chinese Solaris.

Simplified Chinese Solaris System Administration Guide, SunSoft, Inc., part number 802-3081-10.
Describes the features of Simplified Chinese Solaris system administration.

Glossary

7-bit dirty

The term applied to operating system commands that interpret ASCII metacharacters (those with the eighth bit set to 1) in specialized ways. For example, some commands simply masked off the eighth bit, while others used it as a flag of some sort. Opposite of *8-bit clean*.

8-bit clean

A term applied to a platform or operating system that supports a common method of representing characters in the various European languages; specifically, 8-bit character sets such as ISO Latin-1, as opposed to the 7-bit ASCII character set used in the U.S. Solaris commands that support 8-bit character data or that are not concerned with processing text are said to be "8-bit clean." To support the notion of a native-language application environment, a number of Solaris commands that process user input (text) have been modified to support 8-bit characters.

ANSI

American National Standards Institute. An organization that reviews and approves product standards in the United States. In the electronics industry, ANSI's work enables designers and manufacturers to create and support products that are compatible with other hardware platforms in the industry. See also *ISO (International Standards Organization)*.

ANSI C

The first standard (ANSI X3.159-1989) for the C programming language, which specifies most of the functionality for the locale mechanism as well as the basic functionality of multibyte and wide character handling.

ASCII

American Standard Code for Information Exchange. The standard 7-bit binary encoding of alphabetical characters, numbers, and other keyboard symbols. Pronounced "as-kee."

AZERTY keyboard

Keyboard commonly used in France. The keys are arranged in a different order from the more generally used QWERTY keyboard. The name comes from the first six alphabetic characters on the upper left, "A," "Z," "E," "R," "T," and "Y." Compare to *QWERTY keyboard*.

bidirectional text

Text that is written from right-to-left horizontally with the exception of numbers, which are written from left-to-right, or when intermixing with other left-to-right scripts such as Latin. This is characteristic of languages such as Arabic, Hebrew, Urdu, and Farsi.

bit

Short for "binary digit." The smallest unit of information stored in a digital memory. Binary digits indicate two possible values: on and off. A single bit is represented in memory as 0 (off) and 1 (on).

Bopomofo

A syllabary for transliterating Chinese sounds, used in Taiwan. Named after the sounds of the first four characters. Also called Zhuyin-fuhao.

byte

A group of adjacent binary digits (*bits*) operated on by the computer as a unit. The most common size byte contains eight binary digits. See also *character*.

callback function

A procedure called when a specific event occurs in an event-driven environment. Also known as a callback.

CAT

Computer Assisted Translation.

category, OPEN LOOK locale

An OPEN LOOK attribute that defines a program's on-screen language and cultural conventions. The categories are Basic Setting, Display Language, Input Language, Time Format, and Numeric Format.

character

A letter, numeral, punctuation mark, control character, blank, or other such symbol. In multibyte-coded character sets, no longer synonymous with *byte*. The linguistic term for character is grapheme; see also *grapheme.*

character classification

The ability to determine a group of characters that share common characteristics (for example, uppercase, lowercase, numeric, and so on). For example POSIX.1 character classifications are dependent on the value of the LC_CTYPE category.

character encoding

The method by which a language's character set is represented numerically. Conventional applications use 7-bit ASCII to represent characters. However, some languages have larger character sets that require more than the 128 character range permitted by ASCII.

character set

A set of characters used to construct the words and other elementary units of a natural language. Character sets can consist of alphabets, ideographs, and/or other units.

coded character set

Longer (and perhaps more accurate) term for *codeset.*

codeset

A list of unambiguous rules establishing a character set and a one-to-one relationship between each character of the set and its bit representation. In short, a mapping between characters and computer code. ASCII is the most common codeset; others are ISO 8859-1, JIS X0208, and Unicode.

codeset dependent (CSD)

Relying on, assuming, or hardcoding a specific codeset in software.

codeset independence (CSI)

The capability of handling any codeset in software.

collating sequence

The order in which lexical data (composed of alphanumeric characters) is sorted for a particular language or locale.

collation

Sorting; using linguistic or cultural rules to order data in a list.

complex text languages (CTL)

Languages whose scripts have one or more of the following characteristics: context sensitive text, composite characters, or bidirectional text.

composite characters

Characters that are composed with a few base elements. This is a characteristic of languages such as Thai, Lao, Vietnamese, and Korean Hangul.

console

Display screen (terminal or workstation).

context-sensitive text

Character text that can assume different shapes, depending on neighboring characters and their placement within a word. This is a characteristic of languages such as Arabic, Thai, Korean Hangul, and Urdu.

contextual writing

See *context-sensitive text*.

country kit

An assemblage, provided by Sun, of local keyboards, power cords, owner's manuals, and so forth, for a specific country.

cursive script

A script with interconnecting characters, such as Arabic and many forms of Indic writing.

decoder

A facility that takes data that has been encoded, or compressed, by an *encoder* and decompresses it. A decoder can be implemented in hardware, software, or a combination of both. The decompressed data may not match the original data set exactly, depending on how the data was encoded.

deshaping

Reverting to the base shape in Arabic or Indic script. Specifically, in Arabic script, letters can take three forms: initial, medial, and final. Going from one of these forms to the base letter is called deshaping. See also *shape determination*.

diacritical mark

A distinguishing mark added to a character, such as an accent mark, which often shows pronunciation.

diphthong

A compound vowel sound, usually but not always represented in writing by two letters, for example, the *ou* in house.

documentation template

A form or structure that writers use to prepare manuals that are consistent in design and organization. There is usually one template for every kind of page, such as a title page template, credits page template, chapter page template, index template, etc. Firm adherence to templates makes it easier not only to give a common look to a set of manuals, but also makes them easier to read, modify, update, customize, and translate.

dynamic messaging

A form of printing strings where the order of phrases can change at runtime. Compare with *static messaging*.

EBCDIC

Extended Binary Coded Decimal Interchange Code. A coded character set consisting of 8-bit coded characters. The EBCDIC coding scheme was developed by IBM for use with its computers as a standard way of assigning binary (numeric) values to alphabetic, numeric, punctuation, and transmission-control characters.

EC

European Community (usually, the EUR12). Sometimes called the ECC for European Commonwealth Community, not to be confused with ECC memory. See *EUR12*.

EC Class 1

All industrialized countries.

EC Class 2

All developing countries.

EC Class 3

All state-trading (formerly Communist) countries.

ECMA

European Computer Manufacturers' Association.

ECU

European Currency Unit. This concept offers the hope of a single currency unit for Europe as an alternative to each country's individual currency. A French gold coin known as the écu was in wide use during the 17th century.

EFTA

European Free Trade Association. Members are Austria, Finland, Iceland, Norway, Sweden, and Switzerland.

encoder

A facility that encodes data for the purpose of achieving data compression. Frequently, the data to be encoded is video data, but any other type of data, including audio, can be compressed as well. Contrast with *decoder*.

encoding scheme

A mechanism for combining multiple codesets into a unified character coding system. Examples are EUC, compound text, and ISO 2022.

end system

An ISO open systems interconnection (OSI) system that contains application processes capable of communicating through all seven layers of OSI protocols. Equivalent in function to *Internet* host. See also *ISO/OSI model*.

entity

(1) ISO open systems interconnection (OSI) terminology for a layer protocol machine. An entity within a layer performs the functions of the layer within a single computer system, accessing the layer entity below and providing services to the layer entity above at local service access points.

(2) In object-oriented programming, part of the definition of a class (group) of objects. In this instance, an entity might be an attribute of

the class (as feathers are an attribute of birds), or it might be a variable or an argument in a routine associated with the class.

(3) In database design, an object of interest about which data can be collected. In a retail database application, customers, products, and suppliers might be entities. An entity can subsume a number of attributes: product attributes might be color, size, and price; customer attributes might include name, address, and credit rating.

EUC

Extended UNIX Code. A coding scheme that allows up to four codesets to coexist in one data stream. EUC supports one primary codeset and three supplementary codesets. The primary character set (codeset 0) is always ASCII. The other three character sets vary, depending upon the locale.

EUC-JIS

Extended UNIX Code-Japanese Industrial Standard. Used by the EUC to mix ASCII, JIS X0201, JIS X0208, and JIS X0212 character sets, which are popularly used in the Japanese UNIX market and which have been adopted by JLE. In EUC-JIS, ASCII is defined as codeset 0, JIS X0208 is defined as codeset 1, JIS X0201 (right half of the table only) is defined as codeset 2, and JIS X0212 is defined as codeset 3.

EUnet

European UNIX network.

EUR12

Member states of the European Communities: Belgium, Denmark, Germany, Greece, France, Ireland, Italy, Luxembourg, the Netherlands, Portugal, Spain, and the United Kingdom.

EUUG

European UNIX Users Group.

file code (EUC file code)

Any coded character set used for file storage, as opposed to in-memory computer processing. Sometimes used as a synonym for multibyte character, but note that file codes and multibyte characters need not be the same. See *multibyte character*.

floating accent keys

Keys allowing a user to type in a composite character without using the Compose key. The user types the floating accent key first, followed by the key for the letter to be accented. Sometimes called "dead" keys.

floating diacritics

Diacritical marks that can be applied to an arbitrary base character, usually to form an accented character.

font

A complete assortment of type in one size and style. For example, Times Roman bold 10 point is a font; Times Roman is a typeface. See *typeface*.

font set

A set of fonts representing the character sets of a language. Standard English has only one character set. Other languages, however, have multiple character sets that require multiple fonts. These multiple fonts are called *font set objects*.

font set objects

A collection of one or more fonts needed to display characters in languages with multiple character sets.

FTAM

File Transfer, Access, and Management. Specified as part of the ISO open systems interconnection (OSI) remote file service and protocol.

GATT

General Agreement on Trade and Tariffs.

glyph

(1) A particular graphic representation of a character. For example, the glyphs "*a*," "**a**," "a," and "ɑ" are all different glyphs for the character "a," the first letter of the Roman alphabet. The linguistic term for glyph is allograph.
(2) In OpenWindows, a picture or graphic representation of an *object*.

GMT

Greenwich Mean Time. Mean solar time of the meridian at Greenwich, England. Used as the basis of standard time throughout most of the world and in most UNIX systems. Same as UCT. See *UCT (Universal Coordinate Time)*.

grapheme

Linguistic term for the smallest unit of writing, such as an ideograph or letter of an alphabet. In alphabetic scripts, the grapheme represents the phoneme in written form, but there is typically no one-to-one correspondence between phonetic and graphemic systems. For example, "f" in *fish*, "ph" in *phobia*, and "gh" in *cough* are all different graphemes that represent a single phoneme. Language can be written in IPA (the International Phonetic Alphabet), but linguists consider these symbols to be transcribed phonemes, rather than graphemes. In the computer field, character is often used to mean grapheme. See also *character*.

GUI

Graphical User Interface.

Hangul

A character set component, along with Hanja, of the Korean writing system. Hangul characters are generated by (typically three) different combinations of the Korean phonetic alphabet, consisting of 51 symbols. See also *Hanja*.

Hanja

A character set component, along with Hangul, of the Korean writing system. Hanja characters are ideographs that originated from the Chinese writing system and are used mainly in formal documents. It should be noted that the mapping of Hangul to Hanja characters is not one-to-one. A Hangul character can have no corresponding Hanja, or it can map to possibly 70 Hanja characters. See also *Hangul*.

Hanzi

Chinese ideographic characters used in the People's Republic of China (PRC) and in the Republic of China (ROC or Taiwan). Composed of multiple strokes, these characters originally represented things or ideas, but many of them gradually lost their representational basis. Hanzi characters are called Hanja in Korea and Kanji in Japan. Including archaic forms, such characters number in the hundreds of thousands.

Hiragana

One of two Japanese syllabic writing systems, the other being Katakana. The Hiragana syllabary consists of over 80 symbols that encompass all Japanese pronunciations.

hyphenation

Separation of words, usually by a hyphen, at the syllable boundary. This helps fit more text on a line, and is unique to western languages.

ICCCM

Inter-Client Communication Convention Manual (ICCCM). An X consortium standard convention for X client communication. Describes conventions for the communications among X clients. This includes such conventions as client-to-client, client-to-window manager, client-to-session manager, and color characterization communication. This document is produced by the MIT X Consortium.

icon

An on-screen symbol that simplifies access to a program, command, or data file. In window systems, an icon is usually a small pictorial representation of a large base window. Displaying objects as icons conserves screen space while keeping the window available for easy startup and access.

ideograph (ideogram)

A written symbol that represents meaning directly, rather than phonetically. Like a *pictograph*, an ideograph may represent an object or activity in writing by giving a pictorial image of that object or activity. But unlike a pictograph, an ideograph may extend the meaning of the image to include abstract concepts associated with the depicted object or activity.

IEC

Information Exchange Character. A character set as defined by ISO. Also International Electrotechnical Commission.

IEEE

Institute of Electrical and Electronics Engineers.

IETF

Internet Engineering Task Force, an ad-hoc Internet standards body.

industry standard

Elements of a computer system hardware or software subsystem that have been standardized and adopted by the industry at large. Standardization occurs in two ways: through a rigorous procedure followed by the *ANSI* and *ISO* organizations or through wide acceptance by the industry.

input method

The algorithm by which users enter the text of a language. Input methods differ for each language, depending on that language's linguistic structure and conventions. For example, the writing systems for some languages consist of multiple character sets that require several keystrokes to create one character.

internationalization

Designing and building products that can be adapted to different languages and regions, conforming to local requirements and customs without engineering changes. The same copy of an application should be able to work anywhere, with the addition of localization data. Eliminates built-in dependencies on certain locale-specific behaviors.

See also *localization*.

Internet

Note the capital "I." The largest wide-area network in the world, consisting of large national backbone nets (such as MILNET, NSFNET, and CREN) and a myriad of regional and local campus networks all over the world. Internet uses the Internet Protocol (IP) suite. To be on the Internet, the user must have IP connectivity and be able to `telnet` to (or `ping`) other systems. Networks with only e-mail connectivity are not actually classified as being on the Internet.

ISO

International Standards Organization. The actual name is International Organisation for Standardisation, but the expansion above fits the acronym better. An international agency that reviews and approves independently designed products for use within specific industries. ISO is also responsible for developing standards for information exchange. Its function is similar to that of *ANSI* in the United States.

ISO 639

The ISO standard for language names. It gives two-letter abbreviations with full names in English, French, and the original.

ISO 646

An ISO 7-bit coded character set for information exchange. Contains 95 graphic characters, most of which are identical to those found in the ASCII set. ASCII (or ANSI X3.4) is the American form of ISO 646.

ISO 2022

An ISO standard for switching among various existing and approved codesets. EUC is a partially conforming implementation of ISO 2022.

ISO 3166

An ISO standard for territory (country) names. It gives two- and three-letter abbreviations with full names in English, plus numeric codes.

ISO 6937

An ISO 7- or 8-bit coded character set for text communication over public and private networks or using interchange media such as magnetic tape and discs. Provides floating diacritics in addition to precomposed accented characters. Not in wide use except for interactive Videotex.

ISO 8859

An ISO 8-bit coded character set consisting of nine different alphabets that are each divided into right and left parts. The left part (characters 0–127) is common throughout and is identical to ASCII. The right half varies according to the Latin alphabet used (Latin-1, 2, 3, 4, or 5, Latin-Cyrillic, Latin-Arabic, Latin-Greek, or Latin-Hebrew). Contains no floating diacritics, only precomposed characters.

ISO 9660

An international format standard for CD-ROM, very similar to DOS, and adopted by the ISO.

ISO 10646

An ISO 16- or 32-bit coded character set that universally represents all modern writing systems of the world. Unicode is the 16-bit form of ISO 10646.

ISO Latin-1

The standard character set for Western European languages, also called ISO 8859-1. See also *ISO 8859*.

ISO/OSI model

ISO's Open Systems Interconnection model. A layered architecture (plan) that standardizes levels of service and types of interaction for computers exchanging information through a communications network. The ISO/OSI model separates computer-to-server communications into seven layers, or levels, each building upon the standards contained in the level(s) below it. The layers, in order from highest to lowest, are: application, presentation, session, transport, network, data-link, and physical.

jargon

Words or phrases that are incomprehensible or outlandish outside of the region or group (for example, a country, or the computer industry, or a particular country's computer industry) that originated it. For example, "grok" in the U.S. means "to understand completely."

JFP

Japanese Feature Package. Font sets, input methods, and translated messages that can be added to International OpenWindows for Japanese support.

JIS

Japanese Industrial Standard.

Kana

Either of the Japanese syllabaries, Hiragana or Katakana.

Kanji

The traditional ideographic Japanese alphabet. Kanji consists of 6,500+ characters and is used in conjunction with Hiragana and Katakana. Individual Kanji characters can have various pronunciations, depending on the context.

Katakana

One of two Japanese syllabic writing systems, the other being Hiragana. Katakana is similar to Hiragana but is reserved for words of foreign origin.

kerning

Reducing the spacing between individual characters so that the overall word is more compact in appearance.

keyboard

Commonly used alphanumeric input device.

keyboard accelerator

A key or sequence of keys on the keyboard, or multiple clicks of mouse buttons, by which users can quickly perform specific menu or application functions without using a menu.

ligature

> A typographic term for the binding together of two or more characters so that they become one character, as in"fi," "fl," "œ," and "æ."

locale

> A specific region definition that can contain linguistic, cultural, and governmental rules and conventions. A locale name as defined by X/Open can be composed of language and territory and codeset information. An end-user's locale preference can be specified by the LANG environment variable.

locale announcement

> A mechanism for setting and querying the locale environment. For example, POSIX.1 uses the `setlocale()` function to specify and determine locale settings.

locale category

> One attribute of a locale, such as character type, date and time format, numeric and monetary conventions, collation sequences, and translated message.

locale setting

> The method by which the language or cultural environment is set.

localization

> The process of adding locale-specific components, translation, and language support to a product and packaging to meet regional market requirements. See also *internationalization*.

localized text handling

> The method by which the native language strings of a program can be displayed in a foreign language without changes to the program's source code. Samples of strings include error messages, menu text, button text, and so forth.

lookup choice region

> A display of the multiple ideographic choices that correspond to one phonetic representation of a word in an Asian language. For example, in Japanese, the user can type in a word phonetically, then display the lookup choice region, and finally, select the appropriate Kanji, Hiragana, or Katakana representation. Compare with *pre-edit region, status region*.

message

Information generated by an application that informs users about usage, process status, errors, and so forth.

message catalog

A file containing messages for a program. Message catalogs are intended for translation into another language.

message log

A history of status messages.

metaphor

A figure of speech containing an implied comparison. Metaphors are difficult or impossible to translate.

MIME

Multipurpose Internet Mail Extensions. An Internet standard for specifying and describing the format of a message. Redefines the format of message bodies to allow multipart textual and nontextual data to be represented and exchanged internationally without loss of information.

mnemonics

Formulas or other aids to help improve the memory. Mnemonics are usually specific to a language and culture and should be avoided when material is being translated.

mnemonic key

A key that represents the first letter of a command and is thus easy to remember. It is often used in conjunction with a modifier, such as Control or Shift, as a *keyboard accelerator*. For example, Control-P could mean print.

mnemonic symbol

A symbol chosen to assist the human memory, for example, an abbreviation such as "mpy" for "multiply."

MNLS

Multi-National Language Supplement. AT&T's MNLS 3.2 Overview specifies international extensions for SVR3.2. Because the current ANSI C wide character support is minimal and because MNLS specifies extensive functionality in this area, JLE/ALE has adopted a superset of

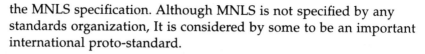

the MNLS specification. Although MNLS is not specified by any standards organization, It is considered by some to be an important international proto-standard.

morpheme

The smallest linguistic unit able to convey meaning, whether a free form (as *pin, child, load, fin*) or a bound form (as *-s* in *pins*, or *-hood* in *childhood*).

multibyte character

Any character taking up more than one byte in computer code. Because 8-bit bytes can only address 255 characters, many codesets require more than 8 bits and contain characters, called multibyte characters, that span two or more bytes. Since some coding schemes contain an ASCII codeset, single byte characters can be considered multibyte. Despite being a linguistic travesty, this terminology is used by the ANSI-C specification. A multibyte character differs from wide character encoding in that the number of bytes representing a character may vary. See *wide character*.

nastaliq

A way of writing Arabic so that each word slopes down from right to left, the last character of each word resting on the base of the text line.

native language

A potentially derogatory term, widely used in the industry because of Hewlett-Packard's Native Language System (NLS). Computer users' native language is the one they prefer to speak. During localization, English or UNIX messages are translated to a target local language.

natural language

The primary language(s) spoken within a particular geographic region. Often used in contrast with *computer language*.

NBS

National Bureau of Standards, now renamed NIST.

NIST

National Institute of Standards and Technology in the USA.

NRC

National Replacement Character set, usually one of the ISO 646 codesets.

object
> (1) In the OPEN LOOK graphical user interface, an item that a user sees.
> (2) A graphics entity. A single image or model defined in 2-D or 3-D space.
> (3) In object-oriented programming, an entity defined as part of the interface.

object layout
> The mechanism by which the location of string objects on a screen is modified to accommodate the changes in string dimensions when a program is internationalized.

OLIT
> OPEN LOOK Intrinsics Toolkit. An Xt-based X11 Window System library under OpenWindows.

on line
> Connected to the system and in operation.

on-line documentation
> A retrieval-based form of documentation provided by many application programs, consisting of advice or instructions on how to use program features. On-line documentation can be accessed directly without the need to interrupt work in progress or to leaf through a manual.

on-line text
> User information displayed on the computer screen, including help messages, menus, forms, prompts, error messages, and so forth.

OPEN LOOK locale category
> See *category, OPEN LOOK locale*.

OSI
> Open Systems Interconnection. An international standardization program to facilitate communication among computers from different manufacturers.

PC-Kanji
> Japanese encoding used by IBM-compatible personal computers, also called Shift-JIS, PCK, or SJIS. Incompatible with EUC Kanji.

phoneme

Linguistic term for the smallest unit of speech that distinguishes one utterance from another. For example, the "p" sound in *pin* is a different phoneme from the "f" sound in *fin*. Phonemes are an aspect of speech, so their pronunciation can vary according to person and dialect.

pictograph (pictogram)

A representation of an object or activity in writing through the use of a pictorial image of that object or activity. See also *ideograph*.

Pinyin

A way of transliterating Chinese sounds into Roman letters, with numbers to represent tones. Used in academia and in mainland China.

pointed Hebrew

A Hebrew writing system that uses vowel marks or cantillation marks or both.

polytonic text

Greek writing in which a variety of diacritics are used.

POSIX

Portable Operating System Interface. An IEEE standard (IEEE 1003.1) that defines a set of operating-system services. Programs that adhere to the POSIX standard can be easily ported from one system to another. POSIX was based on UNIX system services, but it can be implemented by other operating systems.

pre-edit region

A dialog box that displays characters as the user enters them but before the user commits them. Input method conversion then creates screen text in the appropriate writing system. Used for keyboard input in Asian languages with ideographic writing systems. Compare with *lookup choice region, status region*.

process code (EUC process code)

Any coded character set used for computer processing, as opposed to file storage. Sometimes used as an EUC synonym for wide character, but note that process codes and wide characters need not be the same. See *wide character*.

pun

The use of two similar words or sounds with different meanings. Puns are difficult or impossible to translate.

QWERTY keyboard

The most common keyboard layout. QWERTY refers to the top left row of alphabetic keys on this keyboard, which are "Q," "W," "E," "R," "T," and "Y," respectively, from left to right. Compare to *AZERTY keyboard*.

radix

In a radix numeration system, the positive integer by which the weight of the digit place is multiplied to obtain the weight of the digit place with the next higher weight. For example, in the decimal numeration system, the radix of each digit place is 10.

rasterizer

Rendering engine that can support a particular font format.

reengineering

Engineering that is done after a product is developed so that it can be made suitable for localization. This work may include the addition of character sets, redesign for any special screen requirements, and so forth. Should be avoided in fully international products. Not to be confused with the current management fad for rethinking and reorganizing business processes.

regulations

Government rules that govern the use and distribution of a product.

retrofit

To reengineer an existing product by back-porting features from a newer product, perhaps for localization.

RFC 822

IETF standard for 7-bit send mail transfer protocol (SMTP).

RFC 1154

IETF standard for 8-bit extended send mail transfer protocol (ESMTP), not universally accepted.

RFC 1521/1522

IETF standard for Multipurpose Internet Mail Extensions (MIME).

RFC 1866

　　IETF standard for international HTML (HyperText Markup Language).

RFC 1945

　　IETF standard for HTTP (HyperText Transport Protocol).

Romaji

　　A set of symbols used when Japanese words are spelled out in Latin letters phonetically. It is a romanization of Hiragana and Katakana.

screen shot

　　A bitmap reproduction of something that appears on a computer display.

script

　　A writing system. The system could be an alphabet, a syllabary, or a set of ideographs.

SDO

　　Standards Developing Organization. SDOs include IEEE (POSIX), ANSI, ISO, X/Open, and the MIT X Consortium.

shape determination

　　A selection from possible shapes of an Arabic character for use in a particular context. In Arabic script, characters can take either initial, medial, or final forms.

shrink-wrap

　　A transparent plastic wrap covering a package. Used in merchandizing to protect the package from being opened before it is sold. Sometimes generalized as anything that can be put on a shelf and sold.

simplified Chinese

　　Chinese ideographs, used in mainland China and Singapore. About 2,000 characters have been simplified by deleting or changing strokes. See also *traditional Chinese*.

source file

　　A file that can be edited and/or processed by a variety of text or graphics tools. A source file may contain text or artwork. Contrast with a print file, which can no longer be edited.

standard

(1) de jure: A set of technical descriptions formally accepted and endorsed by an SDO. SDOs include IEEE (POSIX), ANSI, ISO, X/Open, and the MIT X Consortium.

(2) de facto: A product that is a dominant market leader.

static messaging

A form of printing strings where phrases are looked up in a message catalog, with no reordering taking place. Because of its simplicity, it is the preferred method for international applications. Compare with *dynamic messaging*.

status region

A dialog box that provides feedback on the state of the input method for Asian languages, some of which have several input methods. For example, in Chinese, users can choose from TsangChieh, Chuyin, ChienI, Neima, ChuanHsing, or Telecode input methods. The status region is part of the frame window and is displayed above the frame footer. Compare with *lookup choice region, pre-edit region.*

syllabary

A writing system in which the smallest unit is the syllable.

text domain

A file that supplies the foreign language equivalent to a native language text string and is used as an argument in the gettext() and dgettext() functions.

trademark

A symbol, word, letter, or the like that is used by manufacturers or intellectual property owners to distinguish a product as theirs. Usually registered and protected by law.

traditional Chinese

Chinese ideographs, used everywhere except mainland China and Singapore, that retain the original forms of Han characters. See also *simplified Chinese.*

translatable text

Natural language text designed for ease of translation; for example, text that is structured in modules, permitting selective translation, and that is free of culturally biased examples, acronyms, and jargon.

translation

> (1) In computer graphics, movement objects along the x, y, or z axis. (2) In programming, the process of converting a program from one language to another; for example, converting the source code of a program written in the C language to object code that represents the same instructions or a close approximation in machine language. Translation is performed by special programs such as compilers, assemblers, and interpreters. (3) During the localization process, the rendering of text in one natural language into another.

translation team

> The group of individuals responsible for creating translated user information. Usually consists of one team leader and several translators.

transliteration

> Translation of a character from upper- to lowercase or from one character set into the corresponding position of a similar character set (for example, Romaji to Hiragana). The result of transliteration is always ambiguous.

typeface

> A family of characters in a particular style, for example, Bodoni, Times Roman, or Palatino. Type is classified according to style, size, class, width, or weight. See also *font*.

UCT

> Universal Coordinate Time. A geographically neutral expression equivalent to Greenwich Mean Time. See *GMT*.

Unicode

> A fixed-width (except for composite characters), 16-bit multilingual character encoding, including Han characters unified from Hanzi, Hanja, and Kanji. Standardized as ISO 10646. Covers all major living languages.

UNIX File System Safe Codeset

> A codeset compatible with ASCII, which prohibits the ASCII slash character and null character as a byte of any other characters. For example, the X/Open File-System Safe UNIX Transformation Format (UTF-8) is a UNIX File-System Safe Codeset.

vocabulary list

A list of potentially troublesome terms in a document, given to a translator before a large job in order to formulate mutually agreeable terminology.

vowel marks

Dots above or below characters in Arabic and Hebrew scripts, which are writing systems composed mostly of consonants.

western numerals

The digits 0 through 9. Also called Arabic numerals, or in Arab countries (oddly enough), Indic numerals. Numerals associated with Arabic writing are different in shape.

wide character

An integral data type large enough to hold any member of an extended character set. In ANSI C programs, it is an object of type `wchar_t`, which is an implementation-defined integral type defined in `<stddef.h>`. There is no direct relationship between display width and wide characters. In EUC, wide characters are often called *process code*, but they are not inherently the same. In Solaris 2.x, wide characters are 32-bits.

word expansion

The ability, based on linguistic rules, to recognize several grammatical forms of a given word. This feature may be used in text search engines, help systems, or as part of a spellchecker.

word separation

The ability, based on linguistic rules, to recognize word boundaries.

writing system

A way of graphically representing a language. Some writing systems, such as Roman and Arabic, have a single script. Others, such as Japanese, have several.

X.400

ISO specification for international message handling systems.

X.500

ISO specification for international distributed information systems.

X/Open

A group of computer manufacturers that promotes the development of portable applications based on UNIX. They publish a document called the X/Open Portability Guide (XPG). The XPG specifies most locale mechanisms documented in this book. XPG Issue 3 incorporates all of POSIX. XPG Issue 4 was recently released with new internationalization features.

X3J11

ANSI standard specification for the C programming language.

XPG

The X/Open Portability Guide. See *X/Open*.

Zhuyin-fuhao

A syllabary for transliterating Chinese sounds, used in Taiwan. Also called Bopomofo, after the sounds of the first four characters.

Index

Symbols

/usr/group 225
/usr/group *see* UniForum
/usr/lib/locale/*lang*/LC_MESSAGES/
        domain.mo 80

Numerics

7-bit dirty 343
7-bit dirty code 58
8-bit clean 230, 343
8-bit clean software 58

A

abbreviations 188
accelerator key mnemonics 230
acronyms 188
addresses, formats 27
aesthetics, international audiences and 187
alcohol-related material, international
        audiences and 187
alphabet, in phonetic systems 15
ambiguity, international audiences and 189
American National Standards Institute
        (ANSI) 221
animals, international audiences and 187
ANSI (American National Standards
        Institute) 10, 221, 343
ANSI C 343
App Builder
        overview of process 126
        primary window 126
        quitting 126

Arabic

        context dependency 17
        context sensitivity 101
        writing direction, numerals 16
        writing direction, script 19
ASCII codeset 37, 296, 297, 300, 344
ASCII standard extensions 34
Asian characters 300
Asian input procedure 302
Asian keyboards 251
Asian languages, character display and
        printing 68
Asian OLIT
        applications, compiling and linking
                328
        archive libraries 139, 167, 328
Athena widgets 167
audible signal, computer 30
automounter 173
AZERTY keyboard 344

B

back-end input method 307
bidirectional text 344
Big 5 40
bindtextdomain() 80
bit 344
bitmap image translation 232
Bopomofo 344
byte 33, 36, 344
byte order 173

C

calendars 24, 25
callback function 344
callouts 186
case
    conversion functions 62
    converting upper/lower 15
CAT 344
catalog descriptor 74
catclose() 74
category, OPEN LOOK locale 344
catgets() 74, 75, 88
catgets() and gettext() 231
CDE (Common Desktop Environment)
    application builder 125
    default locale 121
    input manager styles 161
    interface to input method 138
    standards 147
    support for 286
    VendorShell widget class 138
character 345
character classification 345
character encoding 345
    ASCII 296, 297, 300
    Asian characters 300
    C standard guarantees 63
    Compound Text 297
    EUC 296, 297
    ISO Latin-1 295, 297
    OLIT 314
    text formats, OLIT 132, 151, 314
    X11 151
    XView 296
character set 345
    definition 14, 33
    ISO 10646 218
    MOC 218
characters
    classifying 61
    in codeset space 38
    composing accents 106
    composite 101

composite, creating 109
composites 102
context sensitivity 101
    differentiation from byte 36
    entering with compose key 110
    extents-related functions in X11 155
    kanji 112
    multibyte 154
    occupied space, definition 155
charmap file. OSP 8859-1 199–207
checklist for internationalization 227
Chinese
    character set 19
    hyphenation 20
    input methods 302
    linguistic introduction 19
    script 16
    setting locale in Motif 131
    type-5 keyboard 281
    writing system 19
client-displays 309
code
    8-bit clean 58
    dirty 58
coded character set 33, 345
codeset 345
    ASCII 37
    conversion 215
    definition 33
    differentiation 38
    independence 63
    multibyte 36, 173
    nonletter characters 61
    Unicode 41–43
codeset dependent (CSD) 345
codeset independence (CSI) 345
collating sequence 345
collation 346
collation and formats 52, 54
color, international audiences and 30, 187
committing input 110, 137, 319
Common Desktop Environment See CDE

Common Open Software Environment (COSE) 286

compiling and linking Asian OLIT archive libraries 139, 167, 328

compiling XView 3.2 programs 309

complete localization 6

complex text languages (CTL) 346
  attributes 101

Compose key
  internationalization 110
  sequences 110
  using for composite characters 109

composite characters 346

compound messages 84, 85

compound strings
  converting to/from compound text 136
  in Motif 134

Compound Text encoding 297

compound text facility 136

console 346

Content-Type header field 176

context-sensitive text 346

contextual writing 346

conversion
  between multibyte and wide character representation 64
  between upper and lower case 15
  codeset to another codeset 215
  Kana to Kanji 114
  locale source definitions to database 199
  measurements 27
  multibyte to wide characters (in X11) 154
  noninternationalized declaration 83
  text, dtmail program 128
  to/from compound text 136
  translated message file source to message file object 199
  wide characters to multibyte characters 173

copy editing, style sheets for 188

COSE (Common Open Software Environment) 286

country kit 346

ctype library routines 61

cultural sensitivity 183, 191

currency
  conventions 26
  conversion 27
  formats 53
  presentation order 26
  sizes 27
  specifications 27
  symbols 27
  units 26

cursive script 346

Cyrillic 15

D

Danish type-5 keyboard 257

data representation class requirements 227

date and time formats 52

date formats 24

Daylight Saving Time (DST) 23

dead keys 251

decimal place, indication 26

decoder 346

default font or font set 317

default text format, setting 315

delimiters, word 20

deshaping 347

Deutsche Mark 26

Devanagari 17

DevGuide 291–294
  code generators 291
  element position 293
  element size 293
  Guide Interface Language (GIL) file 291
  OLIT Code Generator (GOLIT) 293
  translation 292
  XView Code Generator (GXV) 292

dgettext() 81

GMT 350
GMT offset 23
grammar
    in translations 189–190
    international audiences and 189–190
grapheme 351
graphics
    guidelines 185–187
    international audiences and 185–187
    international documents 185–187
Greek
    case distinction 15
    punctuation 20
Greenwich Mean Time offset 23
Gregorian calendar 24, 25
GUI 351

H

hands, graphic representations 187
Hangul in Korean 19, 351
Hanja in Korean 19, 351
Hanzi in Chinese 19, 351
hardware
    international graphics 185, 186
    networking issues 170
Hebrew
    bidirectionality 103
    calendar 25
    writing direction, numerals 16
help facility
    displaying localized help files 128
    internationalization 318
Hiragana 15, 19, 110, 112, 137, 319, 351
HTML (HyperText Markup Language) 174, 177, 178
HTTP (HyperText Transport Protocol) 174
humor, international audiences and 184
hyphenation 352

I

i.e., use of 188
I/O class requirements 227

i18n 6
    See internationalization
ICCCM (Inter-Client Communication Conventions Manual) 299, 352
icon 352
ideograph (ideogram) 352
ideographic systems 14
ideographs
    defined 18
    sorting schemes 22
IEC (International Electrotechnical Commission) 219, 225, 352
IEEE (Institute of Electrical and Electronics Engineers) 352
    standards 224
IETF (Internet Engineering Task Force) 225, 352
if, use of for translatability 189
Il8N *See* internationalization
illustrations
    international audiences and 185–187
    specifying locale 186
    translatability 28, 185–187
IM (input method) server 306
IM *See* input method
image translation 232
images 28
imperial system 27
implicit commit 111, 137, 308, 320
Indic scripts 17
industry standard 352
input context
    creating 165
    definition 162
    information about 163
    pre-edit information 164
    status information 164
    using 165
input manager, Motif 139
input method 353
    advantages of using 118
    architecture 306
    Asian languages 302

Spanish 269
Swedish 271
Swiss French 273
Swiss German 275
type 5 253–283
UK-English 277
US UNIX 253
using the compose key 110
keymaps, changing 125
Korean
    Hangul 19
    Hangul, composite characters 102
    Hanja 19
    Johap 40
    linguistic introduction 19
    script 16
    setting locale in Motif 131
    type-5 keyboard 279
    writing systems 19, 302
krona 26
krone 26
Kuten code 114

L

l10n 6
    See localization
LANG and LC_* environment 121, 230
LANG environment variable
    setting in OLIT 313
    setting locale, Motif 131
    setting locale, X11 151
    setting, CDE 122
language
    and territory 233
    complex text 100
    names 234–240
language-specific
    characters in file 122
    data 122
    login 122
    terminal emulator 122
Latin abbreviations 188
layout

explicit 287
implicit 287
object 296
window objects 286
LC_ALL environment 50
LC_COLLATE environment 49
LC_CTYPE environment 49
LC_MESSAGES environment 49, 73
LC_MONETARY environment 49
LC_NUMERIC environment 49
LC_TIME environment 53
levels 1-4 of internationalization 227
library routines
    character testing 61
    EUC codeset-dependent 67
    international 64
ligature 356
lira 26
locale 356
    categories 48
    changing during login 47
    conventions 13–32
    definition 4, 45
    distributed 179
    in extended EUC codesets 38
    initializing 151
    listing installed locales 47
    localized text handling 72
    multilocale computing 180
    multithreaded application 51
    name, format 46
    naming 199
    on distributed networks 179, 180
    setting 49, 131, 151, 295
    setting modifiers 157
    setting, OLIT 313
    standard locale names 233
    steps in defining 198
locale announcement 356
locale category 356
locale setting 356
localedef file, POSIX locale 207–214
localization 356

typographic conventions xxii
typography, international audiences and
      187

U

UCT 364
UDP (User Datagram Protocol) 171
UK-English, type-5 keyboard 277
Unicode 41–43, 364
      definition 41
      in electronic mail 176
      Java language 179
      support in Solaris 41
      use 173
      UTF-8 41
Unicode Consortium 225
Unicode Transmission Format (UTF) 41
UniForum standards 71, 225
UNIX File System Safe Codeset 364
upper and lower case 231
US UNIX type-5 keyboard 253
user interface, *See* interface
user messages 83–87
UTF (Unicode Transmission Format) 41

V

variable names and internationalization 69
Vietnamese
      sorting 21
      word order 22
vocabulary list 192, 365
vowel marks 365

W

wchar_t 36, 40, 173
wcschr() and strchr() 230
wcswidth(3) 98
Web browsers 177
Web page, creating 178
WebNFS 172
week

calendar format 25
first day 25
western numerals 365
when, use of for translatability 189
wide character 365
      API, use of 299
      attributes and functions in XView 296
      attributes, naming conventions 301
      determining code values 40
      encoding 132, 151, 314
      EUC encoding 297
      functions, naming conventions 301
      I/O routines 64
      OLIT 319
      string manipulation 64
      string output in multibyte format 68
      string representation 36
      X11 encoding 154
width of characters, differing 231
WIN_USE_IM 306
window object layout 99
window system features 286
word delimiters 20
word expansion 365
word order 22, 84
word separation 365
word usage
      consistency of terms 188
      general modifiers 188
      in translations 189–190
      international audiences and 189–190
World Wide Web 177
writing style, ambiguity 189
writing system 365
writing systems
      categories 14
      East Asian languages 18–19
      elements 14
      Southeast Asian languages 17

X

X Consortium 226
X/Open 226, 366